Beyond Individualism

TOWARD A RETRIEVAL OF
MORAL DISCOURSE IN AMERICA

Edited by Donald L. Gelpi, S.J.
Afterword by Robert N. Bellah

UNIVERSITY OF NOTRE DAME PRESS
NOTRE DAME, INDIANA

Copyright © 1989 by
University of Notre Dame Press
Notre Dame, Indiana 46556
All Rights Reserved

Manufactured in the
United States of America

Library of Congress Cataloging-in-Publication Data

Beyond individualism : toward a retrieval of moral
disclosure in America / edited by Donald L. Gelpi ;
afterword by Robert N. Bellah.
    p.   cm.
ISBN 0-268-00680-6
    1. Individualism.   2. Community.   3. Social
ethics.   4. United States—Religion.   I. Gelpi,
Donald L., 1934–   .
B824.B48   1989
141'.4—dc19   89-40019

Contents

Preface

Three concerns unify the following essays. In the first place, all of them attempt to criticize the ideology of individualism. In the second place, because all of these essays draw consciously on the American speculative tradition, that tradition itself helps to unify the reflections which follow. Finally, a third motif unifies this volume, namely, the formulation of an inculturated North American theology. Let us reflect on each of these points in order.

All of the essays in this volume attempt to critique one of the dominant ideologies in the United States, namely, the ideology of individualism. In 1840 Alexis de Tocqueville suggested that democratic societies breed individualists and warned against the morally corrosive potential of individualistic patterns of thought. His warning went largely unheeded until the early twentieth century, when the citizens of this nation woke up to discover that somehow the forces of history and of culture had transformed them into a lonely crowd. In the present decade Robert Bellah and the coauthors of *Habits of the Heart* have offered a trenchant analysis of the impact of individualism on the lives and attitudes of contemporary Americans. Bellah and his colleagues have also suggested a strategy for counteracting the moral and social fragmentation that individualism helps motivate by calling for a retrieval of the republican and religious traditions in our culture.

The essays in this volume attempt to begin the process of such a retrieval. As a consequence, they seek not so much to comment on the text of *Habits of the Heart* as to advance the contemporary search for ethical alternatives to individualism. As editor, I therefore offer these essays to the public as an initial indication of the resources which the North American speculative tradition offers for transcending the limitations and ethical impasses which individualism inevitably fosters.

The prospective reader should also know that these essays offer an interdisciplinary approach to the problem of individualism. Its authors represent a variety of speculative disciplines: philosophy, theology, the history of ideas, the history of culture. As a consequence, this collection offers not only a variety of personal assessments of individualism, but also a variety of scholarly approaches to the interrelated ethical questions which individualism raises.

A second factor unifies this collection, namely, that all of the essays draw consciously on the speculative tradition in the United States. Three of the essays, for example, deal with major figures in the development of North American religious thought: Jonathan Edwards, Josiah Royce, and William Ernest Hocking. Royce's philosophy of loyalty reproduces in a more secular, philosophical idiom many of the fundamental insights which Edwards developed in his theological account of "true virtue." Royce's assault on privatized, individualistic morality advances beyond Edwards, however, in its detailed reflection on the conditions for the possibility of shared communal awareness. Hocking, who studied under Royce, developed Royce's philosophy of community into a probing analysis of the moral demands of world citizenship. In other words, because these essays retrieve a developing tradition, similar speculative concerns unify them.

Finally, a third interest unifies these essays, namely, they all deal explicitly with the challenge of theological inculturation. The authors all belong to the John Courtney Murray Group. The Murray Group, a multidisciplinary, postdoctoral seminar, meets annually in order to foster scholarly publication that advances the inculturation of North American Catholic theology. Inculturated theology attempts to express Christian belief in symbols derived from the specific culture in which the gospel is proclaimed even as it uses the gospel in order to challenge that same culture and those who live in it to repentance and to faith. The John Courtney Murray Group has adopted as a strategy for promoting inculturated evangelization the development of a theology which enters into dialogue with classical North American philosophy at the same time that it reflects on important contemporary religious issues. In *The Reasoning Heart: Toward a North American Theology,* the first joint project of the Murray Group, we enunciated the above strategy for theological inculturation. In the present volume we attempt to apply that same strategy to a specific question, namely, individualism.

In editing this volume, I have tried to arrange the essays it contains in ways that enhance their complementarity. For example, in the course of my own reflections on the theology of Jonathan Edwards, I discuss the theology of romantic and marital love. Stephen Rowntree's essay, which follows mine, ponders these human loves from a philosophical standpoint.

In the course of its discussion of sociopolitical conversion, the first essay alludes to the notion of the common good. In the third essay, Andrew Christiansen argues that recent papal teaching about the common good provides an alternative to an individualistic politics of self-interest.

The fourth essay, by Francis Oppenheim, addresses many of the issues raised in the first three from the standpoint of Josiah Royce's philosophy of community. This fourth essay holds a central place in the series and appropriately creates a speculative context for the three which follow it. They each reflect on communitarian issues from a variety of perspectives.

The fifth essay, by John Staudenmaier, for example, examines technology's capacity to create and impose values that both undermine community and foster individualism. His essay suggests the scope of the institutional reform which faces us if we expect to create a new moral environment, or "social ecology," for counteracting the negative consequences of individualism.

The last two essays explore from different but complementary perspectives some of the moral consequences of commitment to the common good of the human community. Carl Starkloff calls for a "social ecology" that respects the cultural pluralism of ethnic minorities in the United States at the same time that it grants them their full rights within the body politic. In the process of arguing his case, he puts into historical perspective the attempt of native Americans to transform their communities of memory into communities of hope. He also examines the moral challenge which oppressed ethnic minorities like native Americans pose to white, middle-class Americans.

In the final essay, John Stacer draws on the work of William Ernest Hocking in order to call Americans beyond national individualism to the responsibilities of world citizenship. In the course of his essay he manages to allude to most of the other essays in this volume.

In an Afterword, Robert N. Bellah assesses the new contribution which this collection of essays makes to contemporary reflection on individualism.

Our essays do not claim to offer a comprehensive retrieval of the North American religious tradition. They do, however, suggest that such a retrieval would point toward a distinctively North American approach to the problem of individualism.

In rejecting the privatization of religion and morality, the best religious minds in this country tend to argue that only commitment to God can ultimately sustain moral commitment to the common good of humanity. They discover in religious commitment a perennial challenge to transcend individual, tribal, regional, and national interests. Those who accept the moral consequences of religious faith, they argue, recognize its capacity to universalize ethical concern by dedicating the "lost individual" to the service of the community of humankind.

North American critics of individualism also call for a discerning, contextual formation of the conscience. They summon individuals to recognize their limited place in the total scheme of things; and they insist on the indispensable role which a balanced affectivitiy plays in the formation of the human conscience. A contrite but optimistic fallibilism inclines the best moral minds in our tradition to espouse a social, dialogic understanding of both speculative and moral thinking that runs in diametrical opposition to the privatization of morality; for, as an optimistic doctrine, fallibilism holds that one has a better, not a worse, chance of reaching a true judgment if one acknowledges one's own finitude, fallibility, and need for correction by others.

Finally, our best moral and religious thinkers insist that human life becomes moral through practical commitment to the good of the human race as such. That commitment needs, of course, to find concrete expression in commitment to specific human communities dedicated to the advancement of the common good of humanity as a whole.

The authors of this book hope, then, that they have made some contribution toward advancing ethical discourse in this nation beyond the impasses into which individualism betrays it. We hope that these essays might serve as a stimulus to further reflection on the important religious and moral questions which individualism raises; and we would welcome the efforts of other colleagues in probing our cultural heritage for alternatives to individualistic modes of thought and discourse. We would hope too that such a retrieval would help point the way to the institutional reforms needed to create the kind of "social ecology" that can effectively free individualistic Americans from the social and moral selfishness that individualism fallaciously rationalizes.

Donald L. Gelpi, S.J.
Berkeley, California
September, 1988

Conversion: Beyond the Impasses of Individualism

Donald L. Gelpi, S.J.

In 1840 Alexis de Tocqueville observed that democracy breeds individualists. Although he recognized a moral affinity between egotism and individualism, he distinguished carefully between the two. He discovered the origins of egotism in blind, selfish instinct. "Individualism," he observed, on the other hand, "proceeds from erroneous judgment more than from depraved feelings. . . . Egotism is a vice as old as the world, which does not belong to one form of society more than to another: individualism is of democratic origin, and it threatens to spread in the same ratio as the equality of conditions."[1]

Tocqueville found in the free institutions of a democratic society a healthy antidote to the self-preoccupation which individualism fosters. He discovered a willingness in Americans to sacrifice a portion of their private interests in the service of the common good. He noted, however, a disturbing American tendency to blend religious and worldly pursuits; and he feared that in the end an individualistic ethos could not only sap public virtues but also betray democratic Americans into crude egotism.[2]

By 1840 Americans had in fact developed two competing forms of individualism. The industrial revolution with its attendant forms of aggressive capitalism had taught the American business community the worldly advantages of utilitarian individualism. The utilitarian individualist views human life as the individual pursuit of power in a world of threatening

1

competitors. Utilitarian individualists expect the social contracts they make to advance their interests by protecting and
increasing their personal wealth and influence. They view life
largely in economic terms. By the middle of the nineteenth century, however, American romanticism had countered a bour-
geois utilitarian individualism with an expressive individualism. Ralph Waldo Emerson functioned as the self-appointed
prophet of this new romantic ethos and found enthusiastic disciples in Henry David Thoreau, Walt Whitman, and scores of
American youth. Expressive individualism holds that at the heart
of each person lies a unique core of intuition and feeling that
demands creative expression and needs protection against the
encroachments both of other individuals and of social institutions. Those who fritter away their personal creative potential
allegedly sacrifice their real personal identity to unthinking social conformity, that perennial "hobgoblin of little minds."

Not every commentator on American mores has viewed its
individualistic tendencies with equal alarm. In 1865 Orestes
Brownson, exulting in the victory of the Union armies over an
"individualistic" politics of states rights, announced confidently
that the United States had been divinely commissioned to realize a great idea. He described that mission as "the realization
of the true idea of the state, which secures at once the authority of the public and the freedom of the individual—the sovereignty of the people without social despotism, and individual
freedom without anarchy."[3]

By the turn of the century, however, and as the United States
moved toward the Great Depression, thoughtful voices began
to suggest that under the impact of nineteenth-century individualism the moral fabric of American life had begun to unravel. In the early twentieth century John Dewey and Josiah
Royce both saw America as a nation of "lost individuals." Dewey
proclaimed nineteenth-century individualism morally bankrupt.
He deplored the sacrifice of individuality to collectivization
and standardization; and he summoned the nation to corporate
commitment to a new kind of social order that would better
coordinate social structures and individual creativity.[4] Josiah
Royce with deeper insight challenged Americans to transcend
individualism altogether through loyal commitment to the human community.[5]

In our own day *Habits of the Heart* has suggested that Tocqueville's foreboding concerning the morally corrosive potential latent in American individualism has proved all too accurate. *Habits of the Heart* describes a culture in serious moral crisis. Its authors—Robert Bellah, Richard Madsen, William Sullivan, Ann Swidler, and Steven Tipton—anatomize the ways in which an aggressive, technological, neocapitalist economy with its attendant forms of individualism isolates persons from one another and from commitment to the common good.[6]

Habits of the Heart argues persuasively that the combined impact of utilitarian and expressive individualism repeatedly betrays the consciences of well-meaning Americans into one moral impasse after another. Individualistic ideologies confront contemporary Americans with false and destructive options in almost every area of their lives: in religion, in married life, in the therapeutic search for emotional integration, and in the political search for the common good. *Habits of the Heart* also suggests a strategy for moving beyond those same moral impasses: a systematic retrieval of our religious heritage as a nation and of the republican strain in our political philosophy, which better reconciles concern for individual rights and the common good than does either utilitarian or expressive individualism.

In this essay I shall begin to test that strategy for advancing the collective conscience of this nation beyond a fragmenting individualism. I shall do so by retrieving some of the fundamental ethical insights of a figure who shaped profoundly the religious traditions of this nation. His thought and writings gave decisive orientation not only to North American religious culture but also to American philosophical reflection on human religious experience. Theologian and revivalist, Puritan divine and pastor of souls, he ranks today in the estimate of many scholars as one of the most creative theological minds this nation has produced. I refer, of course, to Jonathan Edwards.

Edwards did not deal speculatively with the problem of individualism as such; but he did mount a telling theological criticism of one of individualism's chief fruits: the privatization of morality. The first part of this essay examines the reasons why Edwards found privatized moral reasoning inadequate.

One finds those reasons in his theology of conversion and in his account of "true virtue."

One retrieves the past for the light it sheds on contemporary problems. Accordingly, the second part of this essay argues that Edwards's insights have the capacity to enhance a contemporary theology of conversion at the same time that such a theology completes and contextualize Edwards's own theological project. The final sections of this essay then argue that a contemporary theology of conversion, when enhanced by insights from Edwards, provides a comprehensive frame of reference for responding to the moral challenge of individualism.

I. EDWARDS ON TRUE VIRTUE AND PRIVATIZED MORALITY

Edwards's critique of privatized morality flowed directly from his own religious experience. Allow me to quote fairly extensively from his account of his own conversion, for the kinds of religious experiences he there describes hold the key to much of his best religious thought. Edwards depicted his own conversion in the following terms:

> The first time that I remember that ever I found any thing of that sort of inward, sweet delight in God and divine things that I have lived much in since, was on reading those words, I Tim. 1:17. "Now unto the king eternal immortal, invisible, the only wise God, be honor and glory for ever and ever. Amen." As I read the words, there came into my soul, and was as it were diffused thro' it, a sense of the glory of the Divine Being; a new sense, quite different from anything I ever experienced before. Never any words of scripture seemed to me as these words did. I thought with myself, how excellent a being that was; and how happy I should be, if I might enjoy that God, and be wrapt up to God in heaven, and be as it were swallowed up in Him. I kept saying, and as it were singing over these words of scripture to myself; and went to prayer, to pray to God that I might enjoy Him; and prayer in a manner quite different from what I used to do; with a new sort of affection. But it never

came into my thought, that there was any thing spiritual, or
of a saving nature in this.

From about that time, I began to have a new kind of appre-
hensions and ideas of Christ, and the work of redemption, and
the glorious way of salvation by Him. I had an inward, sweet
sense of these things, that at times came into my heart; and
my soul was led away in pleasant views and contemplations
of them. . . .

Not long after I first began to experience these things I gave
an account to my father, of some things that had pass'd in my
mind. I was pretty much affected by the discourse we had together. And when the discourse ended, I walked abroad alone,
in a solitary place in my father's pasture, for contemplation.
And as I was walking there, and looked up on the sky and
clouds; there came into my mind, a sweet sense of the glorious
majesty and grace of God, that I know not how to express. I
seemed to see them both in sweet conjunction: majesty and
meekness join'd together: it was a sweet and gentle and holy
majesty; and also a majestic meekness; an awful sweetness; a
high, a great and a holy gentleness.

After this my sense of divine things gradually increased, and
became more and more lively, and had more of that inward
sweetness. The appearance of every thing was altered: there
seem'd, as it were, a calm, sweet cast, or appearance of divine
glory, in almost every thing. God's excellence, his wisdom, his
purity and love, seemed to appear in every thing; in the sun,
moon and stars, in the clouds, and blue sky; in the grass, flow-
ers, trees; in the water, and all nature; which used greatly to
fix my mind.[7]

Edwards the revivalist found that the converts who responded
to his preaching shared religious experiences not unlike his
own. Moreover, in *Religious Affections,* his most systematic
defense of the conversions which the Great Awakening effected,
he undertook a detailed description of an authentic Christian
conversion.

He argued that any genuine conversion must be effected by
the Spirit of Christ who abides in the souls of converts in order
to sensitize them to the divine beauty incarnate in Jesus and

in the lives of those who resemble him. The Spirit does not create in converts new powers of activity but lays a new foundation within the soul's natural powers for a graced perception of the divine excellence that discovers the divine glory revealed in every created reality.[8]

The action of the Spirit inspires in converts an ecstatic love of God that bears fruit in self-forgetfulness. It orders one's own self-love by ensuring that it not exceed or deviate from God's love for oneself (*RA*, 240–53). Religious enthusiasm for the divine excellence focuses especially on God's moral attributes, or holiness (*RA*, 254–65). This affective perception of divine holiness yields a new understanding of God that teaches the heart to respond instinctively when the Spirit prompts one to live in the divine image (*RA*, 266–91). From this understanding flows a new personal conviction of the reality and certainty of divine things (*RA*, 291–307). The authentic enlightenment of the Spirit also inspires evangelical humility: a hatred for sin and a frank acknowledgement of one's own sinfulness at the same time that one rejoices self-forgetfully in God's saving forgiveness (*RA*, 311–36).

The affective transformation which the Spirit effects in the hearts of converts changes them permanently, enthralling them with the divine beauty revealed in nature and incarnate in Jesus. The Spirit teaches believers to imitate Jesus' love, meekness, and mercy, sensitizes them to the movements of divine grace, and effects a personal healing that endows their lives with a beautiful symmetry and proportion (*RA*, 340–74). Those inspired by the Spirit develop an increasing appetite for divine things (*RA*, 377–83). Finally, and most important of all, authentic conversion bears fruit in Christian practice, in faithful submission to the moral demands of gospel living (*RA*, 384–456).

An insight into Edwards's understanding of the experience of conversion gives concrete meaning to his definition of "true virtue" and makes sense of his repudiation of privatized morality. He defined "true virtue" as "benevolence to being in general."[9] By "being in general" Edwards meant in the first instance God, in the second instance all that God has made; for those who consent to the divine excellence take the divine will as the measure of their consent to every other created reality. Consent to

God, then, both orders and universalizes human moral choices. Edwards wrote:

> There is a general and particular beauty. By a particular beauty, I mean that by which a thing appears beautiful when considered only with regard to its connection with, and tendency to, some particular things within a limited, and as it were private sphere. And a general beauty is that by which a thing appears beautiful when viewed most perfectly, comprehensively and universally, with regard to all its tendencies, and its connections with every thing to which it stands related. The former may be without and against the latter. (TV, 2–3)

Any human choice that falls short of such universal moral concern fails to qualify as true virtue. It may express the natural desire of some limited good, or it may cling sinfully to some creature in opposition to the divine will.

True virtue embodies the love of benevolence.[10] Benevolence causes the heart to incline to the well-being of the beloved and to rejoice in the beloved's happiness (TV, 6–7). Because true virtue expresses in the first instance benevolence toward God and toward all those realities to which God consents benevolently, it consecrates the virtuous to promote God's own intentions, to seek his glory. "Though we are not able," Edwards argued, "to give any thing to God, which we have of our own independently; yet we may be the instruments of promoting his glory, in which he takes a true and proper delight" (TV, 16).

As an expression of benevolence toward God that imitates God's own benevolent consent to his creatures, true virtue springs from the heart. We consent to doing the right thing not as some obligation imposed upon us externally but as something that attracts and lures us because of its inherent excellence and value. The divine excellence incarnate in Jesus and manifest in creation possesses the mind and draws us affectively in the deepest center of our personal reality. We perceive the infinite, all-encompassing reality of God as supremely desirable and want nothing so much as to do whatever pleases him.

Edwards contrasted truly virtuous conduct with both selfishness and with the natural judgments of the human conscience. Let us consider each of these contrasts in turn.

Edwards recognized a natural beauty in finite created reality "which consists in a mutual consent and agreement of different things, form, manner, quantity, and visible end or design; called by the various names of regularity, order, uniformity, symmetry, proportion, harmony, etc." (*TV,* 28). Quite correctly, however, he looked upon mere natural symmetry and proportion as inferior to moral excellence (*TV,* 31). Moreover, he argued that many human acts which consent to created beauty may have the appearance of true virtue but fall short of the reality.

Seeming virtue may, for example, actually mask human selfishness. Edwards wrote:

> Self-love, as the phrase is used in common speech, most commonly signifies a man's regard to his confined private self, or love to himself with respect to his private interest.
>
> By private interest I mean that which most immediately consists in those pleasures, or pains, that are personal. (*TV,* 45)

Selfish interests seek the fulfillment of personal appetites and the avoidance of personal aversions. They desire secondary beauty and dislike the contrary deformity. The selfish rejoice in being honored and dislike hatred and contempt. Self-seeking comes naturally to all creatures. As a consequence, one cannot assume that every natural affection or aversion seeks to promote the public good or avoid public evil. Edwards correctly faulted the moral theorists of his day for painting a naively optimistic portrait of human nature and its alleged spontaneous desire for virtue. Even love of other persons, he argued, may root itself most fundamentally in self-love rather than in genuine benevolence; for those motivated by self-love may perform the same deeds as the truly virtuous but for vicious and utterly selfish motives (*TV,* 45–60).

Edwards contrasted the consent of true virtue not only with the seeming virtue of the selfish egotist but also with choices inspired by the natural conscience. He argued that natural moral choices fall short of the full ethical potential which the graced heart enjoys and exercises. The natural conscience seeks to act self-consistently and to reward or punish human acts according to their deserts. It recognizes the difference between virtue and vice; but because it remains focused on finite created goods without ascending in love to the source of all goodness, the natural conscience judges moral actions accurately but super-ficially. It judges correctly specific instances of moral good and evil, but it lacks an insight into the divine will that grounds and contextualizes the attractive excellence of particular virtu-ous acts. Moreover, the natural conscience understands duty, reward, and punishment; but it grasps duty with the head rather than with the heart. Hence, the natural conscience consents to virtue "without seeing the true beauty of it" (*TV,* 69, 90).

The natural conscience curbs human sinfulness but falls short of true virtue because it does not spring from benevolence to being in general (*TV,* 94–96). Nor can the natural conscience, left to its limited resources, effect the reconciliation of all crea-tures to one another in God. Only true virtue—cordial con-sent in love to the God whose will orders all finite human choices to the ends he desires—can effect that universal reconciliation; for God alone enjoys the natural capacity to consent to the whole of being. Finite creatures acquire that capacity only by consenting to God, by conforming their consent to his (*TV,* 100).

II. COMPLETING EDWARDS'S THEOLOGICAL PROJECT

The Puritan tradition in which Edwards stood had modified the extreme pessimism that had characterized Calvin's own un-derstanding of the relationship between human nature and di-vine grace.[11] Puritan divines like Edwards recognized positive value in human reason and in the natural workings of the hu-man conscience. As a consequence, one discovers in Edwards's theology of true virtue a convergence between his own thought and a traditional Catholic understanding of the relationship between nature and grace. In traditional Catholic thinking grace heals, perfects, and elevates the natural powers that hu-mans possess. Edwards, in his account of the relationship be-tween true virtue and the natural conscience, espoused a simi-lar position.

In Edwards's theology the traditional Calvinist doctrine of human depravity has mellowed into a sober, realistic assess-ment of the limitations and selfishness that characterize human moral reasoning and conduct. The spontaneous egocentrism of the human conscience betrays it all too easily into vicious-

ness. It therefore needs the healing of divine grace if it ever
hopes to cultivate true virtue. In addition, its natural limitations prevent it from grasping the full significance of virtuous
conduct. Human reason opens only a finite window on the
world. The reasoning conscience can as a consequence grasp
the inherent goodness of specific virtuous acts and the inherent evil of vicious ones; but it lacks the contextualizing, uni-
versalizing insight which comes from consent in faith to divine
beauty incarnate. The action of the Spirit of Christ therefore
elevates the natural conscience by creating within it a new foundation for moral reasoning, namely, a heart attuned to the
movements of grace and sensitized to the excellence of Christ-
like behavior. Grace perfects the conscience by conforming it
to the divine will, by teaching it to love created goods only as
much as and in the way that God loves them.

Because the graced conscience also acts within a truly universal context, it recognizes that nothing can lay claim to true
value except in relationship to the rest of reality. True excellence expresses integration into the cosmic order of things willed
by God. As a result, grace also raises the natural conscience
to the ultimate level of socialization.

In other ways, however, Edwards's theology and the Catholic tradition both challenge one another. Catholic theology quite
correctly rehabilitates human nature even more systematically
than Edwards did. Catholic thought discovers in natural virtue positive value, not just the negative goodness that Edwards
found there (*TV*, 91). Catholic theology also recognizes a natural human potential to ascend from reflection on creation to
the reality of its Creator. Edwards's theology, on the other
hand, correctly challenges traditional Catholic theology to recognize the limited particularity of natural judgments of conscience. Radically finite in its perceptions, human moral judgment, left to its own resources, never attains to the universality
of divine moral consent, even when the natural conscience aspires to such universality. Moreover, Edwards also challenges
Catholic theology to insist on the absolute primacy of God's
self-revelation in Jesus over any naturally derived conception
of the deity.

I have undertaken the preceding retrieval of Edwards's accounts of conversion and of true virtue out of the double con-

viction that they can enhance a contemporary theology of conversion and that such a theology, so enhanced, can mount a comprehensive critique of moral individualism. Let us then reflect on the ways in which contemporary reflection on conversion and Edwards's thought mutually enrich one another. That reflection will, however, require of the reader a shift in mental gears. Until now we have focused on Edwards's theology of conversion. In the pages that follow we will use his insights and those of contemporary theology in order to probe the experience of Christian conversion itself for an insight into its dynamics.

A contemporary theology of Christian conversion provides a larger frame of reference within which to situate Edwards's theocentric ethics of faith; for the former recognizes in a way that Edwards did not that religious conversion exemplifies only one kind of conversion. In addition to religious conversion one must speak of affective, intellectual, moral, and sociopolitical conversion.[12]

By conversion I mean the decision to take responsibility for some dimension of one's own experience. What, then, does such a definition imply?

Experience divides into *what* we experience and the *way* in which we experience what we experience. When we take responsibility for the way we ourselves experience reality, we undergo personal conversion. Personal conversion comes in four forms: affective, intellectual, moral, and religious. The affectively converted take responsibility for the health of their emotional growth. The intellectually converted take responsibility for the truth or falsity of their personal judgments and for the adequacy or inadequacy of the frames of reference in which they reach those judgments. The morally converted take responsibility for seeing to it that their judgments of conscience conform to sound ethical norms. The religiously converted take responsibility for responding to some historical self-revelation and self-communication of God on the terms that God himself sets. In other words, the religiously converted respond to God in faith.

The personally converted take responsibility, then, for the motives and consequences of their own personal decisions. The sociopolitical convert, by contrast, takes responsibility, within the limits of realistic possibility, for influencing the decisions of others, especially for influencing the decisions that give shape to the large, impersonal institutions that influence human life and experience. Sociopolitical converts do what they can in order to ensure that the decisions and policies of large institutions express and foster an integral fivefold conversion. In this sense, sociopolitical converts take responsibility not so much for the way they themselves respond to reality as for influencing as effectively as possible the way in which social reality itself develops.

Sociopolitical conversion deprivatizes personal conversion in two ways. First, it confronts the convert with The Others — with persons, groups, and vested interests in human society that promote other value systems and emerge from other social contexts than those already familiar to the convert. Sociopolitical conversion thus ensures that all subsequent personal growth advances in confrontation and dialogue with personal and institutional forces that challenge the convert's own presuppositions. Second, sociopolitical conversion culminates in personal dedication to some cause of universal moral import, that is, a cause which seeks to effect the common good. The common good demands that all individuals and groups contribute to and benefit from the goods of society in a ready and adequate manner. The promotion of world peace, the elimination of world hunger, the defense of the rights of minorities and of the oppressed exemplify the kinds of causes to which I refer.

All five forms of conversion commit one to responsible behavior. By that I mean that converts recognize that they must show readiness, when required, to render to themselves and to others an account of the motives and consequences of their actions. The converted have interiorized sound norms for measuring emotional, intellectual, moral, and religious growth and for assessing the justice or injustice of human institutions. They account to themselves for their own behavior when they actually measure their conduct against those norms. In addition, however, the converted recognize that true responsibility also takes into account the ways in which one's personal choices affect for good or ill the lives of others. In this sense, an integral, fivefold conversion completes the process of socialization that childhood begins. In other words, until one has experienced all five forms of conversion, one languishes in some form of adolescence, whatever one's age.

A contemporary theology of conversion contextualizes Edwards's thought by insisting on the need to look upon religious conversion as only one of five possible conversion experiences. Edwards's account of Christian conversion, however, enriches a contemporary theology of conversion by suggesting the need not only to distinguish the kinds of conversion from one another but also to speak of different dynamics within the total process of conversion. By a dynamic within the total process of conversion I mean the way in which one form of conversion conditions another. More specifically, Edwards's descriptive account of Christian conversion suggests that, within the total process of conversion, it mediates between affective and moral conversion. One form of conversion mediates between two others when it sets them in a relationship to one another that they would not otherwise enjoy.

Edwards saw clearly and correctly that conversion begins in a heart capable of responding to the attractive excellence of reality. The converting Christian consents to the divine excellence incarnate in Jesus and in people whose lives resemble his. That consent, however, has important moral consequences, for it commits one to living in Jesus' image. When one translates these insights into the language of a contemporary theology of conversion, one asserts that within an integral, fivefold conversion religious conversion mediates between affective and moral conversion.

Edwards's theology of true virtue also suggests a second dynamic that Christian conversion contributes to the total process of conversion; namely, it transvalues the forms of conversion that occur naturally. Here two terms need clarification: *natural conversion* and *transvaluation*.

A conversion occurs naturally when it transpires in abstraction from the historical self-revelation and self-communication of God. Affective, intellectual, moral, and sociopolitical conversion can all occur naturally. The pain born of emotional conflict may force one to take personal responsibility for dealing systematically with one's neuroses in complete abstraction from God or religion. The experience of error, malice, or injustice may lead one to an intellectual, moral, or sociopolitical conversion untouched by religious concerns.

When affective, intellectual, moral, or sociopolitical conversion occur naturally, they need transvaluation in faith. We transvalue a reality, an emotion, an image, or a concept when, having used it in one frame of reference, we begin to use it in another that endows it with new meaning. For example, after humanity had discovered the spherical rather than the flat character of the earth, the term *earth* still meant "the hard surface on which I walk"; but it acquired new connotations from being understood in a new geographical frame of reference.

Every conversion creates a strictly normative frame of reference. Religious faith derives its norms from insight into the claims that the historical revelation of God makes on human life and conduct. It therefore provides a normative frame of reference that encompasses and transcends those created by the other forms of conversion, for religious faith encompasses every dimension of natural human experience and leads it to fulfillment in God. The religious convert needs, then, to understand how the encounter with God transforms human affective, intellectual, moral, and social development. When one reevaluates the insights of natural conversion in the light of faith, one transvalues them.

I find the idea of transvaluation implicit in Edwards's insistence that the action of the Holy Spirit endows human consciousness with new sensibilities that cause it to see old, familiar realities in a new light. I find it too in his insistence that Christian faith so universalizes the human conscience that it demands the reevaluation not only of sinful choices but also of the limited insights of natural prudence.

How, then, does Christian conversion transform the strictly normative insights born of the other forms of natural conversion? In order to answer that question, one needs to understand, as Edwards saw, the practical, moral consequences of Christian conversion. Edwards correctly realized that those consequences demand the imitation of Christ. Here again, however, a contemporary theology of conversion can complete and develop his seminal insights by exploring in greater detail than Edwards himself did the moral cost of discipleship.

The Gospels all tell us that Christian conversion draws one into Jesus' own religious experience of living as a child of God. One lives as a child of God in Jesus' image by submitting to the reign of God that he proclaimed. A careful examination

of the Gospels will, moreover, show that entry into the Kingdom makes very specific moral demands on converts. In sum-
moning his disciples to repentant, converted living in his image, Jesus enunciated not a rational ethics, but a morality of
faith.

More specifically, Jesus demanded of his followers a trust
in God's providential care of them that freed them to share the
physical supports of life with other persons, especially with
those in greatest need. This willingness to share one's possessions with others as an expression of one's faith in God transforms the purpose of labor: the converted Christian labors, not
in order to amass personal possessions, but in order to avoid
burdening others and to have something to share with those
less fortunate.

The sharing that Jesus demanded of his disciples envisaged,
moreover, the creation of a community of sharing. It involved
more than almsgiving. Instead, Jesus encouraged his followers
to welcome into their homes the poor, the marginal, the outcast. Christian sharing, therefore, seeks to bring into existence
an all-inclusive community in which no one is excluded in principle and in which the sharing of life's physical supports advances not on the basis of merit only, but on the basis of need.
The sharing that takes place within Christian communities must
also express the mutual forgiveness of its members, and that
mutual forgiveness tests the authenticity of personal and shared
prayer.[13]

Christian conversion, then, commits one to living by a set
of moral values that strikes at the very heart of individualism.
Moreover, a theology of conversion that takes into account the
two dynamics that Edwards discovered in Christian conversion
can draw upon a Christian ethics of discipleship in order to
mount a telling critique of an individualistic ethos.

The retrieval of a New Testament ethics of discipleship transforms Edwards's definition of true virtue as cordial consent to
being in general from an abstract ethical norm of dubious practical applicability into a set of specific moral ideals capable of
luring and judging the human conscience. Moreover, a sound
insight into the demands of gospel living also makes it clear
that a genuine Christian conversion transcends the concerns
of narrow, denominational sectarianism, since the converted

Christian lives committed to reach out in compassion to anyone in need, regardless of race, creed, or class.

In the section that follows I shall argue that the first dynamic
of Christian conversion frees the conscience from choosing, as
individualism demands, between internal and external religion.
The remaining sections of this essay will then examine how
the transvaluation in faith of natural conversion resolves other
moral contradictions inherent in an individualistic ethic. Section 4 will argue that affective conversion, when transvalued
in faith, requires the repudiation of what *Habits of the Heart*
calls "the therapeutic attitude." Section 5 will show how an
intellectual conversion transvalued in faith requires the speculative critique of individualistic ideologies. Section 6 will demonstrate that a moral conversion transvalued in faith frees the
conscience from the paradoxes of privatized love. Section 7
will attempt to show that a sociopolitical conversion transvalued in faith requires that human institutions submit to the
demands of divine justice. Let us reflect on each of these points
in turn.

III. BEYOND INTERNAL AND EXTERNAL RELIGION: THE MEANING OF RELIGIOUS ASSENT

Most contemporary Americans seem content to practice a
privatized religion (*HH*, 220–22). Privatized religion confronts
contemporary American religionists with a false option between
"internal" and "external" religion. Internal religion seduces one
into worshiping the apotheosis of oneself. External religion reduces faith to a matter of facts, not feeling, and erects legally
imposed doctrinal barriers against the threat of religious chaos.
In other words, internal religion collapses the world and even
ultimate reality into oneself, while external religion degenerates into legalism and fundamentalism. Both forms of religion
hold freedom and individuality as central values. Neither offers a language that can mediate between the self, society, the
natural world, and ultimate reality (*HH*, 235–37).

A second insight into the first dynamic of Christian conversion suggested by Edwards's theology offers to contemporary
Americans a religious alternative to both internal and external
religion. Christian conversion begins in a heart sufficiently healed

of neurotic anger, fear, and guilt that it can respond to beauty. When the confrontation with unconscious rage, guilt, and fear occurs in faith, we call it repentance. Repentance sensitizes the converting Christian heart not only to natural beauty but also to the divine beauty incarnate in Jesus and in those whose lives resemble his. Moreover, as Edwards saw, consent to the divine beauty in response to the action of God's Spirit culminates in the determination to submit to the demands of Christian discipleship; and cordial consent to God incarnate endows genuine religion with an ecstatic self-forgetfulness that unmasks the self-adoration of internal religion as empty idolatry.

The moral determination to live by gospel values demands as well the renunciation of religious legalism. Jesus left his disciples not with a set of laws to be obeyed mindlessly and rigorously but with an ideal of communal living. The Christian convert appropriates that ideal as worth espousing personally for its inherent beauty, for the truth and goodness that it embodies. That ideal gives moral identity to the Christian Church. Once appropriated personally, the moral vision of Jesus stands in judgment on the convert's subsequent behavior as a member of the Christian community, even as it judges the conduct and institutions of that community as a whole. Moreover, the ethics of discipleship which Jesus proclaimed replaces the law as the basis of Christian conduct because it demands all that legal piety does and more.

Moreover, a sound insight into the first dynamic of Christian conversion—namely, its capacity to mediate between affective and moral conversion—provides a way of talking about the self, society, and nature that both discloses their mutual interdependence and relates them to the ultimate reality of God. Nature discloses the glory of God and provides the resources for building a community of free sharing in faith. The divinely proclaimed ideals of gospel living lure the heart by their beauty and stand in judgment on both personal and institutional sin.

IV. THE HEALING OF THERAPY: TRANSVALUING AFFECTIVE CONVERSION

The French worry about their livers, the English about catarrhs, and Americans about their psyches. American culture offers a therapy for virtually every emotional problem. Our therapeutic culture promises to free individuals to get in touch with their own wants and interests and to liberate them from the artificial constraints of social roles, from the guilt-inducing demands of parents and other authorities, and from the false promises of illusory ethical ideals like love (*HH,* 101–02). A therapeutic culture replaces obligation and commitment with full, open, honest communication among self-actualized individuals. It urges people to replace self-sacrifice with self-assertion. It portrays problems in human love relationships as excessive and unrealistic demands upon one's personal autonomy. It convinces people that they need not change but can demand of others love and acceptance as they are (*HH,* 98–102).

Instead of raising moral questions, a therapeutic culture teaches individuals to understand how they feel about persons and situations. It shows them how to make their interpersonal relationships "work" in ways that promote their personal self-fulfillment. It replaces ethical concerns with the improvement of communication skills. Finally, it encourages people to cultivate "communities of interest" where friendship and caring networks promote one's own mental health but where the cult of privacy breeds finally isolation and loneliness (*HH,* 122–38).

No one seriously questions the usefulness of psychological therapy. One can, however, legitimately question the individualistic ideology which a therapeutic culture inculcates. A contemporary theology of conversion does precisely that. In calling for affective conversion, contemporary theology summons every adult to emotional honesty and to the responsible cultivation of healthy affective attitudes. Sound therapy seeks to promote both of these ends.

In addition, however, a contemporary theology of conversion, when embellished with insights from Edwards, demands the moral transvaluation in faith of natural affective conversion. One should never, of course, confuse moral and religious imperatives with affective ones. In point of fact, each kind of conversion creates a different kind of "ought." The laws of healthy emotional development differ from the laws of logic, of morality, of faith, or of just social conduct. When faced with an emotional difficulty, we only confuse matters if we ig-

nore its specifically emotional character and treat it as a speculative, ethical, religious, or social problem. Having said so
much, however, a sound theology of conversion would nevertheless insist that the other forms of conversion must condition the human search for emotional health; for unless they
do, the full human integration that therapy seeks to effect will
never happen.

Moreover, as Edwards saw two centuries ago, the natural
conscience, left to its own devices, can achieve limited moral
insights into reality, insights that the consent of faith expands
and contextualizes. To love one's neighbor as oneself does not
require that one measure others' needs by one's own. Instead,
it requires that one stand in other people's shoes, understand
their needs and situation, and then treat them as one would
like to be treated if one were they. Because both moral and religious conversion summon individuals to such ethical self-
transcendence, they demand the transvaluation of any search
for emotional healing informed by a therapeutic attitude which
inculcates egocentric narcissism.

The vast majority of serious emotional problems flow from
a failure to deal properly with the negative emotions of rage,
fear, and guilt. The more we repress these affections the more
they distort human conduct in unconscious and destructive ways.
When, on the other hand, we face repressed negative attitudes
and integrate them into our conscious personality in life-giving
ways, then compulsive aggression, defensiveness, and self-hatred
yield before the healing power of love.

Christian conversion transforms natural affective conversion
into repentance, for it demands that one regard the rage, fear,
and guilt that distort human behavior in violent and destructive ways not merely as obstacles to one's own personal satisfaction but as potential obstacles to union with God. Repentance, moreover, holds out the hope of divine forgiveness and
reconciliation.

As a consequence, Christian conversion also demands that
the emotionally troubled look ultimately not to therapy but to
God to effect their healing. As the founders of Alcoholics Anonymous saw both clearly and correctly, giving over an emotional
conflict to one's "higher power" not only advances the healing
process but in many instances makes it even possible.

V. THE CHRISTIAN CRITIQUE OF INDIVIDUALISM

Not only does a contemporary theology of affective conversion call for the healing of therapeutic individualism, but it also looks to the intellectually converted to critique the other destructive ideologies that isolate individuals in order to exploit and dominate them. The intellectually converted have advanced beyond naive fundamentalism. They recognize that no one is handed truth on a platter. They acknowledge as well that the human mind comes to truth within the limited frames of reference it constructs. As a consequence, the intellectually converted take pains to critique not only the truth or falsity of specific propositions but also the adequacy or inadequacy of the frames of reference within which individuals and communities choose to think.

As we have seen, however, the second dynamic that Edwards's thought introduces into the conversion process demands that the intellectually converted Christian derive norms of ultimate moral adequacy from faith, from a sound insight into the way in which God himself has said his children ought to live. That means that the Christian conscience measures institutional justice and injustice by a New Testament ethics of discipleship. *Economic Justice for All,* the pastoral of the United States Catholic bishops on the economy, illustrates the way in which the demands of Christian discipleship stand at odds with economic individualism.

In their pastoral the bishops draw broadly on both the Bible and Christian tradition to provide moral norms for assessing this nation's economy. From the Hebrew tradition they derive the principle that all people are created in God's image and enjoy an inalienable dignity as human "prior to any division into races or nations and prior to human labor and human achievement."[14] God, the bishops insist, created the goods of the earth to be shared by all (*EJA,* 34). God also came to the aid of the oppressed people of Israel in order to form them into a community covenanted to him and sensitive to the cries and suffering of the poor, the alien, and the oppressed. Through the preaching of the prophets God called Israel again and again back to just and compassionate living (*EJA,* 35–40).

The bishops correctly situate the teachings of Jesus within

a Hebrew theology of creation, covenant, community, and the prophetic denunciation of injustice. They insist that Christian discipleship requires a preferential option for the poor and that the shared hope of Christians requires that they struggle now, as Jesus did in his day, against the forces of oppression and injustice (*EJA,* 41–45).

The bishops root Christian morality in the two great commandments "to love God with all one's heart and to love one's neighbor as oneself" (*EJA,* 64). Concern for justice flows from fidelity to these two commandments, because the norms of justice seek to secure the minimum levels of care and respect which all persons and communities owe one another (*EJA,* 68). "Basic justice demands the establishment of minimum levels of participation in the life of the human community for all persons" (*EJA,* 76).

Having enunciated fundamental principles of justice, the bishops then attempt to establish a set of moral priorities which ought to ground economic activity. First and most fundamentally, they call for a concern on the part of persons and institutions for the common good, for ensuring that all have the opportunity to contribute to the shared life of the human community and to participate in its benefits. Concern for the common good requires a preferential option for the poor, the marginal, and the dispossessed, since they most of all lack access to a just share in the goods that sustain and humanize life. The bishops, therefore, give highest moral and economic priority to fulfilling the basic needs of the poor. They call for the inclusion of the marginal in the economic process and for the investment of wealth, talent, and human energy in projects that will especially benefit the poor. After concern for the poor, the bishops place next highest moral priority on economic policies that strengthen and stabilize family life (*EJA,* 84–93).

Although the bishops argue their position in part from principles derived from the natural law, the social order that they describe roots itself ultimately in Jesus' proclamation of the reign of God and in consent to the communal ethics of discipleship which he required of his followers. As that consent transforms and transvalues human moral reasoning, it gives rise to a strictly theological critique of individualism and of other ideologies that divide and oppress the human race. Moreover, theological documents like *Economic Justice for All* and *The Challenge of Peace,* the Catholic bishops' pastoral on nuclear disarmament and the arms race, illustrate dramatically the power which religious communities of shared memories possess to generate a moral vision capable of counteracting the ethically corrosive influence of individualism and of the other ideologies of isolation, exploitation, and oppression that infect our culture.

VI. BEYOND PRIVATIZED "LOVE": MARRIAGE AS SACRAMENT

The individualist looks approvingly on love relationships that "work" or that "feel good." As a consequence, contemporary Americans who define love individualistically find themselves impaled on the horns of a cruel moral dilemma. They seek in human love an experience of intimacy, mutuality, and sharing at the same time that they regard love as the quintessential expression of individuality and freedom. In loving another they want a relationship both absolutely free and totally shared.

By thus defining love individualistically, contemporary Americans create for themselves a formula for certain frustration. On the one hand, the sharing for which they long threatens to swallow up their individuality by demanding the abandonment of personal interests and desires. On the other hand, those who "lose" their identities by giving of themselves to their beloved have presumably forfeited their ability to contribute to the love relationship as fully autonomous individuals (*HH,* 91–97).

Individualism also distorts the way in which many contemporary Americans approach marriage. The utilitarian individualist looks upon the marriage contract as an agreement between two individuals acting in their own self-interest. The expressive individualist seeks in it a relationship full of shared, authentic commitment (*HH,* 107).

The evangelical tradition in this country offers a contemporary alternative to an individualistic understanding of love and marriage. Evangelicals tend to deny any relationship between love and emotion. They fear that emotion provides too unstable a foundation to build a permanent human relationship. They define love as a matter of deeds rather than of feelings, as the willingness to sacrifice oneself for others (*HH*, 93–97).

Does a contemporary theology of conversion suggest a middle ground between evangelical stoicism, on the one hand, and individualistic egotism masquerading as love, on the other? I believe that it does, for it requires the transvaluation of human love in the love of Christ.

In approaching human love we need, first of all, to recognize the varieties of human loving. The gift love of which the evangelicals speak exemplifies only one way to love — a fundamental way of loving, to be sure, but in the last analysis only one way. The ecstatic love of the contemplative and the needy love of the child exemplify two other fundamental ways in which humans love one another.

Other forms of human love combine these elemental kinds of loving. The love of affection that binds members of a family together blends the love born of need with gift love. Friendship unites contemplative love and gift love: friends appreciate one another and share common interests and ideals besides supporting one another and, if necessary, sacrificing themselves for one another. Romantic love blends contemplative love with the love born of need. Romantic lovers tend to idealize the beloved at the same time that they need one another desperately.[15]

Genuine marital love blends friendship, romantic love, and affection. A recent study of successful marriages shows that they root themselves more in friendship than in romance, although both partners have come to a shared understanding of the place of sex in their relationship. In successful marriages the spouses like one another as persons, commit themselves to one another for the long haul, and want their relationship to succeed. They find one another more interesting as the years go by. They value marriage as an institution. Successful spouses can laugh together, confide in one another, and know how to express and receive affection. They feel pride at one another's achievements. They also share a common vision of life and enjoy sharing interesting ideas and enthusiasms. Finally, in successful marriages spouses look upon marriage as sacred.[16]

Because natural marital love blends friendship, romance, and affection, it expresses gift love. Successful spouses give themselves to one another in a relationship of mutual friendship and support. Moreover, marital love derives its contemplative dimension from romance. Successful spouses find one another genuinely beautiful and create ways of communicating that to one another.

A Christian theology of conversion, when embellished with insights from Edwards, requires that the love of charity transvalue the natural goodness present in marital love. Charity blends in faith the three elemental forms of love: contemplative love, gift love, and the love born of need. Christian love, as Edwards saw, springs from the contemplation of the divine excellence incarnate in God's perfect gift of himself to us when he became human, died for us, and sent us, even in our sinfulness, the gift of his Spirit. In addition, however, the love of charity encompasses the love born of need. Christians confront one another in community as mutually needy individuals. The more advantaged minister to those with the greatest need, but they do so in the knowledge that they themselves have needs and will one day need to accept gratefully and lovingly the ministry of others.

Charity, moreover, derives its moral content from the moral teachings of Jesus. The love of charity seeks to bring into existence communities of sharing in faith that reach out spontaneously to the neediest. The love of charity demands, moreover, that Christians forgive one another with the same gratuity as God has forgiven them in Christ. Charity demands too that the humane sharing of life and of the things that make it possible express that mutual forgiveness. Finally, Christian love looks to God as its source and turns in prayer to the Spirit of Christ for an understanding of the practical demands of loving others in Jesus' image.

Finally, because Christian marriage roots itself in a charism, or gift, of the Spirit of Jesus, one must look upon it as a divine call to ministry. That ministry occurs within the family itself as its members respond from their hearts to the ideal of Christian living that both possesses their hearts and stands in judgment over their conduct. In addition, families minister to others in Jesus' name through hospitality and other forms of practical ministry.[17]

Clearly, then, a contemporary theology of conversion points the way beyond the moral impasse created by the attempt to

understand human interpersonal relationships individualistically. That theology unmasks the moral selfishness inherent in
any purely utilitarian or expressive interpretation of love and
marriage. It also suggests a more comprehensive interpretation
of human love and marriage than the evangelical tradition ordinarily offers. Indeed, the transvaluation of natural marital love
in the love of charity suffuses both marriage and the family
with sacramental significance, for natural events take on sacramental meaning when they reveal the working of divine grace.

VII. CONVERTED CITIZENSHIP

Political thought in this country offers six identifiable strategies for understanding the public, or common, good. It contrasts the establishment and the populist strategies, neocapitalism and welfare liberalism, the administered society and
economic democracy. Let us recall the salient traits present in
each of these contrasts.

Around the turn of the century both populists and the economic establishment offered analogous understandings of the
common good. The elite members of the economic establishment attempted to construct humanitarian institutions to parallel the new corporations that had enriched them. Populists,
by contrast, espoused an egalitarian ethos that sought to expand the control of government over the economy. Nevertheless, both Andrew Carnegie and Eugene Debs saw work, welfare, and authority as tightly interwoven strands of American
life. Both sought an inclusive democratic community. Both stood
committed to efficiency, rationality, and science (*HH*, 267–70).

Welfare liberalism responded to the breakdown of the big
corporations during the Great Depression. It looked to government to espouse the cause of the underdog and to ensure
full employment, worker safety, the reindustrialization of America, and the protection of the environment. Neocapitalism developed in reaction to welfare liberalism. Neocapitalism looks
on the nation as an economy rather than as a polity. It privat-
izes concern for the poor and looks to the free market to integrate the national society. It also conceives of community as
the voluntary association of individuals. Both welfare liberal-

ism and neocapitalism seek to empower individuals to pursue
their private ends through the use of governmental structures,
even though the two positions employ different means to achieve
that goal (*HH*, 263–66).

One may also discern the contemporary emergence of two
other contrasting conceptions of the public good: the administered society and economic democracy. The proponents of
the administered society call for social groups—including business, labor, and government—to work together to promote stable
international economic growth: but they would tighten the hold
of corporate business on the collective life of the nation. The
defenders of economic democracy look to government to democ-
ratize the economy. They call for economic decentralization and
for popular control of the nation's economic structures (*HH*,
267–70).

Does a contemporary theology of conversion point the way
toward civic virtue that goes beyond individualistic strategies
for achieving the common good? Once again, I believe that it
can. As we have seen, a contemporary theology of conversion
distinguishes five forms of conversion in all: on the one hand,
the four kinds of personal conversion—affective, intellectual,
moral, and religious—and on the other hand, sociopolitical
conversion.

Sociopolitical conversion extends morality beyond the concerns of human interpersonal relationships into the realm of
institutional reform. In the process of so doing, sociopolitical
conversion deprivatizes the other forms of conversion. It does
so in two ways. First of all, sociopolitical conversion culminates in personal commitment to some public cause of universal moral import, like world hunger, nuclear disarmament,
justice for minorities and for political prisoners. Second, sociopolitical conversion confronts the convert with The Others—
with individuals and groups within the body politic alien from
one's personal experience, individuals and groups that challenge one's personal presuppositions and vested interests.

A contemporary theology of conversion, when embellished
with insights from Edwards, requires that Christian conversion
transvalue sociopolitical conversion. Christian conversion does
so by replacing rational conceptions of political, economic, and
social justice with Jesus' vision of the Kingdom. That vision

measures the justice or injustice of human social institutions. In other words, to the extent that human institutions fail to incarnate trust in God, a preferential option for the poor, the marginal, and the dispossessed, and mutual reconciliation in the active pursuit of peace, to that extent they fall short of the justice to which God summons us in Christ. That justice includes concern for the common good, a concern for creating the social conditions in which all persons and groups can contribute to and share in the benefits of society in a ready and adequate fashion.

Moreover, for the converted Christian, commitment to the realization of God's reign on earth as in heaven relativizes every other political and economic commitment. Those who executed Jesus understood well the revolutionary implications of this theme in his teaching.

The six traditional American conceptions of the public good described above fall woefully short of the universal moral concern which Christian conversion demands. Not only do they conceive the common good in categories tinged by individualism, but they also approach the problem of the common good within the confines of a narrow nationalism.

Only a conception of the common good that encompasses the whole of humanity can provide an adequte ethical foundation for a genuine renewal of civic virtue. The North American bishops understand this truth well when they join the pope in deploring the lack of an international political authority powerful enough to secure the global common good, when they fault this nation for so restricting aid to the Third World that it degenerates into "selective assistance based on an East-West assessment of North-South problems" (*EJA,* 259). The bishops show a similar universal moral concern when they fault our government for lagging behind other nations in promoting the cultural, economic, and political development of Third World countries, when they call for a global system of finance, when they challenge private investors to recognize their global moral responsibilities, and when they call upon the United States to exercise leadership in solving global economic problems instead of promoting the lethal trade of arms to nations that can ill afford to buy them (*EJA,* 248–321).

Of the six American versions of the common good, neo-

capitalism contradicts traditional Christian values most bla-
tantly, for it enshrines utilitarian individualism at the heart of
national policy and virtually absolves the government of its
responsibility to work for the common good in economic matters. Welfare liberals may overdraw the role government plays
in regulating the economy, but they at least recognize the importance of that role. In the last analysis, however, all six versions offer a partial account of the common good. In effect
they replace the moral concept of the common good with a
particular strategy for achieving it. In *Economic Justice for
All,* the American Catholic bishops show greater wisdom. They
present the pursuit of the common good as a moral ideal and
therefore remain free to espouse a variety of economic strategies for achieving it.

VIII. CONCLUSION

If Americans hope to escape from the ethical impasses into
which individualistic patterns of thinking betray them, they
need to find new ways to think and talk about personal and
social realities. In this essay I have tried to suggest that a theology of conversion offers a viable alternative to individualistic
modes of ethical perception. I have attempted to derive from
the thought of Jonathan Edwards an insight into two dynamics that Christian conversion contributes to the total process
of conversion. I have suggested that when a theology of conversion takes account of those dynamics it possesses the speculative wherewithal to move beyond the moral impasses into
which individualism betrays the human conscience.

One can, of course, mount a rational criticism of those same
moral impasses. The logic of the preceding analysis, however,
leads one to question the ultimate adequacy of such a rational
critique. Religious commitment endows human life with ultimate meaning. Moreover, in the person of Jesus the reality of
God stands normatively revealed within human history. Ultimately, then, the cultivation of true civic virtue in Edwards's
sense of *true* requires, as he saw two centuries ago, cordial consent to divine beauty incarnate.

If so, however, a contemporary retrieval of the American religious tradition which addresses with any adequacy the short-comings of utilitarian and expressive individualism requires finally far more than abandoning individualistic patterns of speech. It requires more than polite, academic discussions of American civil religion. The gospel imperative, "Repent and believe the good news," lies at the heart of our religious tradition, despite its pluralism. Ultimately contemporary Americans will find their way beyond the ethical malaise into which individualism has betrayed them only by submitting to that imperative. Such a national conversion of heart would indeed create a very different kind of social ecology from the one in which we presently languish. It would effect precisely the kind of national moral experiment for which the American bishops call in *Economic Justice for All* when they challenge contemporary Americans to a collective search for the common good (*EJA,* 4).

NOTES

1. Alexis de Tocqueville, *Democracy in America,* trans. Henry Reeve, 2 vols. (New York: Collier, 1900) 2:104.

2. Ibid., 104, 129–34.

3. Orestes Brownson, *The American Republic: Its Constitution, Tendencies, and Destiny* (New York: P. O'Shea, 1865), 4–5.

4. John Dewey, *Individualism Old and New* (New York: Capricorn, 1962).

5. Josiah Royce, *The Philosophy of Loyalty* (New York: Macmillan, 1908).

6. Robert Bellah et al., *Habits of the Heart: Individualism and Commitment in American Life* (Berkeley and Los Angeles: University of California Press, 1985), 278–81. Hereafter referred to as *HH.*

7. Cited in *Jonathan Edwards: A Profile,* ed. David Levin (New York: Hill and Wang, 1969), 26–27.

8. Jonathan Edwards, *A Treatise Concerning Religious Affections,* ed. John E. Smith (New Haven, Conn.: Yale University Press, 1959). Hereafter referred to as *RA.*

9. Jonathan Edwards, *The Nature of True Virtue,* ed. William K. Frankena (Ann Arbor: University of Michigan Press, 1960), 3. Hereafter referred to as *TV.*

10. For a lucid discussion of Edwards's theory of true virtue, see William C. Spohn, S.J., "Sovereign Beauty: Jonathan Edwards and

the Nature of True Virtue," *Theological Studies* 42 (September 1981): 394–421.

11. See Perry Miller, *The New England Mind: The Seventeenth Century* (Boston: Beacon Press, 1961).

12. Cf. Bernard Lonergan, *Method in Theology* (New York: Herder and Herder, 1972), 235–92; Donald L. Gelpi, S.J., *Experiencing God: A Theology of Human Emergence* (New York: Paulist Press, 1978), *Charism and Sacrament: A Theology of Christian Conversion* (New York: Paulist Press, 1976), *The Divine Mother: A Trinitarian Theology of the Holy Spirit* (New York: University Press of America, 1984), "The Converting Jesuit," *Studies in the Spirituality of Jesuits* 17 (May 1985), "Religious Conversion: A New Way of Being," in *The Human Experience of Conversion,* ed. Francis A. Eigo, O.S.A. (Villanova, Pa.: Villanova University Press, 1987), pp. 175–202; Walter Conn, *Conversion: Perspectives on Personal and Social Transformation* (New York: Alba House, 1978), *Christian Conversion: A Developmental Interpretation of Autonomy and Surrender* (New York: Paulist Press, 1986); and Robert M. Doran, *Subject and Psyche: Ricoeur, Jung, and the Search for Foundations* (New York: University Press of America, 1977), *Psychic Conversion and Theological Foundations: Toward a Reorientation of the Human Sciences* (Chico, Calif.: Scholars Press, 1981).

13. For a more detailed discussion of the theological foundations for these insights, see Gelpi, *Experiencing God,* 259–323; *Charism and Sacrament,* 27–62; *Divine Mother,* 183–213; "Breath Baptism in the Synoptics," in *Charismatic Experiences in History,* ed. Cecil M. Robeck, Jr. (Peabody, Md.: Hendrickson Publishers, 1985), 15–43.

14. National Conference of Catholic Bishops, *Economic Justice for All: Catholic Social Teaching and the U.S. Economy* (Washington, D.C.: National Conference of Catholic Bishops, 1986), 31–32. Hereafter referred to as *EJA.*

15. Cf. Otto Bird, "The Complexity of Love," *Thought* 39 (June 1964): 210–20.

16. Jeanette Lauer and Robert Lauer, "Marriages Made to Last," *Psychology Today,* June 1985, 22–26.

17. See Gelpi, *Charism and Sacrament,* 157–86; *Gaudium et spes,* 47–52.

"Johnny Loves Mary Forever": What Therapy Doesn't Know about Love

Stephen C. Rowntree, S.J.

Americans think and talk about love in two very different ways.[1] The less commonly spoken language, the evangelical Christian, understands love "as a firmly planted, permanent commitment embodying obligations that transcend the immediate feelings or wishes of the partners . . ." (*HH*, 93). The more commonly spoken language, the "therapeutic," understands love as a feeling and justifies relationships "only so long as they meet the needs of the two people involved" (*HH*, 108). The therapeutic interpretation of love is so popular because it harmonizes with American individualism, especially the view "that social bonds can be firm only if they rest on the free, self-interested choices of individuals" (*HH*, 109).

We have good reason to fear the atomizing tendencies of modern politics and economics, based as they are on individual rights and individual self-seeking respectively. With Rousseau and Tocqueville, we ought to see love and marriage as essential antidotes to these tendencies.[2] But the therapeutic view of love, which makes self-seeking the essence of love, threatens these antidotes. Self-seeking might then spread unchecked.

In this essay I hope to show what is wrong with a therapeutic account of love. I will argue that it distorts romantic love's essential nature. I will claim that romantic love typically leads to making commitments, to sharing interests, and even to having children. The therapeutic interpretation is blind to these developments. To make this argument I will draw on philosophical descriptions of romantic love's unfolding as emotion.[3] I share *Habits of the Heart*'s underlying account of authentic human development. I will appeal to the authors' teleological theory to show why commitment, shared interests, and parenthood are good for humans.[4] I will acknowledge the valid insights of the therapeutic account but ground them more adequately.

If my argument is correct, romantic love's development is an antidote to isolating individualism, widely available and not dependent on religious faith. Individualistic Americans commonly speak only two languages of love. I articulate a third, preferable to both the evangelical Christian and the therapeutic, because it is more adequate to the experience of love itself. To arrive at this conclusion, I will first sketch the therapeutic account of love and then describe at length romantic love's development. My description will correct therapeutic errors and incorporate therapeutic truths. I acknowledge that my claims about romantic love are bold. They require both nuancing and defense. Baldly stated they sound too good to be true.

I. THE THERAPEUTIC INTERPRETATION OF LOVE

Without question, the therapeutic interpretation of love is widespread. The "Living" sections of daily newspapers carry frequent articles filled with therapeutic principles on how to handle "relationships." Drugstore book racks are filled with self-help books advocating therapeutic views.

The therapeutic interpretation of love has several themes. Feelings are central. "Feelings define love . . . permanent commitment can only come from having the proper clarity, honesty, and openness about one's feelings" (*HH,* 98). Obligations and love conflict. This contrasts with what *Habits of the Heart* takes to be the evangelical Christian view, according to which obligation founds love and marriage (*HH,* 93). The therapeutic attitude "begins with the self rather than with a set of external obligations" (*HH,* 98). It implies that marriage, as an institution having a public structure with defined rights and duties into which couples "enter," alienates rather than unites: "External obligations can only interfere with the capacity for love and relatedness" (*HH,* 98).

Another central therapeutic principle holds that self-love comes first, then love for another. "Before one can love others one must learn to love one's self" (*HH*, 98). The therapeutic view grounds self-love in autonomy. In order to achieve self-love and self-acceptance, I must free myself from anyone else's standards. For insofar as I measure myself against standards set by others, I may well fail to measure up. Since standards set by others may conflict, when they do I must inevitably fail to satisfy some people's expectations. If, however, I only seek to meet my own expectations and I sufficiently moderate these to what I can achieve, I can succeed and hence feel good about myself.

Therapy aims to foster the autonomy that grounds self-love. The therapist encourages the client to express all feelings, however negative, aggressive, or outrageous. The therapist responds nonjudgmentally to whatever is revealed. The therapist's unconditional acceptance encourages the client to acknowledge and take responsibility for all of his or her actions and feelings.

According to the therapeutic interpretation, love consists in the *sharing of feelings* by such independent, self-reliant, and self-loving individuals: "sharing of feelings between similar, authentic, expressive selves—selves who feel complete and do not need others and do not rely on others to define their own standards or desires—becomes the basis for the therapeutic ideal of love (*HH*, 100). Love thus models itself on therapy (*HH*, 100). In the ideal relationship each partner listens and accepts the other's feelings, and in turn reveals and shares his or her deepest feelings. "Both partners in a relationship become therapists in a reciprocal exchange" (*HH*, 101).

A relationship is justified in the therapeutic view because it meets the needs of the two people involved (*HH*, 107). When it no longer meets their needs, the relationship must end. As one of my students wrote recently, "Commitment, what does it mean? Does it mean forever no matter what happens, or does it mean loving and caring for as long as the relationship is advantageous to both persons?" The answer seemed so obvious it did not need stating.

We would do well to regard the language of mutual self-interest in this interpretation of love as an intrusion from economic and bureaucratic spheres. Self-interested individuals making mutually advantageous bargains with one another define the essence of the market economy. People now begin to think of love in similar terms. Marriage and family were once thought to be structured on principles opposed to the economic sphere, a "haven in a heartless world" (*HH, 85–90*). But now heartless self-seeking invades marriage and the family. Because "a kind of selfishness is essential to love," self-sacrifice seems incompatible with love, according to the therapeutic account (*HH, 109–10*).

Since the central content of love consists in sharing of feelings, one obligation binds: the obligation to be open (*HH, 101*). Because of this, an inability or unwillingness to share ends a relationship. When mutual revelation of feelings stops, love's essence disappears.

Such are the fundamentals of the therapeutic interpretation. While they obscure much in romantic love's development, they do contain some truths. My account of love's development will show both the errors and the truths of the therapeutic account. I will argue now that it misses romantic love's movement toward making commitments, sharing interests, and having children, and it correctly identifies communication as integral to love.

II. ROMANTIC LOVE'S DEVELOPMENT

Romantic love has been the basis for marriage in America since at least the nineteenth century. Men and women get married because they love one another, not because of their families' economic or political interests. Marriage for love and "individualism" are inseparably joined. Where you find one you find the other. "Romantic love is a quintessential form of expressive individualism" (*HH, 73*).

What distinguishes romantic love from love of parent, school, God, and so on is its sexual nature (*RL, 3*). Romantic love involves an interest in the beloved as man or woman, as sexual being. The feelings associated with "falling in love" or "being in love" are feelings of attraction to the other as sexually embodied.

A. Commitment to an Irreplaceable Other

While rooted in our embodied condition, this feeling is *not the experience of a drive or physical need*. Being in love is not

like being hungry or thirsty. The person in love desires only
the particular person he or she has fallen in love with. David
desired Bathsheba and would have rejected any advice such as,
"Why bother with her; why not Nicoah? She's available. You're
putting yourself to much too much trouble. You can surely get
what you want more simply." In contrast, when one is hungry
or thirsty, any food or drink will satisfy these needs. Even if
one wants a steak one does not want a *particular* piece of steak
from a *particular* steer. Any piece of sirloin of equal quality
will do. Romantic love is a "social feeling" or a "particularistic
emotion," a "feeling whose object is not anything of a certain
kind, but some particular individual" (*RL,* 39). The intentionality of the emotion is interpersonal. A particular individual
Roberta is in love with a particular individual James. Thus
when someone announces he or she is "in love," the obvious
question is, "with whom?"

Because romantic love's object is some particular individual,
the therapeutic focus on love as "meeting needs" may distort
a central ingredient. What meets a need is ordinarily nonspecific
and nonparticular. If I need a date for a dance, any of several
people might suffice. Or if I need someone to share my feelings
with, any sensitive and empathetic listener will do. When I need
a therapist, I need a qualified person, but I do not need any
particular therapist.

As long as one is in love, one is turned toward and related
to a particular individual. A special relationship with this one
person exists. The lover focuses attention beyond himself and
on the beloved. The lover is moved to action. He wants to be
with his beloved. He tries to ingratiate himself with her, to charm
her, to win her love in turn. Often this effort dominates his life.
His whole life becomes concentrated on winning her. Such a
relationship filled with concern for the beloved contrasts sharply
with any deal I may make in the market with an agreeable buyer
or seller. Insofar as the therapeutic language articulates love
in market terms, it distorts and obscures the richness that lovers experience. Lovers are no longer isolated egos, but connected and entwined partners.

While romantic love focuses on a particular person, the connections involved go beyond the bond between two individuals.
Van de Vate shows that the development of romantic love involves participation in a public, shared social and cultural prac-

tice. This is so because the crucial moment in the development
of romantic love is the declaration of love. To say "I love you"
to another person is to perform *a public linguistic act that has
a history and meaning given by one's culture.* According to Van
de Vate, this declaration commits one to a course of action,
what he calls a "policy." When John tells Marsha, "I love you,"
she does not understand him to be telling her about his particular feeling at that moment:

> Should she discover him, moments later, embracing Rosie, she
> will conclude he lied when he said he loved her, and he will
> not be able to justify himself by saying feelings come and go
> (although feelings do just that). What she takes him to have
> promised is not a sudden flush of feeling, but an enduring com-
> mitment to action, a policy. To be sure this policy originates
> in a feeling and depends upon that feeling, but it is supposed
> to be a far more lasting and reliable affair. (*RL,* 15)

A person has little control over particular feelings. When feeling depressed, one cannot will euphoria. One can control action. The depressed person can go exercise, for example.

The declaration of love comes after a period of action carefully calculated to elicit the response, "I love you too." It is an
art to generate a responding love in the beloved. Advice-to-the-
lovelorn columns testify to the intricacies and perils of this ritual.

A declaration of love is the offer, then, of a certain kind of
commitment. If it is reciprocated, a mutual commitment may
take place. Mutual obligations and commitments take effect
only when the declaration of love is returned. "When Marsha
says, 'I love you too, John,' she promises to adopt a policy that
intermeshes with the policy John promises, and we may say
that a compact or contract or agreement is formed, a set of
mutual obligations and expectations" (*RL,* 15). Persons who
have assumed mutual obligations by declaring love to one another may be unfaithful. But they violate a commitment in so
doing and should feel guilty. Each knows what's been prom-
ised and what violates the commitment.

The development from the feeling of love to the mutual declaration of love is the development from psychological state to
culturally relative and conditioned social practice. As social practice, romantic love resembles a game of baseball or a liturgy.

The expectations, standards, and norms that constitute romantic love must be taught and learned just as one learns how to play baseball or how to say Mass.

A principal task of adolescence is learning the rules and rituals of love. Magazines, novels, popular music, and television shows all teach teenagers how feelings of love are to be expressed. Peer groups also help hand on the rules and rituals, which change and develop from year to year and from generation to generation.

Since romantic love is a social practice involving shared standards, norms, and expectations, obligations and love are not absolutely opposed. The therapeutic interpretation mistakenly claims love and obligation are absolutely opposed. It thinks of love's obligation as necessarily "external." It overlooks the possibility that lovers might willingly assume obligations in order to fulfill their own deepest desires.

The therapeutic account is not alone in opposing desire and obligation. The Kantian tradition in philosophy, for example, finds the clash of inclination and duty at the heart of morality. According to this view, spontaneous inclinations and desires do not arise from reason. They lack, therefore, the universality characteristic of valid moral judgments. Inclination and duty surely *may* clash. My duty not to injure my neighbor clashes with my inclination to strangle him for playing loud music at 4:00 A.M.

Must *all* inclinations and desires, however, clash with duty? The saint wants to nurse the plague-stricken. Parents want to give their children the best. Lovers want to bind themselves to one another. Kierkegaard's Judge William claims that love and duty harmonize:

> [W]hen this [duty] appears before it, it is not as a stranger, a shameless intruder, who nevertheless has such authority that one dare not by virtue of the mysteriousness of love show him the door. No, duty comes as an old friend, an intimate, a confidant, whom the lovers mutually recognize in the deepest secret of their love. (AV, 149)

Lovers do not automatically make commitments. If they do not make a commitment, however, their love ends. They have missed a chance for a richer life since love constitutes an essential ingredient in full human development. Lovers are not "empty selves," but "constituted selves" (*HH,* 152) through and in their mutual love. Those who refuse to commit themselves thereby impoverish themselves.[5]

Because romantic love leads to commitments that shape lovers' future actions, it requires more than momentary action. The lovers' joint project involves temporal continuity. It develops a history. This history may be relatively brief, however. Romantic relationships may last a year or two and then break up. Many people have been involved in several of these short-term relationships. They hardly provide the "communities of memory and hope" (*HH,* 152–54) that our authors see as essential to authentic human development.

On the other hand, romantic love frequently does lead to marriage. While not a sufficient condition for marriage, it is surely a necessary condition in our kind of society.[6] Being in love motivates acceptance of the heavier and much more specific commitment of marriage, which can be a genuine community of memory and hope. As Van de Vate observed:

> In modern Western societies, romantic love is supposed to lead to monogamous marriage. . . . Here the prescription is simple enough: when in love, get married. . . . Two persons of the opposite sex live together, share property, have sexual intercourse, bear and raise children, and provide one another approval and emotional support, cherish one another's family ties. . . . (*RL,* 49)

It is a fact about Western societies that romantic love is the basis for marriage.

Is marriage based on love more than a cultural peculiarity of individualistic societies? Can we interpret marriage as the fulfillment of romantic love's immanent purpose? In particular, can we understand marriage's permanent, "till death do us part" commitment as realizing romantic love's teleology? Judge William tries to do so. He claims that falling in love is based on an immediate unreasoned response to beauty (AV, 21). But he thinks desire for a particular person based on beauty may be simple lust.[7] According to him, "[W]hat distinguishes all love from lust is that it bears an impress on eternity" (AV, 22).

Judge William makes no metaphysical or religous claim here.[8] He is drawing attention to something lovers feel. It is the feeling expressed by a graffito I recently saw on an overpass: "Johnny Loves Mary Forever." In the present, love must seem to be without end. And to think of its future end is to destroy its present existence. Scruton observed: "While I love, I can have no plans for the extinction of love's purpose; to have such plans is to have ceased to love."[9] Robert Solomon agrees. While disputing my claim that romantic love develops into marriage, he nonetheless believes that it includes "the desire and the hope" that it endure.[10] The multimillion declarations that Johnny loves Mary, therefore, all implicitly include what the unknown Johnny made explicit. Love is always experienced as "forever."

This "eternity" of romantic love (granted its reality) is a fragile thing—even a ridiculous thing. Sensual beauty fades, and with it my love. Once I was in love with Mary Anne, another time with Patricia. As Judge William explains, "But since this assurance [of eternity] is founded upon a natural determinant, the eternal is thus based upon the temporal and thereby cancels itself. . . . It shows itself to be an illusion, and for this reason it is easy to make ridiculous" (AV, 21–22).

Romantic love aims to last forever, but it is bound to alter because it is based only on the accident of fluctuating sensuous beauty. As a mere feeling, it is passively determined and changes as its object changes. If it is to last, love must be transformed. Commitment transforms it so its immanent purpose may be realized. The initial love can be maintained only if a commitment is made. To realize its impulse to eternity, romantic love must acquire a history.

For humans live in time, and the eternity we can attain in time is the eternity of being the same in each successive instant. Judge William describes this as "internal history," which involves "an eternity in which the temporal has not vanished like an ideal moment, but in which it is constantly present as a real moment (AV, 140). To become eternal, love must maintain itself instant by instant, minute by minute, hour by hour, day by day, week by week, month by month, year by year. "[T]he gist of the matter is to preserve love in time. If this is impossible, then love is an impossibility" (AV, 140).

Judge William interprets the day-in, day-out fidelity of spouses as the truly heroic achievement. Speaking of a husband faithful for fifteen years, the judge says:

> He has not fought with lions and ogres, but with the most dangerous enemy: with time. . . . He alone, therefore, has triumphed over time. . . . The married man, being a true conqueror, has not killed time but has saved it and preserved it in eternity. (AV, 141)

The husband must daily and hourly continue his fight to maintain his love for his wife, and so likewise she. As Judge William concludes: "Conjugal love has its foe in time, its triumph in time, its eternity in time" (AV, 141).

Judge William claims that "the healthy individual lives at once both in hope and in recollection, and only thereby does his life acquire true and substantial continuity" (AV, 144–45). It is precisely those who are married who have this union of hope and recollection, while bachelors, he claims, "are for the most part addicted either to hope or to recollection" (AV, 146).

Judge William thus finds in the unfolding of romantic love, especially its impulse to eternity, the basis for marriage's "till death do us part" commitment. The acquisition of eternity in time through day-in-and-day-out acts of love involves a balance of memory and hope. Such a commitment constituting a community of memory and hope is necessary for authentic human development. For *continuity* of identity is essential for full, rich selfhood (*HH,* 139) and marriage's balance of hope and recollection provides precisely this "true and substantial continuity" (AV, 145). As Phyllis Rose observed, marriage's appeal is largely "narrative": "the clear cut beginnings and endings it offers, the richly complicated middle."[11]

Lovers may realize the impulse to eternity if they commit themselves to marriage. They jointly achieve shared community and more fully developed selves. But decisions are requisite to achieve these goods. The "I do" of the wedding day is only the first of many. Judge William's account of married love agrees with the often stated insight that couples must work at a relationship. Husband and wife must realize they have pledged to love anew each day. If this promise is not redeemed daily, their marriage may fall apart. The mere words said at the altar guarantee nothing.

Judge William calls love between husband and wife "conjugal love." As we have seen, he claims this love realizes romantic love's inner tendencies. Others have vehemently disagreed. Byron states the objection succinctly: "Love is heaven, marriage is hell."

The opposing argument also appeals to the experience of romantic love, especially its initial stages. At first, romantic love involves ardor, excitement, and intensity. The lover seems to have fallen for an altogether extraordinary creature. "He is the handsomest, smartest, greatest man alive." "She is the most beautiful, the cleverest, the most wonderful woman in the world." All of life seems wonderfully transformed. If we take the initial intoxication and excitement as the essence of romantic love, marriage, no doubt, seems its polar opposite. For those who value intensity, excitement, and novelty above all else, the first stages of love are the most treasured. Rather than settle into the routine and realism of marriage, they seek over and over again to recapture love's initial ardor and intoxication. If such is love, marriage indeed is hell![12]

What about ardor, intensity, excitement? Are these the highest values? Clearly they are not in the account of authentic human development examined so far in this paper. To be a fully developed self requires, rather, continuity of identity through time. Conjugal love does leave behind romantic love's intoxication. But marriage means gain and not loss, because the historical continuity of love is better than the momentary excitement of passion, and because enduring relationships enrich the self, while ephemeral ones impoverish it.[13]

B. Sharing Interests

Another major problem of the therapeutic interpretation of love concerns the sharp distinction drawn between self and other. Some have seen a solution to this problem also in a close examination of romantic love's unfolding. Thus J. M. F. Hunter, who sees the declaration of love as the critical moment in love's development in the same way as Van de Vate, claims it involves a commitment to *identity of interests:* "The interests of the two become as one. . . . When we profess love, we can be expected to give ungrudgingly and to treat the loved one's interests as if they were our own."[14] Roger Scruton sees romantic love, what he calls "erotic love," as a union of love and desire. And like Hunter he claims that central to love are shared interests. He explains that when interests truly are shared, the beloved's good is experienced as it if were one's own good. The opposition of self and other is thus overcome:

> The friendship of esteem becomes love just so soon as reciprocity becomes community: that is, just so soon as all distinction between my interests and your interests is overcome. Your desires are then reasons for me, in exactly the same way, and to the same extent, that my desires are reasons for me. . . . Thus he who loves aims at the other's good, in just the same way that he aims at his own good.[15]

The therapeutic attitude toward love cannot justify self-sacrifice. The notion of love's shared interests explains how love can and does involve sacrifice for others. The authors of *Habits of the Heart* noted the evangelical Christian's acceptance of self-sacrifice but observed: "Many others were uncomfortable with the idea. It was not that they were unwilling to make compromises or sacrifices for their spouses, but they were troubled by the ideal of self-denial the term 'sacrifice' implied" (*HH,* 109).

However, they go on to attribute to their respondents a view that seems precisely to have appreciated how shared interests do overcome the self-other dichotomy: If you really wanted to do something for the person you loved, they said it would not be a sacrifice in such a case. But why would my painful efforts to get in condition so I could eventually enjoy better health not be called sacrifice? And if I identify my interests with those I love, then I could willingly sacrifice myself for their interests as I do for my own. The therapeutic attitude seems to imply that self-sacrifice is not really self-sacrifice unless it is contrary in all senses to the self's good. This misunderstands the primary way in which the self-other dichotomy can be overcome. As MacIntyre shows, the sharp opposition between altruism and egoism emerges only when the notion of shared goods (or shared interests) is lost.[16] Granted the pursuit of shared goods no longer defines the realms of work and politics, it is not surprising that shared goods persist in love relationships. For here the notion has its original and obvious home. Even among individualistic Americans, we find the persistence of a sense of shared interests among those who otherwise have great difficulty in thinking how self and other can be joined. Again I have argued that closer attention to the elements of romantic love (here the commitment to making the beloved's interests one's own) involved in the declaration "I love you" reveals what the therapeutic interpretation with its language of love as ful-filling individuals' needs conceals: in love the dichotomy of self and other is overcome, for when people love one another they share common interests.

My account, like the therapeutic, makes communication cen-tral to marriage. Lovers who have committed themselves to one another and who wish to share common interests must com-municate freely and openly with one another. They cannot make their beloveds' interests their own if they do not know them. They must also come to mutually acceptable agreements about issues such as division of work both inside and outside the home. Initial conflicts of desires may well exist. Marriage commits spouses to work them out.

Judge William thus argues that "candor, open-heartedness, revelation, understanding — these constitute the life principle of marriage, without which it fails to be beautiful or even moral." Since self-disclosure is the "life principle" of marriage, the in-ability to communicate about oneself is an absolute impedi-ment to marriage: "When the individual life is so complicated that it cannot reveal itself," the individual must not marry (AV, 118–19).

My account also agrees with the therapeutic view that hus-band and wife must love one another unconditionally. They ought to accept one another as they are, faults and all. My ac-count emphatically *disagrees,* however, with the therapeutic claim that lovers are "firmly autonomous individual[s]" with-out need of one another's love (HH, 99). Lovers are deeply dependent on one another for their happiness and well-being.[17] The person who loves another beyond all others bestows an irreplaceable affirmation of the other's *unique* worth. A thera-pist's unconditional positive regard, which is shown to all cli-ents without distinction, has effects altogether different from what lovers bestow on one another. And to lose one's lover is to lose this unique affirmation.

Because lovers' common interests mean that each experiences the other's good as one's own, the beloved's suffering—or worse, loss—is experienced as one's own suffering or loss. Lovers are hostages to fate. Their happiness is bound up with their beloved's. The death of a beloved always causes deep loss and grief. To be invulnerable and immune to such suffering, one must transcend love for particular, inevitably vulnerable and fragile persons. In Plato's *Symposium* the ascent to the ocean of beauty teaches that true self-sufficiency, true independence in love requires transcending loves for any *particular person.*[18] Therapeutic love, insofar as it leads to independent selves who have no need for one another, means the death of love.

To argue that dependence is an intrinsic feature of love is not to deny that dependence can be excessive. Lovers should not lose themselves in one another. Sharing interests does not mean that lovers give up their own wants. The logic of love's shared interests implies that lovers have and assert interests. Only then can both identify and take as his or her own the other's interest. Moreover, a long tradition of love and friendship insists that both flourish most fully between equals.

C. HAVING CHILDREN

I have so far argued that romantic love develops into marital commitment and shared interests. For most Americans, however, marriage also means starting a family (see note 25). Becoming parents would seem to be an obvious way in which men and women develop richer identities.[19] Parents have in their children concrete ties to the future and multiple responsibilities in the present. Parents, as a result, develop fuller, more richly constituted selves than nonparents, other things being equal.[20]

Some have claimed romantic love's "long-term project, which will resolve the tensions and fulfill the ancillary wishes and needs that arise in the experience of the basic intentional structure"[21] also includes having children. Contemporary Catholic sexual ethics, for example, makes a claim akin to this. It holds that love and procreation are the two coequal and inseparable ends of sex. The argument I am about to examine differs, however, in being based not on biological teleology but on emotional teleology.[22]

The seer Diotima's argument in the *Symposium* linking love to procreation anticipated the argument that makes procreation part of love's goal. Diotima helps Socrates to realize that since love desires to possess the good not just temporarily but forever, it expresses itself in procreation.[23]

That the previously noted "eternity" of romantic love can be achieved in time not merely through commitment, but also through having children who will live on after parents have died, seems an obvious conclusion to draw. Diotima's argument suggests this precise connection.

Hegel formulates another argument that children are integral to romantic love's development. Like Judge William, Hegel argued that romantic love develops into marital commitment. But he went on to claim that even married love is incomplete because it is only "a unity of inwardness or disposition." Outwardly husband and wife are two separate bodies. But in their children, the couple's love can take embodied form. As Hegel puts it:

> It is only in the children that the unity itself exists externally, objectively, and explicitly as a unity, because the parents love the children as their love, as the embodiment of their own substance.[24]

National survey data show a very high incidence of both desires for children and actual childbirths.[25] Such widespread desires and high percentage of couples having children might be read as some evidence that having children completes romantic love's project.

Parents also develop links with wider communities. Their children's education, recreation, and artistic activities tie parents into numerous organizations shared with other parents. Parents serve on school boards, belong to Parent-Teacher Associations, and teach religion classes. Frequently such organizations get involved in local politics, for example, to increase school funding or improve recreational opportunities. Parents of school-age children are thus commonly involved in many voluntary organizations beyond the narrow circle of the family. In fact I am amazed at both the extent and the intensity of parents' engagement in groups outside the home. I find the claim that the "family is no longer an integral part of a larger moral ecology tying the individual to community, Church, and nation" (*HH*, 112) at best an overstatement, at worst simply false.

If romantic love's immanent development includes having children as expression and prolongation of that love, then it provides yet another counter to isolating individualism. I am by no means claiming that love's development is the only explanation of why married couples have children. But in any case they do, and their doing so involves rich social bonds both with their children and with other parents. Having children is a strong antidote to isolating individualism.

III. CONCLUSION

I have argued at length that romantic love develops into marital commitment to an irreplaceable other. I also tried to show that it leads to a joining of interests that overcomes the dichotomy of self and other. Finally I have claimed that it even develops into parenthood. I grant that choices are necessary to achieve these ends. People may choose at times not to realize some or all of them. These ends appeal to people, I have argued, because they seem to be ways to realize love more fully. Since love is a central constituent of full human development, such choices are good choices.[26]

If this phenomenology correctly describes romantic love, it reveals aspects of romantic love that the therapeutic interpretation conceals. Lovers who commit themselves eternally to one another acquire a temporal continuity of memory and hope, rich and complex connections with one another in sharing interests, and with the future and other parents in having children. It suggests that *within romantic love itself* are antidotes to isolating individualism, antidotes overlooked by the therapeutic and evangelical Christian interpretations of love. My interpretation of romantic love's development suggests a third language of love and, as such, is an important complement to our authors' account. They do not find *within love* antidotes to therapeutic dissolution. This paper has tried to do precisely that.

If romantic love and marital love as I have interpreted them are alive and well in the United States, these bulwarks against isolating and self-seeking individualism remain strong.[27] What is the evidence? The continuing high percentage of persons marrying (93 percent of males, 95 percent of females), a high degree of marital satisfaction (approximately 90 percent of men and women surveyed by Caplow were either "very satisfied" or "satisfied" with their marriages), and high rates of remarriage (75 percent of divorced men and 67 percent of divorced women remarry) are evidence that love as described flourishes.[28]

On the other hand, among contemporary Americans one finds an "increased tolerance of people who reject marriage as a way of life" (*HH*, 110).[29] Caplow found a dramatic increase in toleration of *all* kinds in contemporary Middletown. But this theoretical tolerance for *others* who might reject marriage is no evidence that a high percentage of people reject marriage for *themselves*. The percentage of people actually marrying suggests the opposite.

The high rate of divorce might also suggest a weakening of romantic love and an upsurge of isolating individualism. However, an equally plausible argument is that the high divorce rate testifies to romantic love's power. Thus marriages that fail to achieve love's goals, such as free and open communication and agreement to have children, are dissolved. The formerly married then seek to achieve love's goal.[30] The high divorce rate, then, may be evidence that today's persons insist on realizing romantic love's goals and will be content with nothing less.[31]

Some read contemporary sexual liberation as a strong threat to romantic love.[32] Insofar as sexual liberation focuses primarily on individuals' sexual pleasure, no doubt it is. But even those who argue for sex without commitment generally argue that sex with love is better. The unanswered question is whether one can have *both:* might not sex for pleasure threaten sex for love? Characteristic modern discussions of sex (Havelock Ellis, Alfred Kinsey, Masters and Johnson) do think of sex separated from love.[33] Such interpretations, like the therapeutic, do threaten romantic love's development.

To what extent language *can* disrupt romantic love's development, and to what extent it *does,* remain open questions. With Caplow, I read the evidence optimistically. Romantic love is alive and well. As it unfolds people are encouraged to make choices

that bind them together. They resist the threat of becoming
isolated and empty selves.

NOTES

1. Robert Bellah et al., *Habits of the Heart: Individualism and
Commitment in American Life* (Berkeley and Los Angeles: Univer-
sity of California Press, 1985), esp. chap. 4, "Love and Marriage."
Hereafter referred to as *HH*.

2. For an account of this as Jean-Jacques Rousseau's central
theme, see Allan Bloom, "Rousseau on the Equality of the Sexes," in
Justice and Equality Here and Now, ed. Frank S. Lucash (Ithaca, N.Y.,
and London: Cornell University Press, 1986), 68–88. Tocqueville incorporated and developed Rousseau's ideas, according to Bloom.

3. Emotions are not simply raw and bodily feelings, like acid
indigestion, but mental states defined by their objects. Emotions also
involve tendencies to action. Thus I become afraid when I see a wolf
running toward me and I am moved to run or to protect myself in
some other way. If I realize the "wolf" is actually a dog on a long
leash, my fear disappears immediately and my course of action
changes. Roger Scruton's *Sexual Desire: A Moral Philosophy of the
Erotic* (New York: Free Press, 1986) applies this basic understanding of emotion to sexual arousal, sexual desire, and erotic (what I
am calling "romantic") love. I draw on Scruton and other applications of this approach, especially Dwight Van de Vate's *Romantic
Love: A Philosophical Inquiry* (University Park, Pa.: Pennsylvania State
University Press, 1981), and Soren Kierkegaard's pseudonym Judge
William, "The Aesthetic Validity of Marriage," in *Either/Or,* 2 vols.,
trans. Walter Lowrie, rev. and foreword by Howard A. Johnson (Princeton, N.J.: Princeton University Press, 1971), to articulate the immanent development of romantic love. To anticipate the form of argument to be made, note, for example, the following from Scruton: "The
intentionality of sexual desire, like the intentionality of any other social attitude, involves distinct stages of development. . . . In delineat-
ing the fulfillment of a state of mind, one is recommending a long-
term project, which will resolve the tensions and fulfill the ancillary
wishes and needs, that arise in the experience of the basic intentional
structure" (*Sexual Desire,* 241). Internal references to Van de Vate's
Romantic Love will be abbreviated *RL;* references to Kierkegaard's
"The Aesthetic Validity of Marriage" will be abbreviated AV.

4. Bellah and his coauthors accept the argument that authentic
development means the realization of distinctive human potentials.

Central to a fully realized life, "the good life," in this account, are relationships with others. An unloving human is a stunted human. I emphatically agree.

Therapeutic theory and practice misunderstand basic constituents of the good life. For example, "the ideal therapeutic relationship" is "one in which everything is completely conscious and all parties know how they feel and what they want." This is what the authors label "complete psychological contractualism," which "leads to the notion of an absolutely empty relationship. And this empty relationship cannot possibly sustain the richness and continuity that the therapeutically inclined most want . . ." (*HH,* 139). Above all else, freeing oneself from commitments frustrates authentic human development. The "absolutely free self" turns out to be the "absolutely empty self." Persons who "want not empty but rich and coherent selves" (*HH,* 139) thereby thwart their deepest desires.

Habits of the Heart draws throughout on Alasdair MacIntyre's account of the teleological tradition. This tradition makes a normative account of human development, the human "telos," central to moral argument. See MacIntyre's *After Virtue,* 2nd ed. (Notre Dame, Ind.: University of Notre Dame Press, 1984).

5. See note 4 above.

6. Family historians debate the origins of marriage based on love. Alan MacFarlane claims to find it in England all the way back into the Middle Ages. See his *Marriage and Love in England: Modes of Reproduction 1300−1840* (Oxford: B. Blackwell, 1986). Lawrence Stone argues that it emerges there much later. See Stone's *The Family, Sex and Marriage in England (1500–1800),* abridged ed. (New York: Harper Colophon, 1979). Individualism is the critical influence in all accounts. Marriage for love, therefore, seems to have characterized the city of Rome in the reign of Augustus and in the later empire.

7. Lust means use of another person sexually for self-centered purposes. Lust in this sense takes many forms since sex can express numerous desires and emotions other than love. The rapist, for example, uses sex to dominate and degrade. Teenagers may use sex to establish their status with peers of the same sex. One may have sex to hurt oneself, to assert independence, to get revenge. The possibilities are almost inexhaustible. Utilitarian individualism tempts people to reduce sex to lust. The opposite of lust is sex that expresses love.

8. Romantic love and married love do raise religious questions. For example, Christians who understand marriage as a sacrament believe God communicates himself/herself through it. They also believe God empowers and sustains married love. As noted, the *Habits* team interviewed evangelical Christians who think of faith in God as essential for marriage. Since, however, I am trying to argue that mar-

riage completes a basic human emotion, the theological implications of love are outside my present aim.

9. Scruton, *Sexual Desire,* 231.

10. Robert Solomon, *Love: Emotion, Myth, and Metaphor* (Garden City, N.Y.: Doubleday, Anchor Press, 1981), 205.

11. Phyllis Rose, *Parallel Lives: Five Victorian Marriages* (New York: Vintage Books, 1983), 19.

12. Rousseau makes the conflict between romantic love and married love one of his central themes. For example, in *La Nouvelle Heloise* Julie marries Wolmar but loves St. Preux. For an excellent treatment of Rousseau's views on this and related topics, see Joel Schwartz, *The Sexual Politics of Jean-Jacques Rousseau* (Chicago and London: University of Chicago Press, 1984).

13. Nor do such relationships necessarily become boring. As we've noted, each day brings spouses a challenge to love one another in a vital way.

14. J. M. F. Hunter, *Thinking About Love and Sex: A Philosophical Inquiry* (New York: St. Martin's Press, 1980), 74–76.

15. Scruton, *Sexual Desire,* 230.

16. "It was in the seventeenth and eighteenth centuries that morality came generally to be understood as offering a solution to the problems posed by human egoism and that the content of morality came to be largely equated with altruism. For it was in that same period that men came to be thought of as in some dangerous measure egoistic by nature; and it is only once we think of mankind as by nature dangerously egoistic that altruism becomes at once socially necessary and yet apparently impossible and, if and when it occurs, inexplicable. On the traditional Aristotelian view such problems do not arise. For what education in the virtues teaches me is that my good as a man is one and the same as the good of others with whom I am bound up in the human community. There is no way of pursuing my good which is necessarily antagonistic to you pursuing your good because *the* good is neither mine peculiarly nor yours peculiarly—goods are not private property. Hence Aristotle's definition of friendship, the fundamental form of human relationship, is in terms of shared goods" (MacIntyre, *After Virtue,* 228–29).

17. The therapeutic recognition that self-acceptance requires positive affirmation by another—hence the purpose of therapy—testifies to the interdependence of persons. But this dependence of our sense of self on others is not left behind after therapy. Granted, we do need to develop a sense of independence from others' opinions. But the solution to the problem of unthinking, fearful conformity to the crowd's demands need not be rejection of all standards beyond my own preferences. To follow reasonable norms (in principle shareable

by others) may make me an outcast and prophet, or may make me a popular hero. But looking to whose standards I am to follow rather than to which standards are reasonable mistakes the real issue.

18. For a brilliant study of love's fragility and Greek responses to this problem, see Martha Nussbaum, *The Fragility of Goodness: Luck and Ethics in Greek Tragedy and Philosophy* (Cambridge: Cambridge University Press, 1986). For Nussbaum's discussion of the *Symposium,* see chap. 6, "The Speech of Alcibiades: A Reading of the *Symposium.*" The problem of the dependence involved in romantic love is also a central theme of Rousseau. See Schwartz, *Sexual Politics of Rousseau,* chap. 4: "Sexual Dependence and the Individual," 74–113.

19. The index listing for *family* in *Habits of the Heart* has four entries, none about a couple's decision to have children. See *HH, 339.* The authors acknowledge that having children (as well as getting and staying married) "are now matters of choice rather than things taken for granted" (*HH,* 110).

20. Compare Erik Erikson's well-known claim that "generativity" is essential for full human development. Erikson chose this term rather than creativity or productivity to express the idea "that the ability to lose oneself in the meeting of bodies and minds leads to a gradual expansion of ego interests and of libidinal cathexis over that which has been generated and accepted as a responsibility. Generativity is primarily the interest in establishing and guiding the next generation or whatever in a given case may become the absorbing object of a parental kind of responsibility" (*Childhood and Society* [New York: W. W. Norton, 1950], 231). As Erikson's definition suggests, generativity need not be physical, but can be "spiritual." I cannot pursue this topic here except to say that teaching the young, for example, involves ties to the future responsibilities in the present similar to parents'.

21. Scruton, *Sexual Desire,* 241.

22. Many have found insurmountable problems with the argument from biological teleology. Perhaps the argument from emotional teleology may more easily be grasped and accepted. For a controversial restatement of the argument from biological teleology, see Pope Paul VI's 1968 encyclical on birth control, *Humanae Vitae* (Of Human Life), in *Love and Sexuality,* ed. Odile M. Liebard, vol. 4 of *Official Catholic Teachings* (Wilmington, N.C.: McGrath Publishing Co., 1978), 288–95. For problems with biological teleology, see the reactions to *Humanae Vitae* in William H. Shannon, ed., *The Lively Debate: Response to Humanae Vitae* (New York: Sheed and Ward, 1970).

23. "'The only object of man's love is what is good, don't you

agree?' 'Certainly I do.' 'May we then say without qualification that
men are in love with what is good?' 'Yes.' 'But we must add, mustn't
we, that the aim of their love is the possession of the good for themselves?' 'Yes.' 'And not only with its possession, but its perpetual possession?' 'Certainly. . . .'

"'Now that we have established what love invariably is, we must
ask in what way and by what type of action men must show their
intense desire if it is to deserve the name of love. What will this function be?' . . . 'The function is that of procreation in what is beautiful, and such procreation can be either physical or spiritual.' . . . 'All
men, Socrates, have a procreative impulse, both spiritual and physical, and when they come to maturity they feel a natural desire to be-
get children, but they can do so only in beauty and never in ugliness.
There is something divine about the whole matter; in procreation and
bringing to birth the mortal creature is endowed with a touch of im-
mortality'" (Plato, *Symposium,* trans. W. Hamilton [Hammonds-
worth, England, and Baltimore: Penguin Books, 1951], 86).

24. G. W. F. Hegel, *Philosophy of Right,* trans. T. M. Knox (Oxford: Oxford University Press, 1952), 117. The basic idea is comprehensible, I think, apart from the complexities of the Hegelian system, though obviously only in this context is it fully comprehensible.
It's not surprising that the grandest of teleological systems interprets
the dynamics of love, marriage, and family in teleological terms.

25. Caplow et al. compared Middletown's families with national
surveys. National studies show that over the past 50 years an increasing proportion of the population became parents. "Of women born
in 1890, 22.5 percent remained childless; of those born in 1930, only
5.5 percent did so. . . . [I]n the last two decades, parenthood has become almost universal for those who marry and . . . since 1950, first
pregnancies have occurred closer to marriage. . . . National sample
surveys dating back to 1936 demonstrate a rather remarkable stabil-
ity in the desire for children during recent decades. Men and women
show similarity over time in the numbers of children considered ideal
for persons in their circumstances. In her summary of 25 years of such
surveys, Judith Blake (1966) found virtually no support for families
with no children. . . . Neither was the one-child family accepted as
an ideal by an appreciable number of respondents. Families of two
to four children were preferred by the overwhelming majority, with
preferences for three and four children predominating after 1948. . . .
Since 1961, preferences have shifted toward smaller families. The majority of couples in a 1976 survey chose two or three children over
four or more. But there was no appreciable increase in support for
childlessness or for the one-child family. In the 1970s, only 8 to 10

percent of all married couples were childless; an additional 10 percent had only one child. The expectation of childlessness rose from
2 percent in 1970 to 5 percent in 1975, a small trend overemphasized
by the mass media," Theodore Caplow et al., *Middletown Families*
(Minneapolis: University of Minnesota Press, 1982), 298, 301.

26. I believe romantic love so interpreted is fully compatible with
women's equality. Nothing I have said was meant to imply women's
subordination. I believe it implies, rather, full equality for women.
For a discussion and response to the argument that romantic love is
inherently sexist, see Robert Solomon, "Beyond Sex and Gender (Love
and Feminism)," in his *Love: Emotion, Myth, and Metaphor*, 278–98.

27. I am not claiming that romantic and marital love counter all
forms of isolating individualism. Family commitments must be com-
plemented by engagement in wider social and political causes. A family's exclusive focus on itself is part of the problem of isolating individualism, as Tocqueville correctly observed. Hegel also understood
the family to be a relatively narrow and essentially incomplete form
of social union. He agreed with Tocqueville that family members need
to participate in the wider political life: "But because it is only as a
citizen that he is actual and substantial, the individual, so far as he
is not a citizen but belongs to the Family, is only an unreal impotent
shadow," G. W. F. Hegel, *Phenomenology of Spirit*, trans. A. V. Miller
(Oxford: Clarendon Press, 1977), 270. "Unreal impotent shadow,"
however, *overstates* the limits of the family.

28. For the percentage of the population that marries, see Caplow et al., *Middletown*, 388 (Appendix A, Table 12.2); for high degree of marital satisfaction, see *HH*, 317 (note 18) and Caplow et al.,
Middletown, 124–28 and 360–61 (Appendix A, Tables 4-8, 4-9).

29. Joseph Veroff, et al., *The Inner American: A Self-Portrait from
1957 to 1976* (New York: Basic Books, 1981), cited in *HH*, 110.

30. I agree, therefore, that some marital commitments once made
may justifiably be ended. For a detailed discussion of reasons for end-
ing commitments, see Margaret Farley, *Personal Commitments: Beginning, Keeping, Changing* (San Francisco: Harper and Row, 1986).

31. The complete truth is surely complex and unattainable. Some
divorces are motivated by therapeutic self-seeking, some by an attempt
to realize love's purposes anew after having failed. Others are motivated by innumerable additional factors.

32. See Allan Bloom, "Rousseau on the Equality of the Sexes,"
and *The Closing of the American Mind* (New York: Simon and
Schuster, 1987), 97–137.

33. See Paul Robinson, *The Modernization of Sex* (New York:
Harper and Row, 1976).

The Common Good and the Politics of Self-Interest: A Catholic Contribution to the Practice of Citizenship

Drew Christiansen, S.J.

> [A]ll human beings, as they take an ever more active part in the public life of their own country, are showing increasing interest in the affairs of all peoples, and are becoming more consciously aware that they are living members of the whole human family.
>
> John XXIII, *Pacem in terris* (no. 125)

The good-natured optimism of Pope John is legendary. He smiled benignly on the world, blessed humanity, and affirmed its good works. Among other developments in the early 1960s John also looked favorably upon the process of socialization. He was impressed with the growing interdependence of nations, with explosive growth of social organizations, and particularly with the expansion of opportunities for participation in politics. In the terminology of contemporary political philosophy, Pope John viewed the world with the eyes of "a cosmopolitan." He believed every person belonged first to humanity and only secondarily to any particular nation or group. In *Pacem in terris,* for example, he wrote, "The fact that one is a citizen of a particular state does not detract in any way from his membership in the human family as a whole, nor from citizenship in the world community." He also endorsed the priority of universal moral principles, especially human rights, over narrower allegiances. He would have readily assented to the Second Vatican Council's declaration that "in our times a special obligation binds us to make ourselves the neighbor of absolutely every person. . . . " Critics like Reinhold Niebuhr and John Courtney Murray thought him utopian, but nonetheless the Johannine revolution in Catholic social teaching left an indelible mark on the church's mission to the world. The church after John has not departed from his double conviction that it serves humanity by defending the dignity of the human person and promoting the unity of the human family.[1]

While John's corpus of social teaching consisted of only two long encyclical letters, on many counts it made revolutionary changes in Catholic social teaching. In *Pacem in terris,* for example, he broke with the church's use of natural law language to argue for a political morality based on human rights. A historian by training, he was the first to insist on the importance of reading "Signs of the Times." At first a supplement to the customary philosophical reasoning of twentieth-century encyclicals, sensitivity to the signs of the times later moved official theology away from its pretensions to offer ahistorical verities and toward a more sociohistorical interpretation of social issues. In addition, John addressed his teaching on social questions not just to the faithful, but to "all men and women of good will." This appeal to people of conscience stirred interest in church teaching in non-Catholic circles and restored some of the hierarchy's credibility as an interpreter of common morality.

Among John's other innovations, he also reinterpreted the ancient principle of *the common good.* His definition of the term in *Mater et magistra* as "the sum total of conditions of social living, whereby men [*sic*] are enabled more fully and more readily to achieve their own perfection" (no. 65) became a standard reference point for later church teaching as well as for much moral theology. In *Pacem in terris* he went further, extending the applicability of the concept beyond the nation-state to international relations and the solution of common global problems. This he called the universal common good.

The stress he laid in both his encyclicals on human development and his inclusion of human rights, in *Pacem in terris,*
as the primary end of government reduced some, but not all,
of the historic tensions between the Catholic common good
tradition and the political tradition of the Anglo-American
world. The emphasis on human development parallelled the
agenda of post-Millean liberalism; his vindication of human
rights coincided with the long Anglo-American tradition of
political and civil rights. The first undercut the objection that
the priority of the common good in Catholic political thought
subordinated the individual to the group; the second reassured
critics that appeals to the common good were no excuse for
authoritarianism.

John's reconceptualization of the common good was, therefore, a significant step in the *aggiornamento* or updating of
Roman Catholic social practice. It brought official Catholic social theology in alignment with many political developments
in western European societies, and it especially closed much
of the gap between Roman Catholic and Anglo-American political thought on issues of civil rights and political liberty. At
the same time, it sustained some of the traditional differences
with a politics based on self-interest. It affirmed the essential
unity of the human family, defended social responsibility as
the crux of political life, and argued that men and women should
restrain the extensive exercise of their rights in the interest of
justice for deprived groups. Thus, John's conception of the common good represents a meeting point of the deepest social con-
victions of Catholicism with the hard-won insights of western
democracies. Accordingly, the common good is an appropriate
locus of dialogue between Catholicism and the tradition of liberal political thought. It also constitutes a history of reflection
which may help contemporary American society meet one of
its most difficult dilemmas: the tension between a politics of
self-interest and the desire and the need of political community.

American society has suffered a perduring conflict between
its individualist culture, with its moral pluralism and love of
diversity, and its national politics which assumes large-scale
agreement and consensus.[2] While there is considerable participation in many intermediary groups (school boards, professional
associations, neighborhood clubs, social movements, and so

on), sources of national cohesion and political community are lacking. "The fullest conception of civic politics that emerges from the citizens' movements proposes to link local participation to a national dialogue. Politics in this view is a forum within which the politics of community, the politics of interest, and the politics of the nation can be put in a new context of wider possibilities of accommodation and innovation."[3] Such a sensibility may be summarized in the bumper sticker motto: "Think globally; act locally." The problem remains, however, as to how to make such an incipient insight the framework of a political culture. "This view of politics depends upon a notion of community and citizenship very different from the utilitarian individualist view."[4] That view remains the everyday language of political motivation. How will it be "possible that we could become citizens again and together seek the common good in the postindustrial, postmodern age?"[5] The proposal of this paper is that consideration of Pope John's view of the common good may well shed some light on how to achieve the elusive resolution of the tension between individual interest and the public good.

In assessing the impact of individualism on American political life, the authors of *Habits of the Heart* describe six contrasting American conceptions of the common good. They find all of them inadequate.[6] Here I would like to probe the deeper motives of those inadequacies. I would like to explore how the Johannine model of the common good, now the standard in most Catholic social theology, can address what many political theorists have come to recognize as limitations of the political philosophy embodied in American practices and institutions. In particular, I propose that the Johannine concept of the common good is an antidote to the politics of self-interest. It prescribes a mode of political responsibility in which individuals and groups hold themselves accountable for the impact of their actions on other groups within the wider society. Political judgment is weighted by how any policy advances or detracts from all groups sharing in a common quality of life.

This analysis of the common good in John's teaching will also contribute to Roman Catholic theology. A concept as old and as venerable as the common good, one which is easily subsumed into vernacular speech, is subject to many interpretations. In responding to the sudden evolution of official Catholic social teaching over the past thirty years, commentators have frequently contrasted different uses of the term rather than analyzed carefully its meaning and function in papal thought. Even detailed expositions have invoked outdated neo-Scholastic usage of the term. In addition, both within the church and outside it, the concept has been subject to a variety of interpretations based on ideological interests. Sometimes previous theological commitments, sometimes material interests, and sometimes a mixture of the two have colored views on the common good.[7]

Examination of the papal concept of the common good will reveal a more complex, egalitarian public philosophy than can be found solely in the received notion that the common good means "the sum total of the conditions of social living." In addition, I shall contend that newer terms, such as human solidarity and preferential option for the poor, only extend the evident implications of the basic concept. These later elaborations of the idea reveal how papal teaching on the common good challenges the politics of self-interest in the United States in a variety of ways.

I. LIBERALISM IN DECLINE:
THE LIMITS OF POLITICS OF SELF-INTEREST

The liberal political tradition was born out of exhaustion with the wars of religion.[8] The people of the late seventeenth century despaired of resolving their political differences on the deeper issues of life. The conflicts they suffered through engaged issues of religious and moral authority. Who had the authority to settle religious and moral questions: pope, king, clergy, individual conscience? The conflict over authority caused all the more harm because each party claimed to serve the glory of God and of king. The liberal political tradition proposed a threefold solution to the divisive politics of religious moralism. First, government would no longer confuse its policies with God's glory. The connection between politics and the transcendent would be severed. Second, policy would seek exclusively the protection and advancement of material interests. Economic well-being, like physical survival, emerged as one of the few things skeptical liberals could agree upon as an end of government. Indeed, the advantages of material civilization were evident in commercial republics like Venice whose lifeblood was trade.[9] In the third place, these material interests replaced moral concerns as the guiding principle of politics.[10] By the 1950s liberals saw themselves as the triumphant vanguard of human progress. At this high-water mark of liberal politics, the separation of morals from politics was virtually complete. Behavioral social scientists premised their work on a strict distinction between fact and value.[11] Technocratic political scientists proclaimed the final elimination of ethics from politics "an end of ideology."[12] Then, in the late 1960s and the early 1970s thinkers began to question the results of liberal politics.

Theodore Lowi announced "the end of liberalism" because of the inability of interest group politics to deal with the problems of the common good.[13] Robert Paul Wolff exposed "the poverty of liberalism" in meeting common problems because it was so wedded to the satisfaction of private wants.[14] David Braybrooke, Roland Pennock, and Duncan MacRae all proposed that the politics of self-interest needed modification to meet basic welfare requirements of the disadvantaged.[15] Frank M. Coleman argued that building liberal institutions around the principle of self-interest led to an increasingly manipulative, if not coercive, style of politics; and Charles E. Lindblom and Benjamin Barber took the last step in showing how the politics of self-interest undercut democracy.[16] Former liberals turned neoconservatives, like Daniel Bell and Samuel Huntington, agreed that when everyone pursued their self-interest, society became ungovernable and democracy unworkable.[17] (Their solution was to reduce the pressures on government by lowering the demands of newly entitled groups, so that the elite can rule effectively.) It turned out, after all, that liberalism had worked because of a residue of self-restraint and sacrifice inspired by the Christian tradition. With secularization these constraints had fallen away and selfish demand escalated from all sides. When everyone sought their own advantage, the materialist solution of liberal government could no longer succeed. Bell was most honest about how to proceed. He called for a civic-minded self-restraint he labelled *civitas*.[18]

The collapse of the material solution returned political discourse to notions of the public good, to religiously motivated public virtues. But two things were missing: (1) an adequate theory of the common good, and (2) a strategy for preventing religious and moral divisions from leading once again to political conflict. In other words, the question became: How does one pursue the common good within a moderate politics? The evolution of Catholic social teaching on the common good, along with the practice of that teaching in the United States, I shall try to show, suggests that we can in fact pursue the common good within the bonds of civil peace.

II. POPE JOHN'S UNDERSTANDING OF THE COMMON GOOD

THE THOMIST BACKGROUND

In the writings of Saint Thomas, the term *common good* has both general and political meanings. The general philosophical terminology refers to goodness as such, and when it takes into account Aquinas's whole theological world view, God alone can be described as "the common good" since the Godhead is the ultimate end of all creation (*Summa Theologiae* I, qq. V and VI). In politics, however, the term may denote not just the collective good of the group, but also the total good of the members, and "the good proper to the system they constitute." For some contemporary political philosophers, this composite or analogous use of the term may appear inexact. Saint Thomas, however, thought synthetically, not analytically. One must, therefore, ask of him not uniformity in use, but completeness in description. That is, do the varieties of use adequately encompass the multiplicity of shared concerns in political life? The combination of these different meanings makes the common good especially relevant for resolving the impasses in liberal political institutions.

INDIVIDUAL AND PERSON

Thomist readings of the common good have generally diverged over whether the common good in politics may be interpreted in personalist or corporate terms. In other words, does the common good regard the individual as a person with an irreducible dignity which entails certain forms of respect, or does it treat the individual simply as a member (part) of the body politic? Thomas himself seems to have done both. He opposed the common good, on the one hand, to the private good of an individual or faction and, on the other hand, to the good of persons. In the first case, the common good — that is, the good of the whole community — took priority over individual good, the welfare of society over the individual. Accordingly, the individual belonged to a larger social body, and the good of the whole took precedence over individual goods. In other words, individual self-interest ought to take a back seat to the general welfare. On this view, for example, the priority of the common good warrants sacrificing one's life in defense of one's homeland. On the second view, however, the person takes preeminence over the good of the group. In Thomas's mind, as "a person" the individual human being is ordered directly to God and as such exceeds the political community in worth. In Thomas's day this distinction between individual and person served to justify in a single system the differences between the older collectivist feudal model of society, on the one hand, and the emerging freedom of urban society, on the other, with its new social forms and religious lifestyles. It served as a justification for freedom of religious expression.

Twentieth-century Thomists have employed "the good of the person" to defend human dignity and universal human rights. In this sense human rights as features of the person remained in tension with the common good as the collective welfare of the community. In Vatican II the distinction between personal and common good justified religious liberty. The council intended to protect the life of worship from manipulation for other ends. For the church to defend the religious rights of the person in face of political oppression comes as no surprise. It is remarkable, however, that two years before the Declaration on Religious Liberty John had already expanded the field of the personal to cover the full range of human rights. What's more, in an extraordinary turnabout, in *Pacem in terris* the pope insisted that the common good largely consists in the defense and promotion of those rights. Thus, subordination of individuals or groups to the good of the whole seeks primarily to ensure that the whole society, indeed the whole human community, shares in the enjoyment of those rights. The tension between the good of the whole community and the good of the person has been largely, though not entirely, overcome. The difference which remains between the traditional and the post-Johannine conceptions of the common good consists primarily in the insistence of the magisterium on the obligation to ensure that everyone can develop to the full.

POPE JOHN'S CONCEPTION OF THE COMMON GOOD

To explore John's conception of the common good, we need to examine not only (1) his definition(s) of the term, as so much scholarship has done, but also (2) the complex of political relations in which the concept is utilized, and (3) the principles drawn from it and the applications made on the basis of those principles for social and public policy. With this fuller analysis of the common good we shall be better able to articulate the contribution this concept can make to political responsibility in American politics.

1. The Definitions

Mater et magistra 65 provides a working definition of the common good. "The common good," it tells us, *embraces* "the sum total of the conditions of social living." John himself cites this formulation in *Pacem in terris* (58), and it recurs in a key passage of Vatican II (*Gaudium et spes*, 26). This formula, however, is not the only one to be found in John's corpus. For instance, writing of the universal common good, he proposes that "the public and universal authority must have as its fundamental objective the recognition, respect, safeguarding, and promotion of human rights" (*PT,* 139). The phrase *fundamental objective* carries at least as much weight, it appears to me, as the wording of the accepted definition that the common good *embraces* the conditions of social life.

Earlier in the same letter, John had written, "It is agreed that in our time the common good is chiefly guaranteed when personal rights and duties are maintained" (*PT,* 60). Similarly, he comments, "It is also demanded by the common good that civil authorities should make earnest efforts to bring about a situation in which individual citizens can easily exercise their rights and fulfill their duties" (*PT,* 63). Accordingly, John defines common good in terms of recognition and support of human rights. I do not mean to suggest there is a conflict between the standard definition and this second definition in terms of human rights. In fact, no substantial conflict need arise in the demands which, according to John, flow from the two definitions of the common good, whether conceived as "the sum or conditions of social living" or as the realization of human rights. The lists of interests associated with the social conditions formula in *Mater et magistra* and the rights formula in *Pacem in terris* parallel one another.

At the same time, the human rights formula does increase the weight placed on the development of individual persons in the articulation of the common good. Indeed, it becomes clearer than it had in *Mater et magistra* that the good of the whole is conceived largely as the individual's share in the well-being of the society. Individual persons may share differently, but those differences ought to result from differences in widely shared social conditions or from special needs, rather than from differences in status, as the neo-Scholastic tradition had tended to propose since the time of Leo XIII. One can, therefore, make a case that conceiving of the common good as the general enjoyment of human rights in society offers a more comprehensive, accurate, and definitive understanding of the common good than the customary appeal to "conditions of social living."

At the same time, the earlier definition of *Mater et magistra* does introduce some important considerations which ought to be noted. First, the common good concerns "conditions of social living." Second, these conditions seek to ensure human development (or perfection); and third, they contribute to a growing capacity for such human fulfillment. Each term contributes something vital to understanding the relevance of the common good to modern politics.

First, *the common good concerns social living.* The Catholic tradition does not regard society as emerging from free contracts of individuals, but rather as a natural circumstance in which all human beings participate. On the one hand, cooperation and the division of labor make it possible for individuals

to attain higher levels of material and spiritual well-being than
they would were they to be left on their own. More significant
still, human fulfillment as well as the higher forms of human
activity, including education and politics, are social in nature.
From a Christian perspective, of course, the law of love fulfills
our human nature. Providing the conditions of social living,
therefore, means guaranteeing the resources, defending the lib-
erties, relieving the impediments, and opening the opportunities to participate fully in one's society. (See below.) The principle of participation in recent Catholic teaching flows from
the ideal of social living.

*The goal of the common good is that men and women be
"enabled more fully and more readily to achieve their own perfection."* While the word *perfection* also has theological over-
tones, as a matter of social policy it means human fulfillment
or development. In *Populorum progressio (Development of
Peoples)*, Paul VI's encyclical letter on international economic
development, he used the term *development* to refer to the same
goals and processes which John refers to as perfection. As I
noted earlier, in this sense the term has some affinity with John
Stuart Mill's assertion in *On Liberty* that the strength of society can be measured in terms of the individual development
of its members. Catholic teaching can adapt to this idea because of the eudaemonism embedded in traditional Catholic
ethics. It still parts from liberal individualism, however, in seeing individual development subject to moral and social principles as well as to individual choice. One may not choose just
any life plan out of personal preference. One's choices are limited both by morality and social responsibility. Still, the common aim is human flourishing. The end of all economic activity, John taught—in line with the teaching of his predecessor
Pius XII—is "that everyone in the community can develop and
perfect himself." According to the encyclical, development consists in utilizing natural talents and augmenting personal autonomy, but it also entails cooperating with others, collaborating with government in its efforts to balance diverse interests,
and building up community.

*Finally, the customary definition of common good as "con-
ditions of social living" involves an evolving standard of well-
being.* It appeals, not to any absolute level of entitlement, but

rather to those standards which enable people to develop "more fully and more readily." It does not invoke a basic needs standard, though basic need would represent an absolute minimum of conditions of development. Neither does it speak of a decent family living in the way previous social teaching had. In John's vision of society, the complexification of institutions and social conditions makes possible a better standard of living for everyone (*Mater et magistra* 46–49, 54, 61–63; hereafter, *MM*). As societal conditions evolve, so do the common possibilities of members of that society (and even of the global community). Social responsibility—the sense of the common good—demands that everyone enjoy the benefits of an improving quality of life. "Accordingly, advances in social organization can and should be so brought about," John wrote, "so that maximum advantages accrue to citizens at the same time disadvantages are averted or at least minimized" (*MM*, 64). He was particularly concerned that economic growth foster social development (*MM*, 73). The level at which social policy needs to provide conditions of social living and the shape those conditions will take, however, will differ from one society to another depending on its state of economic and social development (*MM*, 68–72, esp. 71–72).

2. Social Political Functions of the Common Good

The common good provides a principle of justice for society as a whole, not just for government. It affects "the relations of citizens with one another, of citizens and intermediate groups with public authorities and public authorities with one another" (*PT*, 72). Every group within society—unions, professional associations, private health systems, agricultural interests, to name just a few examples—must judge their policies in terms of the common good. Leaders of those organizations and the rank-and-file must ensure that their decisions reflect the interest of the whole community. In this sense, the common good offers a principle of coordination. It represents not just an aggregate of all the goods in society such as the Gross National Product or Social Welfare Function might measure, nor a serial list of a variety of things to be shared in a package of welfare components, but a demand for every individual and group to take into account the impact of actions on other groups and persons in the society.[19] *Pacem in terris* 53 articulates the principle this way:

> Individual citizens and intermediate groups are obliged to make their specific contributions to the common welfare . . . they must bring their own interests into harmony with the needs of the community and must contribute their goods and their services as civil authorities prescribe.

Intermediate groups, moreover, are urged to "pursue the objective" of maximizing advantages and minimizing disadvantages of social development "in a spirit of concord among themselves" (*MM*, 64–65). The contrast with the politics of self-interest could not be clearer. While John does not deny the existence of private and subgroup interests, he does not assume the harmonization of such interests by an invisible hand but their coordination by conscious political decisions of the interested parties.

Pope John illustrates the balancing of interests individuals and groups must undertake in ascertaining the common good with a discussion of wage rates. Minimally workers must be paid a wage sufficient for them and their families "to lead a life worthy of man [sic]." In making their demands, workers and unions must also weigh, however, individual contributions and the economic conditions of the business. But John goes further still. They also need to weigh the needs of each community and especially overall employment. Finally, they ought to bear in mind "the common good of all peoples" (*MM*, 71). Clearly the common good requires something very different from the promotion of national interest through the private pursuit of self-interest.

The common good does not rule out the pursuit of self-interest, but it severely constrains it by taking into account the interests of other groups and the overall good of society. In effect, when they participate in politics or act in the market, citizens and social groups must act with the same responsibility as government officials "to promote the common good of all, without preference for any single citizen or civic group" (*PT*, 56).

What appears a principle of impartial justice is, however,

basically a principle of inclusion in the general welfare of the society as a whole. The principle also promotes the interests of the disadvantaged members of society "who are less able to defend their rights and to assert their legitimate claims" (*PT*, 56). As a principle the common good provides a rule of societal justice, not just of political justice. While government has the obligation to make adjustments to compensate for the disadvantages suffered by marginalized groups, everyone must recognize that privilege undermines the common good. *Mater et magistra* 79 lists averting the rise of privileged groups "even among workers" as a requirement of the common good.

The bias of the principle against privilege, whether on the part of individuals or of interest groups, appears most clearly in John's insistence on the elimination of class distinctions. From the time of Leo XIII to Pius XI, while Catholic social teaching defended the interests of workers and the poor, it also assumed that different standards of living were appropriate to people in different roles either because of social status (Leo) or social function (Pius). While John was no leveler demanding flat equality, he nonetheless deemed inequities of class incompatible with the common good. In advocating a more equitable distribution of wealth within nations in *Mater et magistra,* he did not rest content to leave the question settled at the level of a general rule that economic growth should be accompanied by social development. He went on to add, "Toward this end, vigilance should be exercised and effective steps taken so that *class differences arising from disparities of wealth not be increased, but lessened so far as possible*" (*MM,* 74; emphasis added). In considering the shift in capitalism from an agricultural to an industrial economy and later from an industrial to a service economy, he took an even firmer stand. In transforming economies, the common good seeks *either to eliminate or to keep within bounds the inequalities* which exist between different sectors of the economy (*MM,* 79; emphasis added)." The control and elimination of inequality stands, by almost any analysis, as a strong standard of egalitarian justice. The bias against privilege entails a preference for a more egalitarian society.

Pacem in terris, as we have seen, switched the immediate focus of John's concern from just socioeconomic development to human rights. The encyclical, however, made a significant correlation, on the one hand, between inequality and rights violations and, on the other, between the restriction of inequality and the protection of rights. John asserted that socioeconomic inequalities make it exceedingly difficult for people to exercise their rights. "Experience has taught us," the pope wrote, "that, unless (governmental authorities) take suitable action with regard to economic, political, and cultural matters, inequalities between the citizens tend to become more and more widespread, especially in the modern world, and as a result human rights are rendered totally ineffective and the fulfillment of duties is compromised" (*PT,* 63). In identifying the growth of socioeconomic inequality as the source of rights violations John had identified a sign of the time which would appear over and over again in later years in the social teaching of the Council, of Pope Paul VI, and of Pope John Paul II.

Pope John had also put his finger on the vital connection between socioeconomic inequality and fundamental forms of injustice. The correlation between inequality and deprivation of rights entailed that the common good functions not just as a principle of extensive distribution (*PT,* 64), but also as the point of leverage for an egalitarian critique of privilege. "It should not happen," the pope wrote, "that certain individuals or social groups derive special advantage from the fact that their rights have received preferential protection" (*PT,* 65). Rights, however important, should not elevate one far above one's peers. The common good entails a norm of relative equality, therefore, because when inequalities go unchecked it becomes difficult, if not impossible, to guarantee even basic rights. While John holds on to some counterpoised principles (such as sustaining individual initiative), the burden of his teaching holds in check the advantages gained by any set of individuals or groups for the sake of the full development of everyone in the community (*MM,* 74).

John's writings abound with requests for one social group to reconsider its advantages in light of their impact on others. For example, John, from a peasant background himself, showed special concern for the welfare of farmers and agricultural workers. For this reason *Mater et magistra* contains the most extensive treatment of agricultural issues in recent Roman social teaching. Nevertheless, after endorsing agricultural cooperatives so that farmers can pursue their own interests, John has this advice: Farmers "should strive to bring their rights and interests into line with the rights and needs of other classes, and to refer to the same common good" (*MM*, 146–47; also see *Gaudium et spes,* 66; hereafter, *GS*). Again, writing of worker participation, John argues that laborers, and not just management, enjoy representation on regional and national economic councils (*MM*, 99). Addressing the issue of international relations, he warns developed nations against perpetuating a situation of advantage through their foreign aid. Disinterested aid, he argues, "will help much toward shaping a community of all nations, wherein each one, aware of its rights and duties, will have regard for the prosperity of all" (*MM*, 174, 169–174). The common good, therefore, clearly requires that any one group—whether citizen, interest groups, or governments—restrain its own interests for the sake of common advancement.

For the sake of the common good, people may even be expected to give up to some degree rights they already enjoy. Pope John taught that "one of the fundamental duties" of government "is to coordinate social relations in such a fashion that the exercise of one man's [*sic*] rights does not threaten others in the exercise of their own rights," (*PT,* 62); but Paul VI took the striking step of affirming that on the principle of the common good, people ought even to forego some of their rights for the sake of equal advancement of other people. "[T]he more fortunate should renounce some of their rights," Paul wrote, "so as to place their goods generously at the service of others" (*Octogesima adveniens,* 23; hereafter *OA*). According to David Hollenbach, self-restraint with respect to one's own rights or government restraints on the full exercise of some rights of some citizens should not force people to give up basic rights.[20] The basic guarantees protected by right are inviolable. Rather, more people should enjoy a common level of rights protection. Political elites, for example, might be asked to surrender some of their influence for the sake of wider popular participation in public forums. In addition, one may tolerate a lesser degree of realization of one right for the sake of attaining necessary levels of another right. Limits might be established on market transactions, for example, to insure that the basic needs of everyone in society go satisfied. In Robert Nozick's phrase, the common good represents an "end-state" theory which measures justice by social outcomes rather than by rules of fair play alone.

Nowhere is the difference between the common good and the politics of self-interest so evident as in this question of the (self-)limitation of rights. While the Anglo-American political tradition has granted rights less generously than Catholic social teaching, it has enforced the rights it has permitted more stringently. On the whole, it has tended to make those rights absolute, with no possibility of coordinating them with one another or with other social goods. An individual may pursue a right based on his or her self-interest without concern for the effects on others. Ironically, the church does not turn an unsympathetic ear to the neoconservative claim that when everyone seeks entitlement society becomes ungovernable. Catholic social teaching has consistently criticized the unbridled pursuit of self-interest. The differences lie in the structure of sacrifice. Catholic social teaching puts priority on the universal enjoyment of rights at a common level, whether in satisfying basic needs or in advancing further entitlement like the right to higher education. The burden of sacrifice, therefore, rests on the advantaged to make concessions for those less well off. Neoconservative theories, however, ask self-restraint and sacrifice of newly entitled "individuals" so the old elites may continue to rule effectively.

Concern for the common good, then, holds each part of society accountable to the rest. As Vatican II would later say, "Every social group must take account of the needs and legitimate aspirations of other groups, and even of the welfare of the entire human family" (*GS*, 26). Such accountability has many sides, but government has a special responsibility to consolidate the diverse groups in a society behind the common good. Politics, if you will, ought to mirror the common good as a process of social responsibility.

Here we underscore two points about contemporary Catholic teaching on government. First, government should coordinate the interests of all groups. While John held the traditional view that political authority makes the final judgment of the common good, he put emphasis on the moral leadership of public officials. "[C]ivil authority," wrote John, "must appeal primarily to the conscience of individual citizens, that is, to each one's duty to collaborate readily for the common good of all" (*PT,* 48). As far as possible, political authorities ought to respect the workings of subgroups and subordinate organizations within society (*MM,* 53). Government does not seek, in the first instance at least, to prescribe for others what they must do, but in the words of Paul VI, "to encourage, stimulate, co-ordinate, supplement and integrate" the initiatives of private citizens and intermediate groups (*Populorum progressio,* 33; hereafter, *PP*). Government's authority for setting goals and choosing policy solutions derives from the fact that it holds the ultimate responsibility for achieving the common good, but it should exercise such authority "to stimulate all the forces engaged in this common activity" (*PP,* 33). Contemporary political theorists sometimes regard Catholic social teaching as statist because it appeals for government intervention or state regulation of the economy. These appeals, however, constitute the exception, and need to be seen in the context of leading a cooperative political process based on moral leadership. The government's primary responsibility consists in bringing various sectors of society together to support one another. As a rule, individual and group autonomy and state coordination should counterbalance one another. A government should act directly and on its own chiefly when the several sectors of society withhold support or when cooperation fails to bring about the desired result.

Second, it follows that government has a special role as the agent of last resort. It must act either when others have failed to act or when the actions they have taken have failed to realize a just result. In particular, it has a special responsibility to look after those who are excluded from the general prosperity of the wider society. "Considerations of justice and equity," wrote John in *Pacem in terris,* "can at times demand that those involved in civil government give more attention to the less fortunate members of the community, since they are less able to defend their rights and to assert their legitimate claims" (56).

A preferential option for the poor therefore agrees with the common good as articulated in more recent Catholic social teaching, when such a policy aims at including a marginalized group in mainstream society. Vatican II expressed the same intention when it declared that "everyone must consider his every neighbor without exception as another self," for "in our times a special obligation binds us to make ourselves the neighbor of absolutely every person, and of actively helping him [sic]" (*GS,* 27). The U.S. Catholic bishops applied this principle to the American context when they proposed in their pastoral letter *Economic Justice for All* that "[p]ersonal decisions, policies of private and public bodies, and power relationships must all be evaluated by those who lack the minimum necessities . . ." (90). In short, government serves the principle of subsidiarity not only by respecting the autonomy of various social groups, but also by upholding the dignity of the poor when they have been denied access to the banquet of life.

III. AN ALTERNATE POLITICS

The common good requires a different vision of political life from that defended by the American political tradition with its politics of self-interest. The common good replaces the pursuit of individual interest with the promotion of a common quality of life. Instead of the continual quest of advantage, the politics of the common good looks to the advancement of all sectors of society. Where liberalism thrives on competition, the common good prospers by cooperation. Where the American political tradition encourages people to consult their interests in an adversarial way, the common good requires self-limitation for the sake of everyone's profit. The common good, therefore, does not offer some vague guiding principle for political life. Instead, it embodies a distinctive vision of how to conduct politics.

The U.S. Catholic bishops' two recent pastoral letters, *The Challenge of Peace* (1983) and *Economic Justice for All* (1986), exemplify the processes of common good politics. The letters seek to build consensus on nuclear weapons policy and to encourage economic cooperation. *The Challenge of Peace,* recognizing that "today the possibilities for placing political and moral limits on nuclear war are so minimal that the moral task

. . . is prevention," urges that "as a people, we must refuse to legitimate the idea of nuclear war" (133). Accordingly, the bishops write to contribute to a public consensus which will say no to nuclear war (139). "Especially in a democracy," they write, "public policy . . . can, through a series of measures, indicate the limits beyond which a government should not proceed" (140). They continue, "We seek to encourage a public attitude which sets stringent limits on the kind of actions our own government and other governments will take on nuclear policy" (141). Finally, they commit themselves to taking part in a national debate, along with public officials, analysts, private organizations, and the media, on "the limits beyond which our military policy should not move in word or action" (141; also 195).

In short, the bishops regard public debate on the grave moral issues entailed by nuclear war and deterrence as an integral part of democratic politics. Various actors will take part in that debate; but, in keeping with the common good tradition, the debate seeks to formulate a shared consensus as to the limits under which government leaders, the military, and weapons scientists can go in formulating policies which affect the future welfare not only of American society, but of the whole of humanity as well. The common good of humanity, not the imperatives of international power politics, nor the technological imperatives of the military-industrial complex, should determine the direction and limits of defense policy in the nuclear age. The guidelines for policy need to emerge from public policy debate in which the church functions as one actor among many.

Economic Justice for All, the 1986 pastoral letter on Catholic social teaching and the U.S. economy, suggests a similar program of political action. The bishops plead for "a common moral vision" (22–24), urge the adoption of an American experiment in economic rights (83), and encourage collaboration across the customary adversarial boundaries (management/labor, public/private) which have divided groups according to their separate interests, in "a partnership for the public good" (295–325). The bishops' proposals for collaboration across sectors and regions, between institutions, and in the international arena recognize that we can achieve the common good through

participatory processes which themselves encourage cooperation. Catholic social teaching has always insisted that achieving the common good requires the participation of all parties.
But the detail with which the bishops explore the avenues of
collaboration highlights the need for a match between cooperation as the means and a common life as the end. Gandhi insisted that one can achieve moral (peaceful) ends only by moral
(peaceful) means. Similarly, one can achieve the common good
only with cooperative means.

In a number of recent works, Dennis McCann has taken
up the question of how society or the church discerns for itself
what the common good requires.[21] In his *New Experiment in
Democracy,* he has proposed that, whether within the church
or society, public discussion in an effort to determine "gener-
alizable interests" provides the proper way to identify the moral
requirements of the common good. For McCann contemporary social teaching needs to define the common good more
clearly as "the good to be pursued in common." McCann's re-
phrasing tries to suggest that the common good needs to be
understood in procedural as well as substantive terms. In other
words, the principle of the common good does not offer an
already-out-there, ready-to-be-grasped norm of justice but rather
a set of goals to be arrived at through open debate and public
consensus. True politics cannot be pursued merely by consult-
ing one's own interest, like a hungry man filling his stomach
or an accountant looking for a higher quarterly return. Rather,
politics, as the highest form of social living, entails "critical
self-reflection" so that we can identify "what all can want."

McCann, I believe, makes an important contribution to
Catholic theology by suggesting that public dialogue plays an
essential role in identifying the common good.[22] More particularly, we need open discussion, as in the case of the bishops'
pastoral letters and particularly in the 1976 Call to Action, in
order to foster the development of Catholic social teaching itself. That tradition, however, already makes several recommendations about the conduct of politics which need consideration. Based on my earlier analysis of John XXIII's conception
of the common good, I would like to name several principles
for a politics of the common good. I propose them as guidelines for citizens, political leaders, and voluntary associations

in fostering a politics of the common good. Before considering these norms, however, I would like to ponder the way ethical principles function in American politics today. For the common good offers not only different principles but a different way of conducting ethical politics.

Rights, Debatable Policies and Ideals: The Graded Salience of Moral Norms in Politics

In doing applied ethics, moralists find it both necessary and useful to distinguish between various levels of moral responsibility. Some versions of public decision making, Bentham's for example, disallow ethical questions from being considered in the public arena at all. But as a rule, the Anglo-American political tradition has tended to treat moral issues like economic interests. In the politics of self-interest, moral concerns do not differ from other concerns. They count as interests among other interests which, like any other cause, need to exert political power to be heard. Their valence in the political process depends on market demand, voter preference, or political influence. Even when it does not disallow moral discourse altogether, as Bentham and the Philosophical Radicals did, it labors under a serious drawback, because it cedes no prima facie priority to moral principles.

In recent years, however, moral and political philosophy in discussing the place of ethics in public decision making has begun to include alongside the interest model an alternative called the rights and duties model. According to this approach, certain basic rights and duties set limits on political trade-offs. The rights and duties model distinguishes between rights and ordinary political bargaining. Rights are nonnegotiable and, therefore, set a limit to justifiable political action. Thus, the right to life and bodily integrity proscribes murder, torture, and physical intimidation from the range of permissible actions in the political arena. Once settled, however, as, say, civil rights were in the sixties or environmental duties were in the seventies, rights and duties impose routine limits on the practice of everyday politics. The rights and duties model, therefore, prescribes a limited field of action which excludes ordinary politics and mandates or proscribes certain kinds of action.

Some political philosophers go further and argue that not just rights, but welfare concerns, qualify as matters of public good and need to enjoy a normative status in public debate and political bargaining. Both the rights and duties model and the welfare model agree that ethics seeks to establish basic constraining norms for the common life. Beyond those limits, the proponents of both views hold that politics should remain open to bargaining and to the pursuit of interest. The resulting moralized politics stands divided between a field of strong ethical controls where politics has considerably less flexibility for action, on the one hand, and the range of ordinary, everyday politics where morality has little bearing, on the other. It follows that ideal programs for social reform have no specified role in politics. Individuals may pursue ideals in concert with like-minded folk, but ideals do not provide proper matter for legislation.

The use of such distinctions is not fatuous. The exclusion of ideal morality from politics has special significance. In the first place, given the existence of moral disagreement, distinctions between weightier rights and obligations, on the one hand, and other good, but less necessary, goals, on the other, establishes a coexistence between morals and politics. That is to say, morals can impinge on politics without preempting the whole political arena. Within the range of political activity pluralism in morals is permissible, and political or negotiated solutions to disagreements are possible. When not every moral issue carries equal weight, conditions favoring civil discourse and mutual respect increase.

There is, of course, no absolute barrier one way or the other. Normative principles—such as liberty, justice and equality—are like political principles, both contested and contestable. So, individuals or groups will sometimes question moral settlements on rights just as leading black scholars today question busing for the sake of school integration and even integration itself as a means to equal education.[23] Abortion continues to be agitated in public policy debate. Nonetheless, a distinction between harder, less debatable ethical norms and softer, more debatable ones serves to limit the range of ethical disagreement which can effectively be brought to the public arena. In addition, public consensus about the stricter norms, like nondiscrimination and integration, should lead to compliance with those norms. At the same time, acknowledgement of a range of disagreement should stimulate both respect for other positions in political debate and a self-denying spirit which enables partisans of any one view to accept the need to persuade others of their position over an extended period of time if their moral ideas expect to reach basic, common acceptance. The United States Catholic Conference's formulation of a "Consistent Ethics of Life" under the leadership of Cardinal Joseph Bernardin seems to work within this framework.[24] It aims at building consensus by showing the rational and practical consistency between the Catholic position on abortion and a range of other issues on which there is already substantial agreement in American society.

I would urge a second reason for distinguishing grades of importance for ethical norms; namely, that it makes good moral sense, even if not all the norms any individual would like to see legally enforced are publicly recognized at any given time. Both Catholic social teaching and recent liberal political theory recognize, for example, the priority of basic needs over other sorts of welfare concerns. Need provides a rational norm of distribution which takes precedence over notions of private advantage. Similarly, in the conduct of warfare, the prohibition of direct attack on civilians binds stringently both in Catholic teaching and in international law. As a practical matter, setting priorities facilitates the conduct of policy, because not every moral claim requires honoring at the same time, or to the same degree.

Finally, the lower political salience of moral ideals finds warrant in the fact that the wholesale transformation of society can only be a very long-term goal. In the attempt to effect social transformation, the perfect can become the enemy to the good. In addition, a unified, rational scheme of life, since it covers so many aspects of living, tends to threaten pluralism and individual choice. Accordingly, ideals of life should require a much higher standard of agreement before their public adoption. In political life, ideals best serve communities of concern, like the historic peace churches, who contribute to the evolution of public policy by the witness of their lives and by their special perspectives on particular issues.

The Common Good as a Political Ideal

This distinction between basic rights, the politics of interest, and ideal ways of life poses something of a problem for
the politics of the common good, for in some respects the common good represents an ideal vision of politics. I do not mean,
as critics might allege, that it relies unrealistically on a moral
anthropology which regards self-criticism and altruistic action
as possible. (Although I believe that within limits that anthropology is a defensible one, I shall not defend it here. The realism-
turned-pessimism in Anglo-American political thought, which
assumes that one must always act for reasons of self-interest
and that a moral politics lies byond reach, seems to me to have
as much to do with successful intellectual propaganda as with
the facts of political life.) Rather, the problem is that the common good embraces so much of life. It offers an expansive, dynamic norm which requires regular readjustment of public policies. The expansiveness of the concept is particularly captured
in the phrase "the conditions of social living whereby men [*sic*]
are enabled more fully and more readily to achieve their own
perfection" (*MM*, 65). The common good offers an explosive
concept both because "social conditions" potentially cover so
many facets of life and because the goal of human fulfillment
has such elasticity. In Pope John Paul's phrase, the common
good requires "continual revision" of social, economic and political arrangements. It appears to aim at optimal moral outcomes. For this reason, even with the many accommodations
made to Anglo-American political thought by John XXIII, Vatican Council II, and the late Pope Paul VI, the politics of the
common good challenges the perduring intuition of the liberal
political tradition that the inevitability of political and moral
disagreement demands limited government and at most a narrow though strict ethics.

While the common good does admit effective priorities for
urgent demands like the provision of basic needs, Catholic political thought derives its dynamism from the idea that the
general welfare requires the upward readjustment of the moral
norms in society in tandem with changing social developments.
That adjustment seeks to ensure that social developments become available to the society as a whole. From the point of

view of policy ethics, this means that one must redraw regularly the boundaries of moral concern in politics. Accordingly, adoption of the common good as a standard for policy ethics will upset the recent settlement which recognizes a clear but delimited place for ethics in the field of human rights and fundamental duties. Instead, moral concerns may surface almost anywhere. As a consequence, one risks a loss of civility with the politicization of everything in the especially divisive way which attends moral disputes. Promoting a common good ethics in the American ethos raises the possibility of serious social disruption. A shift to a politics of the common good, therefore, ought not be attempted in the absence of the self-reflective, self-denying, and other-oriented attitudes which form a part of the ideal.

III. CIVIC AMITY: THE VIRTUES
OF COMMON GOOD POLITICS

Tradition resolves the divisiveness of an ethical politics, then, by selecting the moral issues which merit public concern. The common good approach addresses the same problem by promoting patience and reserve on the part of political leaders and ordinary citizens in the pursuit of the common good. Consider three cases in recent American Catholic experience. First, Cardinal Bernardin's "Consistent Ethic of Life," as I have indicated, shows an understanding that even on such a serious issue as abortion prolonged polemics and hard-ball politics do not serve the public good. A more long-term and sophisticated moral witness is necessary to build a consensus on the issue. New York Governor Mario Cuomo's refusal to be drawn into the abortion debate on terms set by the most strident parties likewise represents a spirit of constraint which models the kind of civility needed to bring morality and politics together in a democratic contract. Partly too, the American bishops showed a spirit of prudence which sets priorities within a larger scheme when, in *Economic Justice for All,* they decided that they would focus on basic or minimal economic rights and on the inclusion of the poor in the economic policies of the nation rather than applying directly the higher standards of economic dis-

tribution found in Roman teaching. Deference to the strongly
held views of others contributes to the civic amity which is a
precondition of the common good.

While some may view these political stances as mere tactics
and others will see them as compacts with the devil, they express virtuous dispositions essential to a politics of the common good: consideration toward the opinions of others, self-
restraint in pursuing one's own claims, willingness to persuade
others over the long term, a desire for cooperation, a disinclina-
tion to divisiveness, and protective concern for civil peace. What
Vatican II wrote of religious liberty applies also to the introduction of moral issues into politics:

> In the exercise of their rights, individuals and social groups
> are bound by the moral law to have respect both for the rights
> of others and for the duties toward others and for the common
> welfare of all. Men [*sic*] are to deal with their fellows in justice
> and civility.
>
> [God's] truth appears at its height in Christ Jesus. . . . Christ
> is our master and Lord. He is also meek and humble of heart.
> And in attracting and inviting His disciples he acted patiently.
> . . . His intention was to rouse faith in his hearers and to con-
> firm their faith, not to exert coercion upon them. (*Dignitatis
> humanae*, 7; hereafter *DH*)

In the same spirit of political charity Paul VI urged a legitimate variety of possible options in the quest for justice. Paul's
defense of pluralism provides a kind of summary of the dispositions required for a politics of the common good. The
church asks, wrote Paul, "an effort at mutual understanding
of the others' practices and motives; a loyal examination of
one's behavior and its correctness will suggest to each one an
attitude of more profound charity which, while recognizing
the differences, believes nonetheless in the possibility of convergence and unity. The bonds which unite the faithful are
mightier than any which divide them!" (*OA*, 50). While Paul
was writing of political differences among Christians, we need
mutual understanding, self-examination, charity, and belief in
the possibilities for agreement in order to carry out a politics
of the common good in civil society as well. In the absence
of these dispositions, not only will the common good lie be-

yond reach, but nonaligned politics threaten intense social conflict. With such attitudes, however, working for the good of all
may become a genuine possibility. The principle of the common good, therefore, ought to find application not in the abstract, but only in conjunction with the virtues of a common
life.[25]

PRINCIPLES OF THE COMMON GOOD

Finally, we turn to the principles of a politics of the common good. They offer guidelines for both citizens and public
officials. Some principles, such as the priority of basic needs
or the inclusion of disadvantaged groups, will carry greater
weight than others. Nonetheless, the balancing of goods for
the sake of the commonweal raises questions of sufficient complexity to preclude any final lexical ordering of norms. The common good functions above all as a coordinating principle, and
the weight of relevant norms will alter depending on circumstances. The goal of the coordination, however, remains clear:
*Everyone in the society ought to be able to share in an advanc-
ing quality of life.* In the politics of the common good, a society commits itself to the principle that every person should
share in a common quality life, and that as social conditions
improve all share the new developments. This general goal explains how later formulations such as "the preferential option
for the poor" and "the principle of solidarity" function as cognate norms. The option for the poor aims directly at the inclusion of one marginalized group into the mainstream of society.
The principle of solidarity charges privileged individuals,
groups, and nations with making sacrifices, even from their sub-
stance, to close the gap between themselves and the poor. The
two newer formulations aim at implementing the common
good, one by favoring policies which increase participation by
the poor, the other by identifying one form of the self-restraint
necessary to advance the good of all.

As a principle of practice, the common good attempts to
make each individual and social group consider the bearing
of its demands and aspirations on the whole society. Two sorts
of guidelines emerge from recent Catholic teaching for consideration by citizens, intermediary groups, and government. The

first class of rules provides general norms which apply to all levels of social organization:

1. Cooperate with government in harmonizing conflicting interests.
2. Control the inequalities which arise between groups.
3. Support government in its role as advocate of the last resort for disadvantaged groups.

These rules distill recent Catholic teaching on the common good, especially that of John XXIII. While certain other formulations have come to the fore since John's time, the more recent formulations cohere with the common good tradition. They offer principles for realizing the good of the whole society. All the principles of the common good seek to guide the actions of social groups under most circumstances.

The second set of norms offers rules for correction, when social processes or the pursuit of self-interest has led to great disparities between groups, whether in one society or among nations. The following norms apply ordinarily:

1. Seek the good of all without preference.
2. Balance one's own or one's group's interests with consideration for the interests of others.
3. Restrain the use of rights until those rights can be enjoyed by all.

There corrective principles also apply to relations between groups; for example, to business and labor, or to the academy and the community. The activity of government should enhance cooperative activity already under way between various other groups and find solutions when those groups are at an impasse. But the principles apply to the whole of society first, and then to politics. In political life, the principles provide guidance on how individuals and groups can accommodate to one another so that all can share in a life where they can develop to the full.

CONCLUSION

Over the last several decades we can observe convergence between the American political tradition and the common good tradition of Roman Catholicism. The American tradition has come to identify a number of limitations inherent in the pursuit of interest as a principle of social organization and of politics. Some theorists and some public policy analysts have found room for ethics as a kind of marginal constraint, correcting the worst effects of the politics of interest. More recently, others have also become concerned with the control of inequality. In short, the liberal tradition has begun to move closer to a classical politics in which ethics and politics serve one another in the public life.

For its part, Catholic social thought has begun to accommodate itself to some basic concerns of liberal politics. The substitution of human rights for natural law assigned greater value to individual life and development than in older interpretations of the common good. The common good was redefined in terms of its effects on individual persons. The emphasis on personal development also coincided with the goals of J. S. Mill's school of utilitarianism and with the goals of later social reformers. The theme of participation coincided with the goals of democratic practice. So, the tradition of the common good has also moved in the direction of *rapprochement* with liberal political philosophy. Yet the common good still remains an alternative to the politics of self-interest. The shifts have muted differences but not overcome them.

The preceding analysis of the principle of the common good in recent Catholic social teaching has been presented chiefly in the hopes of clarifying the nature of that alternative. At the same time the common good offers not just another alternative. It represents a position which answers at least some of the internal contradictions of the politics of self-interest as they have been identified in recent years. Moreover, the narrowing of differences between the two strains of political thought, the growth on the Catholic side of participation in the definition and regulation of the common good, and the encouragement of attitudes and dispositions which reduce the tensions coming from excessive moralism in the political arena—all these developments illustrate the adaptability of the common good tradition to the moderate politics to which the tradition of liberalism aspires. The time has now come for the advocates of the liberal tradition in America to experiment with the princi-

ple and rules of the common good in order to test whether
they provide solutions to the shortcomings of a politics founded
on self-interest.

NOTES

1. Vatican II's Pastoral Constitution on the Church and the
Modern World (no. 31–43), commonly known by its Latin title *Gaudium et spes,* presents human rights and the service of the unity of
the human family as the two primary ways in which the Church serves
the world. The English text may be found in David J. O'Brien and
Thomas A. Shannon, eds., *Renewing the Earth: Catholic Documents
on Peace, Justice and Liberation* (Garden City, N.Y.: Doubleday/
Image, 1977), 178–284.

2. Robert N. Bellah et al., *Habits of the Heart: Individualism
and Commitment in American Life* (Berkeley: University of California Press, 1985), 196–218, 250–71.

3. Ibid., 218.

4. Ibid.

5. Ibid.

6. Ibid., 256–70.

7. For a survey of the changes which have accompanied Catholic social teaching on the common good since the time of Leo XIII,
see Charles E. Curran, "The Common Good and Official Catholic
Social Teaching" in Oliver F. Williams and John W. Houck, eds., *The
Common Good and U.S. Capitalism* (Lanham, Md.: University Press
of America, 1987). Other contributions to the same volume illustrate
the variety of interpretation to which the concept can be subject in
the public domain.

8. In English-speaking political philosophy, one may write of
liberalism without fear of being misunderstood. Liberalism is the mainstream of Anglo-American political philosophy in which the principle of individual liberty is the unifying bond for a range of cognate
political theories. Thus, liberalism is the mother of thought for politicians on both the left and right of American politics.

In ordinary speech and everyday politics, however, the terms *liberal* and *liberalism* represent only the party on the left of the political spectrum. For that reason, to speak of liberalism can be confusing to the average reader. Accordingly, I have been sparing in my
explicit use of the terms *liberal* and *liberalism,* and instead have used
cognates like *the Anglo-American political tradition, individualist
politics, the American political tradition,* and so on.

A classic survey of liberalism may be found in Sheldon Wolin,

Politics and Vision: Continuity and Innovation in Western Political Thought (Boston: Little, Brown, 1960), chap. 9: "Liberalism and the Decline of Political Philosophy," 286–351. A more comprehensive historical survey and ethical evaluation may be found in Anthony Arblaster, *The Rise and the Fall of Western Liberalism* (Oxford: Basil Blackwell, 1984).

On how Western society turned its back on the quest for glory, see note 9 below.

9. See A. O. Hirschman, *The Passions and the Interests: Arguments for Capitalism before Its Triumph* (Princeton, N.J.: Princeton University Press, 1977), 7–86, on the arguments for a politics centered on commercial prosperity.

10. On the displacement of conscience by interests, see Wolin, *Politics and Vision,* 331–42. Hirschman discusses how the search for glory, whether for God, king, or self, was replaced by the calmer ambition of the pursuit of material prosperity in *The Passions and the Interests,* 63–66.

11. For a review of the separation of fact and value in American social science, see Duncan MacRae, Jr., *The Social Function of Social Science* (New Haven, Conn.: Yale University Press, 1976), chap. 3: "Positivism and the Devaluation of Ethics," 32–76.

12. Daniel Bell, *The End of Ideology* (New York: Free Press/Macmillan, 1960).

13. Theodore J. Lowi, *The End of Liberalism: The Second Republic of the United States,* 2nd ed. (New York: Norton, 1979).

14. Robert Paul Wolff, *The Poverty of Liberalism* (Boston: Beacon, 1968), esp. chap. 5: "Community," 162–95.

15. David Braybrooke, *Three Tests for Democracy* (New York: Random House, 1968); J. Roland Pennock, *Democratic Political Theory* (Princeton, N.J.: Princeton University Press, 1979); and MacRae, *Social Function.*

16. Frank M. Coleman, *Hobbes and America: Exploring the Constitutional Foundation* (Toronto: University of Toronto Press, 1977); Charles E. Lindblom, *Politics and Markets: The World's Political-Economic Systems* (New York: Basic Books, 1977); and Benjamin Barber, *Strong Democracy: Participatory Politics for a New Age* (Berkeley: University of California Press, 1984).

17. Daniel Bell, *The Cultural Contradictions of Capitalism* (New York: Basic, 1976); and Michael J. Crozier, Samuel Huntington, and Joji Watanuki, *Crisis in Democracy: Report on the Governability of Democracies to the Trilateral Commission* (New York: New York University Press, 1975), esp. pt. 3, "The United States," 59–118.

18. Bell, *Cultural Contradiction of Capitalism,* 25–26, 220–82, esp. 244–51.

19. On the socal welfare function and related aggregate measures, see MacRae, *Social Function,* chap. 5: "Economic Ethics," esp. 107–44.

20. David Hollenbach, *Claims in Conflict: Retrieving and Renewing the Catholic Human Rights Tradition* (New York: Paulist Press, 1979), 89–100.

21. Dennis McCann and Charles R. Strain, *Polity and Praxis: A Program for American Practical Theology* (Minneapolis: Winston Press, 1985); Dennis McCann, *New Experiment in Democracy: The Challenge for American Democracy* (Kansas City, Mo.: Sheed and Ward, 1987); and Dennis McCann, "The Good to be Pursued in Common" in Williams and Houck, *Common Good,* 158–78.

22. The recent publication of the draft of a U.S. bishops' letter on women and the church in which much of the text consists of testimony from women suggests further progress in this process of public dialogue in the shaping of consensus even within the church. See "Partners in the Mystery of Redemption," *Origins* 17:45 (April 21, 1988), 757, 759–88.

23. On recent revisionist views of integration, see Derrick Bell, *And We Are Not Saved: The Elusive Quest for Racial Justice* (New York: Basic Books, 1987).

24. For a review and analysis of Bernardin's "consistent ethic of life," see Joseph Bernardin et al., *The Consistent Ethic of Life* (Kansas City, Mo.: Sheed and Ward, 1988).

25. On the need to take principles and virtues together, see Basil Mitchell, *Morality: Religious and Secular: The Dilemma of the Traditional Conscience* (Oxford: Oxford University Press, 1980).

In the case of recent Roman Catholic teaching on the common good, it is particularly important to give some practical priority to the virtues over the principles, as the formulation of the principles are clearly the result in part of reflection on evolving social conditions which in the short term may prove divisive. The substantive norms of justice in recent Catholic social teaching are defensible for social and moral as well as theological reasons; but a consensual process may demand refraining from advancing the hardest demands in more sensitive political contexts. The need to build a common political will goes ahead of pressing specific goals.

In that sense, the U.S. bishops' accommodations to the U.S. political economy in *Economic Justice for All* and their articulation of "the consistent ethic of life" as strategy for building consensus on the restriction of abortions represent models of how to introject substantive normative concerns into political debate.

A Roycean Response to the Challenge of Individualism

Frank M. Oppenheim, S.J.

I. INTRODUCTION

We Americans clearly need a way of talking about individual and community without becoming immediately polarized. American philosopher Josiah Royce (1855–1916) offered an interpretation that integrates these two realities in a harmonious complementarity. As one who has carefully examined Royce's thought for some time, I want in this essay to employ some of Royce's central insights relevant to real individuals and communities and to our talk about them. Royce insisted on the value of genuine individualism even as he campaigned for decades against its self-centered counterfeit. He pioneered a path leading to the kind of community that achieves humanly enhanced goods and better individualizes its members.[1] Perhaps what America needs as it approaches the year 2000 is not so much the therapeutic individualism stemming from William James as the community consciousness nourished by Josiah Royce.

In the decades just before and after 1900, Royce must have struck many Americans as an oddity. The times were filled with social turmoil, floods of immigrants, booming young industries, labor riots, and national muscle flexing in the Spanish-American War. To Andrew Carnegie and his fellow tycoons Royce must have seemed an impractical professor with his head lost in the clouds. To most Harvard students — sons or grand-

sons of those once poor lads who had struggled up the ladder
of American opportunity to sizable fortunes—"Uncle Royce"
seemed an irrelevant teacher. For them, what counted was the
stimulating message of Russell H. Conwell. He was the "successful" preacher who around the turn of the century announced
the same "good news" to six thousand eager audiences. To one
and all his message was: "It is your duty to get rich," "It's all
wrong to be poor," and "The number of the poor who are to
be sympathized with is very small." He explained that sympa-
thy far too often leads us to help the *un*deserving poor (whom
a just God is continuing to punish) rather than the surprisingly
few deserving poor.[2]

Contrary to Conwell's inciting of their desire for wealth,
Royce challenged his Harvard students and public audiences
to grow morally by doing deeds of atonement. He advised them
to guard against the nondiscriminating sympathies of moblike
thinking and "certain [other] limitations of the thoughtful
American public."[3] He called his audience to integrate their
unique individual energies with the nation's common good. To
many, then, at the close of the Gilded Age, Royce seemed "a
really strange duck."

Even in the eyes of many secularized professors and scientists disciplined to agnosticism by their "value-free" methodolo-
gies, Royce surely seemed a misfit in "proper" Harvard. How
could he still preach idealism and wrap it up in biblical language when the pragmatic movement had brushed all that aside
long ago? Did he not know the watchwords of the present Progressive Era were change and individual initiative, not abso-
lutes and community life? How did he dare speak of "atoning
loyalty toward *all* people" when "those on the inside track"
were racing pell-mell for those cash values that many took to
be the intent of James's *Pragmatism?*

Little wonder, then, that Royce found few who actually
grasped his message. Treatment like this, according to a well-
known rabbi from Nazareth, revealed a true prophet. Furthermore, Royce's final years (1910–1916) were marked with increasing tragedy,[4] yet during them he grew interiorly more than at
any other time in his life. This mature period was marked by
astounding intellectual, affective, moral, and religious development. His "Peircean insight" of 1912 transformed his philo-

sophical life and led him to create *The Problem of Christianity* (1913).[5] As Gabriel Marcel soon detected, Royce had finally arrived in this late master work at a new medium and method through which he could convey with ease the message that he had so long been trying in vain to express fully.[6] The "Great Community" of humankind, guided by the "Spirit of the Universal Community," now became Royce's rekindled hope.[7] He discerned some of the structures of this community and contributed to its coming both by finding a "religious mission of sorrow" in his late sufferings and by turning these into atoning experiences. As World War I cast its darker shadows upon widening circles, Royce compared himself to a night watchman who waits eagerly for the dawn (*HGG,* 132–36). He hoped ardently for a brighter day after the war. In this way his intensified struggle with the problem of evil occasioned much inner growth — growth that expressed itself in his mature writings and public service.

Having introduced Royce, I now wish in this essay to respond from a Roycean perspective to the challenge of self-preferential individualism. In doing so, I will shift the focus from middle-class Americans and their values to all members of humankind's great community, lay the foundations needed to replace self-preferential individualism with community consciousness, point to a metaphysics different from "ontological individualism"— an alternate metaphysics in which communities are as basic to reality as are individual persons — and highlight the increased need for deeds of atonement that fit the central mystery of Christianity. In the conclusion, I will use Royce's design to invite each American to take part in creating that kind of "community of memory and of hope" through which we can fittingly enter the third millennium.[8]

II. A ROYCEAN APPROACH TO INDIVIDUALISM AND COMMITMENT

A. Issues in Individualism

In their Preface, the authors of *Habits of the Heart* clearly express their justified concern that American "individualism may have grown cancerous."[9] They then portray contemporary American individualists in vivid and concrete terms. In doing so, they focus on the middle class and demonstrate these Americans' widespread sense of uneasiness, insecurity, isolation, and estrangement. They persistently highlight the underlying question of how to preserve or create a morally coherent life (*HH*, viii). In the present section, then, I want to respond, as a Roycean scholar, to these three topics in order.

1. *Beyond Middle Class Values*

Readers of Josiah Royce know how strongly he urged the further promotion of humankind's great community. As a Roycean, then, I can only concur heartily with the recommendation of the *Habits* team that we Americans cease regarding ourselves as a special creation and that we rejoin the human race. I delight to find that the data reflected in *Habits* clearly reproduce Royce's own sketch of those human selves who naturally lie captive to fearful alienations and anxious isolation. I am also pleased by the authors' recommendation that middle-class Americans need greater sensitivity toward their natural and moral ecospheres. Royce loved and revered nature, responded discriminatively to past generations and their traditions, and felt responsible for future generations (*HGC*, 122–26).

On the other hand, the authors' focus was limited by the need that sociology has to advance empirically. Consequently, they can seem to fall victim to the very disease that they are trying to remedy. For a *fair* understanding of a problem, Royce required that our knowledge of it be marked not only by close personal touch and coherent unity but also by a breadth of range.[10]

We need, then, to attend to how these Americans are affecting and being affected by Japan, West Germany, and other free-market democracies, the Soviet system, and especially that two-thirds of the human race which comprise the Third World. In other words, we need to listen to 95 percent of what is (at least potentially) Royce's great community of humankind.

Furthermore, a still wider context of the middle class deserves notice. Most of us self-preferentially individualistic Americans certainly need a heightened sensitivity toward our natural environment. We also need to carry out Royce's directive that we minded beings open up to "grades of mind above our own" (*BWJR*, 2:759). We need not only to open ourselves to the possibilities of a universal community, its spirit, and this pair's ongoing teaching that calls humankind to more effective bonds of unity; but we also need to exercise practical faith in these three realities (*PC*, 402–5).

Then, too, Royce's metaphysics of a two-leveled universe consists ultimately of individuals *and* communities. Both of these are always developing yet constant in their unique bearing into the future. This "social realism" offers to threatened middle-class Americans a remedy for their myopic individualism. In our therapeutic culture, the individualistic self must both tell itself, "I'm OK!" and support it with "I'm good!" When a person of our middle class feels threatened by America's richest and poorest, and especially by hostile "foreigners," such a self will tend uncritically to join the American chorus, "We Americans are Number One!" This popular slogan, however, hardly hides the personal and national arrogance opposed to the principle that all are created equal. It is out of tune with our Declaration of Independence and with biblical and federalist languages fashioning it. By contrast, Royce's doctrine that graced communities are living realities, greater and nobler than real individuals, suggests that we Americans need a saving humility and an openness to the gifts offered by such communities. His doctrine also confirms the solidarity of each American as a co-member of the human race. Within it all of us are equally "Number Twos" beneath the universal community and its spirit as our governing pair.

Our first probe, then, has revealed some of the limitations of focussing on middle-class Americans. It has prepared us to turn to some limitations in these Americans themselves.

2. Anxious Isolation in Middle-Class Americans

Those who try to promote community—whether at the level of family or neighborhood or city or nation—run into the shotgun barrage of particle-like individuals all shooting off in their own directions. The lives of middle-class Americans exhibit a pervasive "note of uncertainty . . . an anxiety about where we

seem to be headed," a "widespread feeling that the promise of
the modern era is slipping away from us" (*HH*, 276–77). Americans generally feel isolated, uprooted from traditions, and
troubled in conscience about having preferred themselves — as
individuals, groups, or a nation — to the larger common good
(*HH*, 285). Many Americans feel unsafe with the sharp economic and racial inequality surrounding them. They are especially fearful that if they give up their inner dream of private
success in life to promote a more genuinely integrated societal
community, they will lose their individuality and be absorbed
into a stifling collectivity (*HH*, 286).

Work in offices and plants so strains most Americans, and
corrupt practices in business and government so sour them, that
they simply want the comforts of a small utopian town where
they can remain passive and uninvolved in public problems. They
want a safe hideaway, free of "weirdos" and hostile foreigners.
Whether frayed or bored by keen competition, many want off
the speeding escalator of upward mobility. Many prefer to accept dead ends at work or seek early retirement.

Hence, to sum up middle-class Americans' deep feelings that
all is *not* well, the authors of *Habits* draw on an ancient quotation from the historian Livy describing his own decadent Rome,
"We have reached the point where we cannot bear either our
vices or their cures" (*HH*, 294).

Royce pictures American society with equally concrete realism. He goes beyond this, however, when he insists that Americans' experience of "lostness" and of "estrangement from a fuller,
more meaningful life" is only the first of two required steps for
the integral development of persons as human. In brief, things
have to get worse before they get better. Both steps — that of
experiencing the "lost state" *and* that of finding the rich meaning of the "loyal life"— are required to elevate human selves into
the higher life of what Royce calls "man the community." Later
on, I will describe this graced life in the unity of a spiritual
whole that reverences responsible individual freedom. For the
moment let us focus on Royce's first step:

> The saving idea of man the community comes to us through
> two kinds of perfectly human experiences. First, it comes to
> us through the experience of the failure both of our natural self-

> will and of our mere morality to save us. This failure is due
> to the essential defect of the level upon which, by nature, man
> the social individual lives. . . . Individual self-will is due to our
> insatiable natural greed, and is only inflamed by our merely
> moral cultivation. (*PC,* 219)

The isolated individual is awash in feelings of getting nowhere.
Whether setting one's course for oneself or merely conforming
to external behavioral norms, one finds no meaningful life created by living so individualistically. This kind of person either
tries to ignore other persons or, if he or she recognizes them
in society, does so as a unique individual only. Thus, having
increasingly inflamed one's antagonism towards them, one is
goaded into deeper individual cunning in order to outwit those
others still further.

To this sad but familiar picture of widespread alienation,
Royce added another step—one that leads to true freedom:

> Secondly, however, when such experience of the failure of
> a merely individual human existence has done its work, an-
> other sort of experience is needed to reveal to us the mean-
> ing of the life which belongs to the other human level,—to the
> level of the beloved community. This experience is the experi-
> ence of the meaning of loyalty. It is this experience which, while
> always essentially human in the facts that it brings to our no-
> tice, opens up its endless vistas, suggests to us countless inter-
> pretations in terms of our relations to a supernatural world,
> and justly seems to be a revelation of something not ourselves
> which is worthy to be our guide and salvation. (*PC,* 219)

Here is that crowning experience of grace and loyalty that follows upon one's deep sense of personal psychomoral bankruptcy
as a mere individual. Only from that deep existential crisis will
one cry out, "I cannot make sense of my life by myself; I cannot reach a genuinely rewarding life *unless I am united to a
saving community and its Spirit* whose leadership and influence I accept and commit myself to follow by my freed responses and initiatives."[11] The self's psychic alertness both to
call upon and to commune with the whole universe and its Spirit
constitutes the central nerve of a human self's truly meaningful life. As Royce had said earlier, the human self "gains its very

individuality through its relation to God; but in God it still dwells as an individual; for it is an unique expression of divine purpose."[12]

Royce also witnesses that if human selves are to escape their anxious isolation, they must also cooperate in a second step: their graced and free commitment to the higher reality of a genuine community and its spirit. This prompts us to inquire about the right road toward such commitment and the deviant paths leading away from it.

3. *How Can One Create or Preserve a Morally Coherent Life?*

Royce delved to the very foundations of ethical life: that fundamental orientation whereby one loyally loves the whole universe. Royce's mature philosophy centers on universal community and its spirit.[13] This pair uses a temporal process of worldwide interpretation to invite selves of all kinds, especially minded beings, to reach their fuller genuine individuation, and thus to escape the various forms of irrational individualism.[14] Minded selves do this by loyally communicating and operating in genuine communities, and even by entering into the spirit's operation of atoning deeds. These latter heal alienations, provide reconciliations, and foster greater unity between human selves and their diverse communities.

To enter into this saving worldwide process of reconciling interpretation, each human self needs to adopt and promote a certain fundamental attitude of will: to belong to a genuine community rather than to center on oneself. As the two-step experience described above indicated, an isolated human self cannot achieve this "belonging" except as influenced by a saving community and its spirit. The genuine moral life of each person, then, lies in this fundamental interdependence between the human self, its saving community, and its spirit. If the human self regards itself as merely isolated, it perverts its own genuine life.

Moreover, in its temporally processing consciousness, the human self can choose its genuine fundamental orientation. This lies in the self's loyal love of the whole real universe. The context for this basic choice is set by the self's psychic conviction about its past deeds — good and bad — and by its in-depth awareness that it always can betray its genuine selfhood and its community. Aware of the community and its spirit and their invitation, the self also knows it can directly counter its fundamental call to belong to both; that is, it can violate the fitting basic direction of its moral life. By choosing not to communicate and cooperate in a genuine community according to its own unique gifts and character, the human self can "sin against the Holy Spirit," as Royce expressed it using biblical language.

By carrying out a profound analysis, Royce showed that we can take one of three basic attitudes of will toward the universe (*PC*, 348–62). The first fundamental attitude is "the affirmation of the will to live." One recognizes this attitude in the choice to be immoderately self-interested — a choice that marks both utilitarian and expressive individualists. They prefer their individual self over other selves, communities, and public goods. Both the logic and practice of such individualists, however, are self-contradictory. Beneath their present experience of mutually conflicting human wills lies their basic unrejectable desire for an ultimate ideal harmony of wills.[15] Logically, then, one cannot consistently want oneself and all others to prefer each one's individual self and nevertheless desire the unrejectable ideal of an ultimate harmony of all human wills. Practically, one cannot tolerate it if all others fully exercise their aggressive self-preferential attitudes against oneself.

The second basic attitude of will is "the denial of the will to live." In its encounters with other persons and society's demands, a human self is often bumped and bruised. So, the self frequently tends to prefer introversion and to regard its own intense interior life as more real and important than the external world. Its preference to withdraw from external life often inclines it to seek direct mystical union with the All, without any mediation through other human selves. This basic attitude of self-denying withdrawal from the world is found not only in Hīnayāna (or Theravāda) Buddhism, as Royce pointed out, but also in the current trend among Americans to increased privacy, to heightened introversion, and in the extreme instance, to suicide. The inconsistency intrinsic to this second attitude becomes clear since the human self can develop psychologically and morally *only* by interrelating with other human selves and their communities.

The third fundamental attitude of will, "genuine loyalty towards the whole of reality," commends itself as positive, community-building, and self-validating. Royce taught that one "must fall in love with the universe" if one is to begin *genuine* life, philosophy, and religion (*PC,* 269–70, 319). This kind of loyalty is the "*practically devoted love of an individual for a community*" that thus becomes one's cause (*PC,* 41; Royce's emphasis). Such love empowers the genuinely loyal self to interact with the community and its members, to cooperate for the common good mutually hoped for. The neuralgic point of this loyalty is that it be genuine, not merely natural; that is, that it be (at least implicitly) open to *all* minded beings and *all* genuine communities. This requires getting beyond the exclusiveness that usually marks merely natural communities (like families, clans, races, and nations). Usually these exclude outsiders in some arbitrary way. Therefore, an initial trusting openness toward every minded self, as (at least potentially) a member of the universal community of reality, is an indispensable basis for genuine loyalty, the third and only self-validating basic attitude of will.

We have, then, experienced the performatory contradictions intrinsic to the first two basic attitudes of will. However widely embraced by nondiscerning selves, both attitudes corrupt the tap root of moral life in any human self. Hence, the third attitude—namely, genuine loyalty toward the universal community of reality—is the only basic attitude of will that is morally viable. Whatever follows in this chapter, then, presupposes one's fundamental preference for this third attitude of genuine loyalty. Royce held it to be the seed of morality, religion, and sane philosophy (*PC,* 319).

Beyond creating one's authentic moral life, this profound conversion or transformation to loyalty also affects the intellectual, affective, religious, and sociopolitical spheres of one's life.[16] Knowing that genuine morality requires an openness to a community that ultimately is divine, Royce would not settle for a "mere morality." Hence, when one's fundamental attitude of will is genuine loyalty towards the real universe, the "loyal belonging" within this attitude relates one to the "invisible church" and its Spirit. According to Royce, this Spirit continually communicates a life-giving doctrine that each genuinely loyal self is called to make one's own and put into practice by loyal service.

Because of this kind of "belonging," the moral self is just as communal as it is uniquely individual. In brief, then, no communal cause, no self! Royce's communal way of "finding oneself" undergirds the "relation between private and public life"—a relation that is "one of the keys to the survival of free institutions" (*HH,* viii).[17] Royce's position, then, concurrent with America's biblical and republican traditions, identifies both community and individual as coequally ultimate realities. His "special realism" sharply counters the current belief of most Americans that the world's primary realities are individuals only and that all communities simply derive from individuals' choices and so are not ultimate realities. It also counters that materialistic naturalism that degrades moral life in America by stifling the minimal idealism needed for even the possibility of morality and religion.[18] If human selves are not minded beings whose inmost search is for a transtemporal truth and love, and for an absolutely transcendent, minded Being, then morality and religion, as morally and religiously committed people ordinarily understand them, are impossible.[19]

B. The Pursuit of Happiness

Middle-class Americans like to think of themselves as in pursuit of happiness. *Pilgrims' Progress,* John Bunyan's classic that Royce read so frequently, pictures the human person instead as a pilgrim trekking through the wilderness to one's true homeland. Unlike the "pursuer of happiness," this image suggests not only knowledge of our destination but also trial and error along the way. It precludes our nesting by the wayside since here we have no lasting city. It packages both pain and pleasure in our pilgrim experience of wayfaring. This image parallels that of being "citizens of two worlds," offered by Pope John Paul II.[20] In these latter images the goal of the human person contrasts sharply with that suggested by the image of the "pursuer of happiness." Bunyan and the pope do not suggest that our highest human good consists in avoiding pain and pursuing pleasure. Instead, their more adequate images portray that good as lying in a sought-after homeland where our union is harmonious in the life of the Spirit.

Next, concerning procedure, most of our practical and theoretical thinking in the past has consisted either in experiential perceptions or grasps of universal concepts, or in a combination of these two. Both C. S. Peirce and Royce, however, have shown that these cognitive procedures are inadequate (*PC*, 273–319). Percepts and concepts cannot adequately explain the knowings we experience when we interact with people, grasp values, read signs, make logical inferences, and come to know in many other ways. All of these depend upon a third and even more fundamental cognitive procedure called *interpretation*. It breaks through the mediating idea that builds unity of minds and thus creates a genuine "*community of interpretation*." This third basic cognitive procedure is impossible unless it goes *beyond* perceptions and conceptions by sighting a "*third factor*" (or sign) that links disparate minds. Hence our current pressing need to shift our cognitive procedure into the interpretive mode—not merely for reaching further creative insights at the general level, but especially for grasping and being grasped by those concrete, dynamic, interpersonal insights that evoke a direct changing of hearts. Anyone drawn to an interpretation of this latter more direct kind experiences the challenge of making a quantum leap in one's cognitive procedure. Most of us have long-standing habits of relying simply on percepts or concepts or on their combinations, or perhaps of using interpretation to arrive only at general results. Nevertheless, if we enter into the search that occurs when people dialogue and focus mainly on the signs that interacting minds communicate, we will become direct interpreters who form an interpersonal "community of interpretation." By entering into this person-shaping process of interpretation, we contact the living source of a "community of memory and hope" (*PC*, 248).

Americans yearn for the spontaneous emergence of community. Schooled by Emerson and James, they also like to look to the open future and not to the settled past. These popular prejudices make it harder to grasp the wisdom in Royce's prophetic teaching that real community *also* requires a discerning respect for past tradition and a conscious intelligent cooperation in the present. Josiah Royce specified these requirements for creating and maintaining genuine community (*PC*, 229–71). They have become one of his most appreciated contributions to our American wisdom.

Into his stipulated, more precise sense of *community,* Royce inserted the conscious sharing of "psychic extensions." He required that *each of the distinct members of the human group consciously identify oneself with the same, definite, ideally interpreted event or deed of the past or future.* If each potential member does this, there arises a community of memory, or of hope, or of both. Royce's specially restricted sense of *community* had a definite objective structure along with great intersubjective significance (*PC,* 248). Nevertheless, since such communities can be either "genuine" or "merely natural," we need to look more closely at their differences.

To rise to the truly loyal life of a genuine community, members must both fulfill *three conditions and* rise from a first to a third degree in their consciousness of community (*PC,* 253–55, 260, 262–71). The first condition requires each potential community member to *extend the consciousness of one's life*—yes, to the real past and future events of one's own mortal life as a unique individual—but especially, to those events and actions, persons and objects which generally lie beyond one's individual life span. One does this by identifying with and appropriating those items as part of one's own individual life, as ideally extended to those same past or future events that a pluralism of diverse selves also identify with and make part of their lives.

For example, how does a person consciously create one's self-identification as an American? One takes in, *as* part of one's own ideally extended life, the past events of the Declaration of Independence and of Gettysburg. One also takes in, as part of the American self one wants to be, those future days when all citizens of this country will have access to equal opportunity and when big money will not skew due process.

Royce added one qualification to this first condition. Since a genuine community is essentially a "doer of deeds," the only way the idealized events and objects of an individual self can belong to a community is if they are "bound up with the deeds of the community" (*PC,* 254). Such psychic extensions, then, must promote *deeds* of communal service.

This consciously possessed life is both individual and communal in a way specified by Royce's second condition: a number of distinct unique selves can and usually do engage in social communication. The life of the community consists in this exchange of signs by its irreducibly distinct members. Thus each member serves the common life *better* if one intelligently contributes (or communicates) to that life one's own constructive gift in its uniqueness (*PC,* 257).

Meanwhile, other potential members are also making their own ideal extensions and consciously appropriating some of the same idealized past and future events, actions, persons, and objects. They, too, identify these same items as "part of their ideally extended lives." So Royce concluded, "The *third* of the conditions for the existence of the community . . . consists in the fact that the ideally extended past and future selves of the members include at least some events which are, for all these selves, identical" (*PC,* 256; Royce's emphasis). That all these members' past and future ideal extensions coincide in some *same* past and future items creates the basis for these selves' sharing in at least almost the same interpretation of these items with each other.

For example, the Pauline Christians extended their consciousness back to their master's dying and rising as part of each one's own life and then stretched it forward to each one's own future bodily resurrection in the Lord. Since all these individually unique Christians included at least these two events in their ideal extensions, they could, according to the earlier second condition, communicate their nearly identical interpretations of them to one another. As a result, Pauline Christians enjoyed the sense of sharing life together. Each member possessed the same idea or doctrine, interpreted its practical bearing in the same way, and mutually recognized that the other members were making the same kind of ideal extensions to the same events and interpreting them similarly. In this way they formed one body of many members (*PC,* 256–58).

Beyond conditions, however, the conscious life of community has its *degrees* of quality. Even a band of robbers can attain the first degree of forming a "community of memory and hope." When this is enriched by shared understanding, personal identification with the community's life, and mutual acceptance by the other members, then the community has evolved to the second degree. A transformation into the climactic third degree, however, occurs only when *genuine* loyalty animates this consciousness of community. Such perfect quality is as precious as it is difficult to achieve (*PC,* 269). Interpreted in secular terms, this highest degree of consciousness of community enables each member to love both one's particular community and the universal community *as* communities, in addition to loving all its individual members. Interpreted in Christian terms, this degree is marked by that divinely graced *caritas,* which is wholeheartedly practical in serving all the Church's actual and potential members. For this genuine loyalty or *caritas,* however, one must already have fallen in love with the universe (*PC,* 270, 357). But this loyal embrace of the whole of reality only arises if one has, as we saw, adopted the third fundamental attitude of will: loyalty to the ethicoreligious development of all finite persons.

It should be noticed, moreover, that although this sketch of the Roycean conditions and degrees of community life and consciousness is rectilinear, the actual history of any community's consciousness is often wayward, deviant, or even perverted into a "community of sin" and hate (*PC,* 127, 404; *HGC,* 53). According to their degree of deformity, communities of this latter type are even more powerfully destructive of moral and religious life than is the individual traitor. Correspondingly, they call for even greater compassion, reconciliation, and atonement.

We have seen, then, that just as individuals can be either ethically "lost" or genuine, so too communities can be "lost" or embodiments of the universal beloved community. Families, tribes, artists, scientists, nations, and similar groupings form, in their varying degrees, communities of both types: "lost" or genuine; merely natural or graced. In a series of genuine communities, the smaller are supported by the larger, according to a solidarity of subsidarity that serves the further realization of the universal community. Ordinarily, however, communities are mixed, so that the more usual situation is one of conflicting loyalties—for example, people who favor our national interests exclusively versus people who also favor the interests of the whole human family in that "fitting order of effective charity" sketched by Pope John XXIII.[21]

Royce, then, offered a pilgrim image of the human person, which is less misleading and more realistic than "pursuer of happiness." He called us to interpersonal interpretation as a more basic cognitive procedure, highlighted our need for "communities of memory of hope," and became quite specific about the attitudes, actions, and structures needed for such communities. He emphasized the "psychic extensions" in the *self-appropriating act* that makes one a member of a community, since each needs to say meaningfully, "This or that past or future event or person is part of my (ideally extended) life." Royce also stressed self-donation to a communal cause, the heart of his loyalty doctrine. He focused on the *life* of the community which calls each unique individual to receive the influence of the movements and teachings of the community and its spirit. In so doing each member-self will promote both the common good in its distinctive way *and* further its own genuine individualization.

C. PRIVATE LIFE IN AMERICA

Royce's most significant comment apropos to love and marriage[22] may be that a relation between only two persons forms a "dangerous pair." By contrast, a relation between two persons united by a common cause offers hope for increasing union and growth. Royce saw that if two human beings love each other in a merely natural, one-to-one relation, each one's individualistic self-preference will eventually sow hostility between them and ultimately destroy the love of this pair. He named this kind of relation "dyadic" and called it "dangerous" (*HGC,* 63).

Royce indicated the escape route out of this familiar hell of "merely natural" lovers. Will each of them grasp the same ideal together (their "third something" or common cause) and commit themselves wholeheartedly to it? Together will they communicate about it, cooperate toward it, and let this common good mediate and interpret their lives? If so, they will transcend the "dangerous pair" and form community; their love will be interpersonally healthy. Royce recognized that this triangular structure—John, Mary, *and* their shared "cause"—founds community and is indispensable for sound love. He called it a "triadic" relation. Furthermore, if the shared "cause" of John and Mary is in some way open to the universal community (for example, by intending to contribute to the growth of the human race, or by respecting all people), then theirs becomes a *genuine* community of love. It tends to save both themselves and those they influence.

In practice, however, how are Mary and John to tell whether theirs is a dyadic or triadic relationship? They can examine themselves with questions like the following: Have they dedicated themselves to the common life they share? Are they especially sensitive to their "cause" and its demands for mutual communication about it and cooperation to further realize it? Do they respect the worth of others' different ideals insofar as these are also open to promoting the universal community? Besides examining their shared life, both Mary and John must be personally in touch with our complex world. They must be untouchable by its corrupting influences. They must also be sensitively open to the Pedagogue Spirit's directional signs. In one amazing sentence that holds these three needs in balance Royce encapsulated his directives for loving loyally. Having proposed a "Pauline Christian" as his model for any genuinely loyal person, Royce wrote:

> [One] can remain, in spirit, a Pauline Christian, only in case he also learns, while justly recognizing the known world of today, how *not* to confer henceforth with flesh and blood, and how to discern spiritually the things of the spirit, despite the complexities of our modern realm. (*PC,* 376; Royce's emphasis)

Easy perhaps for a philosopher in his late fifties to create this recipe, but how does one learn the art of balancing the three ingredients requisite for loyal love? Royce's response: Practice believing in and experiencing the discernable difference between the "movements of spirits" at work in a merely natural community and those operating in a genuine community (*PC,* 404–5). Then pray for the gift of interpreting the direction in which these various spirits move (*PC,* 319).

By carrying out these Roycean recommendations, one escapes the captivating spirit found in certain therapeutic relations that call one to attend only to the present spontaneous upsurgings of psychic energies and feelings. In contrast to the therapeutic relationships that are hermetically sealed off from other social bonds, Royce used the energies of the real community and its spirit to bring about healing. He even employed each one's feelings of stubborn individualism and instinctual rebellion against society's will and its institutional pressures. Through these feelings, too, one can get in touch with one's own deepest initiative and freedom. Thus, whether experiencing communal or self-preferential feelings, one can ask, Which sort of spirit is moving in the action I'm thinking of doing? or again, Does this course of action truly promote the coming of the universal community? (*PC*, 404–5).

In the light of the answers thus uncovered, one can discern (or "see") whether giving oneself to love in this proposed way fits a practically respectful loyalty for all people and their genuine causes, as well as for one's own truest individuality and community. By such discernment one may discover whether societal forces are merely using oneself in a depersonalizing way, whether they are seductively coopting oneself into a rigid conformism, or whether they are inviting one into free service of the open community. In sum, Royce calls all lovers to exercise a critical discernment of spirits when they choose their "modes of action."[23]

If one already lives in a loving circle, why reach out to the stranger? Why extend oneself to differences that will challenge and invite change? Middle-class Americans often view their career simply as an all-encompassing escalator that lifts them to higher standards of living. Thinking this way, however, they become more fiercely competitive and heighten their psychic tensions. As a result, they increasingly seek therapies for freedom from their anxieties and demand more insistently those alternatives of jet-set relaxations that are longer lasting and sometimes more exotic (*HH*, 120). This one-dimensional view of the middle class has helped produce Americans' therapeutic culture that is detached and "casually relaxed." Based only on a contract to follow procedural rules, this culture excludes both the incentives to reach out to strangers and the objective moral standards governing such reaching out.

In contrast to this one-dimensional, now-centered functionalism, I find that Royce integrates the human self through many pairs of energies. Emergent from community yet always living in it, the unique human individual is energized by the inflowing life of the community as both a second-level reality and as itself a unique minded being with its own life. Moreover, the energy of the particular cause of this community, if genuine, is by its openness paired with and confirmed by the grace of the universal community, which also touches the individual human self. In this self, the energies of appropriated history and hope enrich its present life. Finally, as even infants show by both their imitative behavior and their social contrariness, the twofold energies of this self's social interests and unique initiatives further enrich the life of this uniquely socialized self. For the Roycean self, then, these four pairs of energies make the human self's life "sensitive, discerningly docile, and creative with its own initiative."[24] Its life consists in its "extensions," as Royce calls them, its foundations for reaching out and "belonging."

This inescapable other-relatedness of the human self also becomes evident from Royce's shift to interpretive knowing as the lifeblood of his mature philosophy. Interpretation requires one to view each personal self as *both* an individual *and* a community. By such knowing, then, the human self is uniquely individualized only insofar as it is socially bonded, that is, only insofar as it reaches out and commits itself wholeheartedly to a common cause and to all other member-selves embracing that cause.[25] A Roycean view of the human self's interpretation-based consciousness powerfully counters, then, both utilitarian and expressive individualism. These deviant senses of individualism, however, need first to be grasped in their deeper poisoned root, namely, in the "belief that the individual has a primary reality whereas society is a second-order, derived or artificial construct."[26] This belief is "ontological individualism," the cancer that infects most individualism alive in America today—whether of the utilitarian ("What's in it for me?") or of the expressive ("Just let me be me") varieties. Ontological individualism sharply contradicts "social realism," the belief, namely, that community (or "basic society") is *as* real and fundamental as individuals. Social realism is embedded in America's biblical and republican traditions, as well as in Royce's philosophy. Indeed, the genuine community is nobler than any finite individual because it is the sole source of grace and higher life. He based his philosophy of community and spirit on this doctrine of the "two levels" of reality and of consciousness, and on his definitions of community and individual (*PC,* 139, 194, 218–19). These bases deserve a closer look.

Royce distrusted the many vague senses of the term *community*. He wanted to sharpen his own usage so that it would exclude herds and flocks, transient human gatherings and mobs, and even those groups who simply happen to live in the same place under the same government. "Not every social group which behaves so that, to an observer, it seems to be a single unity, meets all the conditions of our definition," he added (*PC,* 251). His more accurate definition, however, had to cover both "merely natural" and "genuine" communities—his terms that partly parallel what people today call "closed" and "open" societies.

Because Royce achieved a fuller understanding of *community* and *individual* by interpreting each of them alternately as *both* an individual self *and* a community, his technical term "man the mere individual" points to a kind of community as well as a kind of individual person. Thus by "man the mere individual" Royce indicated an individual human self "morally detached" from a genuine community *or* the whole human race viewed as a morally impotent mass of such individuals *or any* communities caught in "their original hatefulness" that lie between the two (*PC,* 404). These were what he meant by "merely natural communities" or "man the mere individual." They are characterized by ethicoreligious deadness (or impotence to integrate knowledge, will, love, and deed). Essentially, such a self—whether a community or an individual human being—cannot move toward the goal of human life. Only through the saving influence of the *graced* universal community (or beloved community) can this "lost individual" or "lost community" become empowered to dedicate itself in loyalty to a genuine community, and thus "belong" to it. Only then can it express this dedication through genuinely loyal deeds that progressively save this no longer mere individual.

Royce felt that his term "man the community" needed even more careful handling. Many miss his meaning here by misidentifying it with a human society or a social institution or a mere collectivity of human individuals. Rather, by "man the community," Royce meant the invisible community of humankind's shared spiritual interests, ideals, and hopes, along with its shared processes of communication and cooperation.[27] Here is Royce's deeper "second level" of humankind's existence and consciousness. His famous "second level," however, is not exclusively human since it is also, "in its inmost nature, a divine community" (*PC,* 72).

Coming to his critically important description of "man the

community," Royce first cleared away the debris of many misleading interpretations:

> And by man the community I mean, *not* the collective biologi-
> cal entity called the human race, and not the merely natural
> community which gives to us, as social animals, our ordinary
> moral training. Nor by man the community do I mean the
> series of misadventures and tragedies whereof the merely ex-
> ternal history of what is called humanity consists. (*PC*, 218;
> Royce's emphasis)

Having brushed aside these senses (that deviated from his target
because they employed primarily biological, cultural, or historical approaches), Royce felt he could safely communicate his
positive meaning:

> By man the community I mean man in the sense in which Paul
> conceived Christ's beloved and universal Church to be a com-
> munity,—viewed as one conscious spiritual whole of life. And
> I say that this conscious spiritual community is the sole pos-
> sessor of the means of grace, and is the essential source of the
> salvation of the individual. (*PC*, 218–19)

Since this genuine community is "viewed as one conscious spiritual whole of life," alienating hostilities and moral inertness
violate this higher life. Rather, fullness of trust and loyal love,
reverent communication and cooperation constitute this shared
life in the unity of the Spirit. Here is a "beloved community,"
strikingly different from the "only too human" and too frequent
"merely natural communities." As mentioned, Royce did not
settle for making abstract hypotheses about possible "beloved
communities." He called each human self to a practical as well
as theoretical *personal faith* in the reality and life of "beloved
communities." Only such deed-doing faith generates the kind
of loyal self-gifting, communication, and cooperation that genuine community life requires (*PC*, 357, 402–5). Clearly, such
life is miles removed from that of either utilitarian or expressive individualists.

D. Religion in Public Life

Royce was reared in an evangelical tradition but as an adult
did not belong to any visible denomination. Throughout his

life he clearly appreciated mysticism despite its immaturity and frequent caprices (*PC,* 216). So one would fairly expect Royce to emphasize sect and mysticism more than church. The Church invisible, however, was his religious homeland, his beloved community. Moreover, he was convinced that since this "Universal Community must be something concrete and practically efficacious, . . . the visible Church had to be organized" (*PC,* 137). So he suggested that those who, unlike himself, belonged to a visible church should test whether it promotes the coming of the universal community. "If your church does not yet fully meet this standard, aid towards reforming your church accordingly" (*PC,* 405). Keenly sensitive to the many scandals and blemishes in the history of the Church, Royce patiently acknowledged the good services of visible churches. This attitude toward the visible Church is almost as awesome as is his wholehearted devotion to the Spirit of the invisible Church (*PC,* 42, 61, 138, 403).

The sectarian dimension in Royce's philosophy of the Christian religion was fostered both by his evangelical upbringing and his recognition of the Church's past debasing alliances. History taught him that when the Church sought support by close unions with governments, business, universities, and other centers of worldly power, it was distracted from its genuine life and work. Hence, he favored that the Church cease currying the favor of the powerful—cease "consorting with flesh and blood"—and rely solely on its inmost Word of God, the "sword of the Spirit," found in its basic Christian doctrine of life (*PC,* 212–13).[28]

Mysticism, as the relatively direct experience of the divine presence, was part of Royce's inner religious life, fostered by his pioneer mother who was herself called a "mystic." He studied it carefully for decades, indicated the shortcoming of its excesses, and branded any individualistic desire for immediacy of the divine presence an immature escapism from the needed route to God that leads through one's neighbors and the human community. He judged William James's exclusive emphasis on individual ecstatic moments of the "alone with the Alone" a "profound and a momentous error" because it discarded communal encounters with the Holy as valid sources of religious experience (*PC,* 40–41). Instead, Royce recommended attention to ordinary everyday mysticism, the finding of God in the glance of a true lover, in a friend's freely helping hand. This source of religious insight he found in

> the mystery of loving membership in a community whose meaning seems divine. . . . Such union of the two levels has its place in our daily lives wherever the loyalty of an individual leader shows to other men the way that leads them to the realm of the spirit. And whenever that union takes place, the divine and the human seem to come into touch with each other as elsewhere they never do. (PC, 140)

Strengthened by such everyday mysticism, disciplined by a sect-like unwillingness "to consort with flesh and blood," and whole-heartedly committed to promote the coming of the invisible Church of all the loyal, Royce witnessed to that kind of balanced, community-centered, religious life that alone can have healthy influence on political life in America.

Royce espoused an explicit supernaturalism rooted in the natural. By his "two level" doctrine, he showed that the healing of exaggerated individualism requires membership in at least the invisible Church *and* a visibly organized community with its specific common cause. These religiously influenced communities of the loyal preserve the body politic from *preferring* either an antireligious naturalism or even an areligious secularism. Thus Royce's doctrine of "social realism," with its emphasis on a "second level" which is ultimately divine, has reinforced the American tradition, "In God We Trust," and showed it to be inescapably vital for the continuance of our culture. For the Roycean self can only be a genuine human self if it is related by loyalty to God.[29]

Most importantly, Royce would stress *atonement.* He made atonement the climactic deed of religious life; for "without atonement, no salvation" (PC, 42, 73). He was keenly aware of the disloyalties to the community committed in his day. He found himself and all the genuinely loyal called upon to design carefully and to carry out courageously those counterbalancing deeds of healing and reconciling service. If alive today, he would, I believe, point out the crying need for atoning deeds in our country, given our many disloyalties to our own children, to the elderly, the poor, particular ethnic groups, and women generally, as well as given our sins against Third World peoples. He would point out that if the Suffering Servant of Israel and Christianity is "the Lamb of God," those who claim membership in his community have to pay the cost of discipleship. The modern mind may regard this idea of atonement as "the strangest, as the most hopelessly problematic" of all the ideas in the life of religion (*PC*, 73). Still, religion's central mystery of losing one's life to find it enhanced in oneself and one's community should not be passed over in practical silence.

III. SUMMARY AND CONCLUSION:
BUILDING A COMMUNITY OF MEMORY
AND HOPE FOR THE NEW MILLENNIUM

What are the main features, then, in this encounter of Roycean thought with contemporary, anxious, and isolated individuals? Royce insistently defended each uniquely individual human self and its distinctive process of individualization as much as he persistently attacked self-preferential individualists who are morally detached from community. Counterbalancing Americans' tendencies to trust mere spontaneity and to look just to the future, Royce required a richer recipe that included critically purified traditions and intelligent structuring of community life.

In addition, Royce proved that loyal love of the universal community is the only non-self-destructive, fundamental attitude of will. This required him to push beyond the concerns of middle-class Americans, to attach himself to humankind's great community, and to investigate the interactions of all the "provincial," national, and cultural groups upon each other.[30]

Moreover, Royce insisted that more be said about community consciousness than cultural analysis can say. Americans need to know *how* to restore community life. Royce provided a blueprint of steps to be taken to check whether each American has done all one can to develop a healthy shared spiritual whole of consciousness, the life of a genuine community.

Still more significantly, within "ontological individualism" Royce scotched the error lying coiled to spring: the assumption that individual human beings are primary and nonderivative. By his discovery of "extensions" in the self's psychological and moral makeup, Royce showed that the source of an individual's life lies in "belonging to community." He also bonded the life of each finite self to the universal community by insisting that genuine loyalty to the processing universe requires one to exercise practical faith in a universal community and its Spirit (*PC*, 342, 362, 403). Convinced by performatory contradictions that the reality of every minded being is constituted by conscious self-presence among "others," Royce stated, "The most important part of my knowledge about myself is based upon knowledge that I have derived from the community to which I belong" (*PC*, 358).

Finally, Royce stressed deeds of atonement as the climactic act of religion, the act that forgives, reconciles, and restores unity to community. He deeply felt how community life was wounded by our various degrees of sinfulness—stretching from mere weakness and ignorance to those deliberately treasonous "sins against the Holy Spirit." What World War I was then doing to the community of nations was only one of Royce's experiences of sinful disloyalties. His intelligent counteractions arose from his own spirit of atonement.[31]

In these major ways, then, Royce anticipated, critiqued and undergirded *Habits of the Heart.* Turning, then, to the future with him, do his directives for building community consciousness offer us sound guidance as we approach the year 2000?

To imagine a world community of hope requires enormous daring in our day. Individuals and nations tremble at the mushrooming nuclear threat. Autocratic governments oppress populations by increasing their use of torture. North-South tensions grow at least as fast as East-West tensions. Meanwhile, illiteracy, drug trafficking, and terrorism spread, largely out of control.

Nevertheless, precisely because we live in such critical times, the stark option confronting us is either to despair of the human race, or to put our hope to work by developing our needed consciousness of global community. As the year 2000 approaches, all of us (more than five billion human selves) have the resources to become a worldwide community. We have far more scientific information and greater technological expertise today than Royce knew of. We need, however, to go beyond this progress by personally sharing our stories with their feelings and thus identifying with the great community. Taking our cue from Royce's stress on the importance of both tradition and hope in community building, we need to communicate about our common past experiences and future hopes. For this, we need, like a skilled juggler of dumbbells, to keep several pairs of polar opposites in rhythmic balance — our memories and hopes, our needs of Roycean "provincialism" *and* of an increased consciousness of "world citizenship,"[32] our needs to use nature industrially *and* to care for ecology if we are to achieve moral integrity through ecological care. Besides alternating and balancing our care and service, we also need to use our imaginations creatively.

Let us, then, *imagine!* Suppose that with Royce we hold a practical faith in the beloved universal community, its spirit, and the interpretive process whereby the spirit draws human selves to take fuller part in this community. Suppose, too, that Royce's directions are correct for forming the consciousness of a genuine community of memory and hope. Then the question arises: *Which "events and deeds"[33] would the modern, educated person select such that every member of the human race could personally and readily identify with them as "part of one's own idealized life"* — whatever be one's race, culture, or creed? To which far-off "events" would any and all of us human beings respond with feeling and conviction, "That, too, is part of my life story"? Looking with the evolutionists to past global events, we can nominate the following points for common conscious convergence:

1. Ejected from the sun long ago, planet earth alone in the solar system has occupied that exceptional kind of orbit which allowed organic life to arise.

2. Eventually, organic life emerged in earth's oceans, and this life gradually diversified into plant and animal organisms. (The breathtaking emergence of these self-organizing, self-ordering, self-healing, and self-replicating organisms can be clearly portrayed as the indispensable basis for the human family today.)

3. Gradually, communities of *human* beings arose. Their members distinctively cared for their especially frail young, created art, buried their dead, sought practical truths for hunting, herding, and agriculture, invented languages, rites, and

artistic forms, and even began generating theoretical systems.

4. Tragically, these human stocks, like the Neanderthals, were wiped out by some cataclysm — such as the end of an ice age.

5. Somehow a new sprout, *Homo sapiens,* arose out of this tragedy and spread over the earth's surface, creating different languages, an alphabet, number systems, customs, and art. The outbreak of wars between tribes and empires, however, revealed in such human beings a lethal tendency to disloyalty toward the human family as a whole (a destructiveness due to lack of love for all humans) and the need of healing from such alienation.

6. Sages such as Moses, Buddha, Confucius, and Jesus arose in various world cultures and religions. They pointed to a divine Spirit at work in the human world, one who could empower human selves to be transformed from self-centered alienation into genuine loyalty to the great community of humankind.

7. The earth's tribes and nations became europeanized by the spread of Western colonization and technology. This provided a network that paradoxically both unified human selves — at least at the functional levels of economic enterprise and scientific advance — yet also violently dominated some groups. (Eventually this was followed, mostly in the 1960s, by the political decolonization of many nations and subsequent efforts at economic decolonization.)

8. In 1840, Samuel Morse patented the telegraph, the first form of electromagnetic communication, which soon developed into almost instantaneous global communications. Evolving humankind seemed to be generating a "second nervous system," but the triumphant spread of wireless, radio, and television was ambivalent. It allowed for global domination by an information system *or* for genuine service of the whole human family's needs for truthful news, education, and unity.

9. In the 1940s scientists harnessed nuclear energy in the atom. This unleashed a tremendous source of power for future world development as well as threats to the very survival of humankind. It cast the shadow of nuclear holocaust on all peoples and added the dread of still not knowing effectively how to handle nuclear wastes safely.

10. In 1948 at San Francisco, representatives of many nations joined their hopes of freeing the human family from war.

Their shared aspirations and ideals created the United Nations'
"Universal Declaration of Human Rights." Hereafter, all members of the human community had a "standard of achievement"
accepted by a public international forum for the defense and
promotion of their basic human rights.

11. With the voyage to the moon in the late 1960s, earth
people were gifted with a television shot of earth from a space-
ship, revealing the "only one earth" that we have (where life,
though frail and imperilled, is alone found).[34] This image calls
human selves to preserve this tiny life center and to hand on
an enhanced earth to future generations, through a courageous
hope that puts universal loyalty into practice by cooperative
deeds.

Regarding each of these eleven events, everyone of us can
say, "That is part of my life" in its roots in history. If everyone
does so and then communicates these self-identifications with
many others, we will be bonded mightily into humankind's great
"community of memory."

To specify the ingredients needed to generate a great "community of hope," however, calls for more imagination. Because
the future is hidden and indeterminate, our ideas of it have to
be vague. Nevertheless, we can point out at least some common, idealizable, future events and deeds that may call forth
common hopes in all of us who share life on this our "only
one earth." To what, then, can all human hearts look forward
as their hoped-for destiny, according to the spirit of the universe? Can they also recognize, beneath an amazing variety of
values in diverse cultures, that there are some transcultural goods
that all human hearts desire?

1. Consciousness of world citizenship can be so effectively
nurtured that more and more people will tolerate nothing less
than the actual observance of those human rights formulated
in the United Nations' Universal Declaration. This hoped-for
degree of consciousness of world community will modify exaggerated claims of unrestricted national sovereignty. Thus, while
the "provincialism" of national peoples and their governments
will flourish in creative dialogue, enough common resolve will
arise to outlaw war, terrorism, and guerilla groups.

2. Round the earth, most men and women want the ongoing exploration of space to be carried out peacefully, so that

its treasures can be used for the peaceful promotion of the human family's life and unity.

3. Many people yearn for a worldwide acceptance of such a "law of the seas" as will effectively provide basic resources in peace to all members of the human family.

4. Another widespread hope is that by cooperation and communication the rich diversities and talents of various nations and cultures become more widely appreciated by more peoples.

5. Again, people long to see the effective educational means (teachers, schools, and reliable communication systems) promoted around the world to enhance the literacy and cultural programs of all peoples.

6. The eradication of prejudices of all kinds — particularly racist, sexist, religious, and class varieties — is a goal longed for by every genuine lover of the human family.

7. People also yearn for the day when basic health services and care are operationally in place for all dwellers on the earth.

8. For eradicating widespread poverty and unemployment, many people search beyond the opposed business blocs of First, Second, and Third Worlds to create one, conjointly cooperating, world economic system that will peaceably distribute material goods and services more equitably throughout the world.

9. Most profoundly, members of all world religions, who already believe that some Spirit of the universe is its guiding center, have two hopes: that they themselves will practice this faith, and that their fellow human beings who prefer atheistic or agnostic positions will join them in practical communication and cooperation by acting *as if* such a Spirit were working in the world (*PC*, 405).

Our earth's more than five billion inhabitants can effectively share their conscious self-identification with these nine "common ideal future events and deeds," just as they can share the eleven suggested past events and deeds. If they do so, there will emerge a common awareness of us human selves as being one body, "one conscious spiritual whole of life," under the intimate, subtle, and loving guidance of the Spirit of the universal community (*PC*, 218). If Josiah Royce were alive today, he would remind us that we now have far more instruments for creating this global consciousness than were present when he identified the structures needed for creating a global "community of memory and of hope." This global communal awareness, in its respect for freedom, would become a powerful remedy for that morally detached individualism which threatens American culture. Promoting this sense of our deeply rooted solidarity becomes the responsibility of each of us. To this responsibility Royce called us about seventy-five years ago. Fifty years later, another American man of wisdom, John Courtney Murray, (whose patronage gathered the writers of the present volume), electrified Americans with the urgency of Royce's call by adding his own prophetic voice:

> If this country is to be overthrown from within or from without, I would suggest that it will not be overthrown by Communism. It will be overthrown because it will have made an impossible experiment. It will have undertaken to establish a technological order of the most marvelous intricacy, which will have been constructed and will operate without relations to true political ends; and this technological order will hang, as it were, suspended over a moral confusion; and this moral confusion will itself be suspended over a spiritual vacuum. This would be the real danger resulting from a type of fallacious, fictitious fragile unity that could be created among us.[35]

NOTES

1. See, as one instance, Royce's chapter, "Individualism," in his *Philosophy of Loyalty* (New York: Macmillan, 1908), 51–98. He here exposes four irrational forms of individualism before he presents his own form of a rational ethical individualism (77–81).

2. See Russell H. Conwell, *Acres of Diamonds* (New York: Harper and Brothers, 1915), 18–21.

3. See *The Basic Writings of Josiah Royce,* ed. and intro. John J. McDermott, 2 vols. (Chicago: University of Chicago Press, 1969), 2:1065–1134. Hereafter referred to as *BWJR.*

4. For the details of Royce's life and its note of increasing tragedy, see John Clendenning, *The Life and Thought of Josiah Royce* (Madison: University of Wisconsin Press, 1985).

5. Josiah Royce, *The Problem of Christianity,* intro. John E. Smith, 1 vol. ed. (Chicago: University of Chicago Press, 1968). Hereafter referred to as *PC.* In Royce's Berkeley lectures in the summer

of 1914, he described this late intellectual breakthrough into the theory of signs and method of interpretation of American logician C. S. Peirce. Shortly before Royce died, he equated the profundity of this insight into Peirce with that of his originating philosophical "religious insight" of 1883; see *The Letters of Josiah Royce,* ed. and intro. John Clendenning (Chicago: University of Chicago Press, 1970), 645.

6. See Gabriel Marcel, *Royce's Metaphysics* (Chicago: Henry Regnery, 1956), 147.

7. In this essay I follow Royce's exact meanings of, and differences between, his late technical terms: "Great Community," "Universal Community," "Community of Interpretation," and "Spirit." I do not, however, follow his now-outdated and sometimes inconsistent capitalizations. Royce's usage of "Great Community" refers to the living, intelligent, organic unity of all *human* selves of all times. (See Josiah Royce, *The Hope of the Great Community* [New York: Macmillan, 1916], 35–42. Hereafter referred to as *HGG.*) His usage of "Universal Community" refers to a similar unity of all *minded* beings whatsoever — finite and infinite — of all eras, past, present, and future, with or without habitat in some galaxy. His usage of "Community of Interpretation" refers to any community that exhibits the triadic logical structure found in the union of a sign-sender, sign-interpreter, and sign-receiver. Similarly, Royce's usage of "Spirit" is strictly analogous, multi-layered, and "capable of exact and logical statement." (See *HGC,* 131, and Frank Oppenheim, "The Idea of Spirit in the Mature Royce," *Transactions of the Charles Sanders Peirce Society* 19 [Fall 1983], 381–95). Except for direct quotations, or where "Spirit" refers to the Holy Spirit, these technical terms will be set in lower case.

8. See *PC,* 248–71.

9. Robert N. Bellah et al., *Habits of the Heart: Individualism and Commitment in American Life* (Berkeley: University of California Press, 1985), p. viii. Hereafter referred to as *HH.*

10. See Josiah Royce, *The Sources of Religious Insight* (New York: Charles Scribner's Sons, 1912), 5–6.

11. See *PC,* 40–41.

12. Josiah Royce, *The World and the Individual* (New York: Macmillan, 1901), 2:286.

13. See Clendenning, *Letters of Royce,* 645.

14. See note 2 above.

15. Royce's early "moral insight" lay in his discovery that within the freely diversified and conflictive wills of human selves there lies the ideal of ultimately harmonizing these wills through a sense of community. See Josiah Royce, *The Religious Aspect of Philosophy* (Boston: Houghton Mifflin, 1885), 162–75.

16. For careful elaboration of this conversion process in its various spheres, see the article by Donald Gelpi in this volume.

17. The authors of *Habits of the Heart* employ, as merely analytic tools, the concepts of the "empty self" and the "constituted self" as extreme in order to center on the real self somewhere in the middle (*HH,* 154). Royce's different interpretive search for the real moral self begins by finding performatory contradictions in the first two basic attitudes of will. Then it discovers positively the self-validating truth that the individual self and community are intelligible only as co-equally ultimate realities that imply each other. Thus Royce's search terminates positively in the third fundamental attitude of will: genuine loyalty, the morally transformed individual's ever-intelligent, whole-hearted gift of itself to the community.

18. On this see John E. Smith's introduction to *PC,* 33–36, esp. 36.

19. See Clendenning, *Letters of Royce,* 586–87.

20. E.g., in his address, "The Role of the Laity in Africa," 8 May 1980, in Accra, Ghana, John Paul II said, "When you faithfully carry out these two roles as citizens of both the earthly city and heavenly kingdom . . ."; see *Origins* 10 (June 5, 1980), 47, #5.

21. See John XXIII, *Pacem in Terris,* (Peace on Earth), ed. and intro. J. Gibbons, S.J. (New York: Paulist, 1963).

22. In her "Love and Adulthood in American Culture," in *Themes of Work and Love in Adulthood,* ed. Neil J. Smelser and Erik H. Erikson (Cambridge, Mass.: Harvard University Press, 1980), 120–47, Bellah's colleague, Ann Swidler, provides a far fuller and richer study of love in American life than space limits permitted in *HH.*

23. See *PC,* 58–59, 83–84, 199, 234–75, and esp. 376, 404–5; also Royce, *Sources of Religious Insight,* 286. For his description of the rise of the ideal of interpretation, see *PC,* 312–13, 318–19.

24. Royce's *Outline of Psychology* (New York: Macmillan, 1903) is built on this threefold description of the human self; see pp. vii–viii.

25. Perhaps the mature Royce's best description of a minded self occurs at the close of his 1916 encyclopedia article, "Mind"; see *BWJR* 2:759.

26. See *HH,* 334.

27. On this see John E. Smith's definition of genuine communities as "*living intelligent, organic unities* combining a many in a one in terms that allow for their development in time and history" (*PC,* 35; Smith's emphasis), or the definition of community in *HH,* 333.

28. For a study of this aspect of Royce's thought, see Frank Oppenheim, *Royce's Mature Philosophy of Religion* (Notre Dame, Ind.: University of Notre Dame Press, 1987), 343, 220–23, 257–59.

29. Royce, *World and Individual,* 2:286.

30. For Royce's significant doctrine of a "wise and wholesome Provincialism," see *BWJR*, 1067–88 along with John McDermott's trenchant introduction, 1065–66.

31. For instance, at the outbreak of World War I Royce put aside his well-prepared lecture for the Philosophical Union at Berkeley and, to fit the crisis, laboriously created and repeatedly redrafted a completely new address, "War and Insurance." Again, in 1915, when Americans clung too passively to neutrality while their fellow citizens were being killed by German U-boats, and when his colleague Professor Munsterberg had by then become Prussia's strongest advocate at Harvard, Royce countered by awakening the sleepers with his prophet-like clarion call, even as he moderated his passion by submitting his proposed actions in atoning obedience to the common good of the United States and of the whole human family. On this see Clendenning, *Life and Thought of Royce,* 376–99, and *BWJR,* 1135–63.

32. On this see John Stacer's pioneering essay in this volume.

33. Here "events and deeds" are taken in Royce's large sense to include the significant persons and tools connected with these events and deeds.

34. See Barbara Ward and Rene Dubois, *Only One Earth: The Care and Maintenance of a Small Planet* (New York: Norton, 1972).

35. Quoted through Robert Bellah's article, "The Quest for Common Commitments in a Pluralistic Society," *Philosophy & Theology* 2 (1987): 30–31.

U.S. Technological Style and the Atrophe of Civic Commitment

John M. Staudenmaier, S.J.

By most measures, 1933 was the worst year in America's long economic history. Unemployment, in the fifth year of a savage depression, reached its highest level, 25.2 percent.[1] Bread lines and homeless wanderers provided the body politic with images of shattering failure in the body economic. Still, visitors to Chicago's International Exposition that year saw no sign of social pain. The dazzling spectacle (boasting "more colored lights . . . than in any equal area or even any city of the world")[2] was dedicated to a "Century of Progress." In the official guidebook's effusive prose:

> the dawn of an unprecedented era of discovery, invention, and development of things to effect the comfort, convenience, and welfare of mankind. . . . An epic theme! You grasp its stupendous stature only when you stop to contemplate the wonders which this century has wrought.[3]

A more blatant example of Depression incongruities would be hard to imagine: overwhelming human suffering juxtaposed with unabashed huckstering. It is tempting to dismiss the exposition's upbeat theme as an example of the escapism manifest in the ubiquitous entertainment movies of the era. Images of prosperity provide some slim comfort in grim times. Such an explanation ultimately falls short, however, because it overlooks ominous undertones found in the fair's iconography and guidebook rhetoric. Three examples suffice. "Science" and

"Industry," the second term a conflation of technology and business, were represented by two forty-foot, aluminum-coated figures frowning down upon entrants to the Hall of Administration. Even more striking, the foyer in the Hall of Science confronted visitors with sculptor Louise Lentz Woodruff's "Science Advancing Mankind." Life-sized male and female figures faced forward with arms uplifted, both dwarfed by a massive robot twice their size. In the words of general manager Lenox Lohr, the robot typified "the exactitude, force, and onward movement of science, with its hands at the backs of the figures of a man and a woman, urging them on to the fuller life."[4] Finally, the sculpture's iconographic message was sternly reinforced by the guidebook's stunning, bold-faced thematic motto: "SCIENCE FINDS, INDUSTRY APPLIES, MAN CONFORMS."[5]

The exposition, in short, exalts science and technology as the twin gods of inevitable progress and at the same time reduces human beings to the status of passive conformity. Some three decades later, historian William Appleman Williams reached a similar conclusion.

> America's great evasion lies in the manipulation of nature to avoid a confrontation with the human condition and with the challenge of building a true community.[6]

Williams's provocative sentence confronts citizens of the United States with the link between their technological style and the national character. He suggests that the American technical dream of conquering the wilderness ("the manipulation of nature") encourages escape from the central civic responsibility, as political as it is uncertain, of negotiating the terms for national community.[7]

In like fashion, communications scholar James W. Carey sees several conflicting dyads—technology versus community and power versus tranquility—as the essence of a peculiarly American dualism.

> The American character since early in its history has been pulled in two directions and has been unable to commit itself to either. The first direction is toward *the dream of the American sublime, to a virgin land and a life of peace, serenity and community.* The second direction is *the Faustian and rapacious,*

the desire for power, wealth, productivity and universal knowl-
edge, the urge to dominate nature and remake the world. In
many ways the American tragedy is that we want both these
things and never seem to respect the contradiction between
them.[8] (emphasis added)

Carey attributes the staying power of this American contradiction between love of serenity and lust for power to a gradual
cognitive shift from an idealization of nature to an even greater
idealization of "the technological sublime."

The dream of the American sublime has never been used to
block the dream of American power primarily because *the rheto-*
ric of the technological sublime has collapsed the distinctions
between the two directions. As a result, America has allowed
technology and the urge for power unrestricted room for expansion.[9] (emphasis added)

For Carey, as for Williams, Americans have substituted the
sweet promise of technological progress for the inherently uncertain process of negotiating community.[10] Implicit in their
interpretation we find the same radical passivity that the rhetoric and iconography of the Chicago Exposition portray so vividly. If "Science," "Technology," and "Industry" operate in the
world as an inevitable and autonomous force, and if that force
is necessarily progressive, providing harmonious community
through the conquest of nature, then citizens of the body politic can pursue their individualistic goals without concern for
the common good. Progress, in short, renders political and ecological activism irrelevant. Autonomous progress will work its
will no matter what individual human beings do about it.[11]

Taken together, these disparate strands of evidence point to
an often-overlooked explanation of those trends in public discourse observed by the authors of *Habits of the Heart.* Based
on extended interviews with over two hundred middle-class men
and women, Bellah and his associates identify radical individualism as the habitual "first language" of contemporary Americans. Their "utilitarian individualism" is identical with the mentality flowing from the ideology of autonomous progress wherein
the individual takes an active role in pursuing private self-interest
while remaining radically passive in the larger civic arena.[12]

The authors of *Habits of the Heart,* like Williams and Carey and Quirk, call attention to a social problem of substantial magnitude. I agree with all of them when they argue that the common good does not, in fact, take care of itself and that the rhetoric of progress, with its individualistic public passivity, must be replaced by an interpretation of technological decision making that takes politics seriously. Indeed, the degree to which the people of the United States lose touch with the republican and biblical traditions that have in the past provided a public balance to private interests marks the extent to which we lose our capacity to imagine ourselves as "a people" at all. If we habitually talk about ourselves as nothing more than an aggregate of individuals we render it nearly impossible to understand our moral and civic lives in terms of the task of negotiating a vision of the common good.[13]

Still, the crisis of individualism is more than a question of language, important as that is. As Williams and Carey and Quirk suggest, the erosion of our capacity to think in terms of a negotiated common good has also been fostered by our technological style and, indeed, by those technologies in which we, as a nation, have chosen to invest and on which we have come to depend. By addressing both these matters — the politically passive rhetoric of progress and contemporary technological style — this essay blends social analysis with historiography. It rests on my conviction that respect for the complexity of technological style is not simply an in-house concern for engineers or historians of technology. Thus, by exploring some of its central dynamics from both a historiographical and a social historical perspective, I hope to add an important dimension to the discussion of individualism and the common good.

As I argued in *Technology's Storytellers,* autonomous technological determinism rests on the radically ahistorical premise that technical designs operate according to their own inevitable laws, that the context of origins has little to tell us about the design decisions that bring new technologies into being.[14] If such progress sustains the American dream then we need look no further to reassure ourselves about the health of our technocratic social venture.

In sharp contrast, a contextual approach to the history of technology challenges progress ideology by situating technical design decisions within the fabric of public decision making. Historians of technology have begun looking to the values, biases, motives, and world view of its designers when asking why a given technology turned out as it did. From the contextualist perspective, technologies are political and cultural as well as technical artifacts. Thus, the historical interpretation of successful technologies engages in social history at a foundational level, especially in a society, the late twentieth-century United States, which has adopted such an extraordinary array of complex systems as the governing structures of its culture.

In *Storytellers* I argued that an overall model for the contextual study of successful technologies includes three stages in the technological life cycle, namely, *the design stage, the momentum stage,* and *the senility stage.* All three reveal the contextual character of the technical design as it moves from the inherent fragility of its time of origin through a period of successful momentum and into obsolescence. I argued further that successful technologies come in clusters, each embodying the same set of values, the entire cluster reflecting the *technological style* of its culture of origin. Finally, I suggested that when historians interpret technological style they must pay attention to three groups as they relate to the technology in question, namely, *the design, maintenance, and impact constituencies.* [15]

In the years since proposing the three-constituency model I have wrestled with its limitations in two areas. On the one hand, its focus on a single successful technology tends to create the simplistic impression that new technologies can be understood without reference to the tradition of technological style that preceded it or to technological styles that did not achieve societal acceptance. On the other hand, *Storytellers'* description of the design, maintenance, and impact constituencies overlooked a crucial dimension of their technological relationships, namely, the fact that members of each technological constituency tend to mask their connection with a successful technology in a kind of social amnesia that helps account for the atrophe of our civic rhetorical traditions (republican and biblical) while fostering dependence on private individualism as our primary language for public discourse.

In this essay I will explore both aspects of the model using the American automobile, whose popularity matches its historical familiarity, as an exemplary case study. After tracing the broad outlines of automotive history from 1900 to the present, I will double back to the nineteenth century, situating automotive history within a larger technical and social context —America's adoption of the ideal of standardization and its correlative turning from a negotiation style for solving technological problems. In conclusion, I will return to the design, maintenance, and impact constituencies in an attempt to explain why their relationships with successful technology prove so elusive.

One final prenote is important. The term *successful technology* means something more than functional efficiency. In the present context the term designates a technology that has achieved so much momentum within its society that the society would experience grave difficulty doing without it. Thus, the American automobile system would be "successful" while dental floss would not.

I. *STAGES OF TECHNOLOGICAL SUCCESS: THE AUTOMOBILE*

1. The Design Stage and the Design Constituency

It could be argued that the design stage of the American automobile lasted until roughly 1910. The previous decade and a half was marked by turbulence and uncertainty, hallmarks of the design stage of new technologies generally. In 1900 it would have been difficult to say just what "the automobile" was. Steamers, electrics, and internal combustion horseless carriages, assembled by a host of small enthusiasts, caught the public's attention as romantic wonderments, but whether any design would achieve the status of a serious and durable transport technology was not yet clear. Bankruptcies were, it seemed, nearly as common as mechanical breakdowns. The Ford Motor Company emerged triumphant from the confusion. The 1908 Model T may well be the most successful single design in American history; its durability and reasonable cost fit the social context almost perfectly.

Profits from the enormously popular "T" permitted Ford to

invest in a radically new production system, the world-famous 1914 moving assembly line. This innovation, more than any other development, created the American automotive style. Instead of bringing individual parts to a fixed station run by a skilled worker, the line used semiskilled workers, each with a single task, while the car moved past them. The innovation caused dramatic increases in production efficiency but carried a high price tag. Ford transferred the judgment about quality from workers to supervisors, and by that rearrangement of shop floor politics the company institutionalized a new form of worker alienation that would affect the quality of auto assembly for the rest of the century.[16]

This shift of adult decision making from worker to supervisor embodies the values and biases of the Ford "design constituency," those members of the Ford team who had access to the crucial design decisions of 1906–1914. Their world view did not, however, spring magically into the historical arena of turn-of-the-century American society. The design constituency emerged from and aptly reflected the social context of its era. Southern and eastern European immigrants made up much of the automobile work force and brought with them all the strangeness of alien lifestyles and foreign languages, and Ford's paternalistic obsession with control fit nicely into a pervasive national fear of immigrant-generated social chaos.[17]

Thus, U.S. automotive technology took definitive shape as a combination of internal combustion vehicle and mass production technology. Its early years were flexible in the sense that the design process was strongly influenced by its social setting, particularly as embodied in the world view of the Ford design constituency. We should not push the concept of flexibility too far, forgetting that new technologies depend on older ones. The Ford style emerged from a century-long technical tradition of machine-tooled metal parts assembly stretching back to the arms manufacturing practices of the U.S. Ordnance Department.[18] Nevertheless, when compared with the next stage in its evolution, the flexibility of the automotive design stage left automotive technology remarkably open to contextual influences. In this sense, we can speak of it as embodying some set of values, as having a style of its own.

The concept of *style* is not, however, limited to individual technologies. Successful technologies, as we noted above, tend to come in stylistic clusters, each one embodying the same overall world view. The ideology of autonomous progress explains this phenomenon by the historically simplistic argument that technological success flows from the inexorable forward movement of the human conquest of nature: the successes of today flow inevitably from the achievements of yesterday. How, then, might we explain clustered technologies in a historically responsible fashion?

The people and institutions with access to the venture capital that new technologies always require—in short, the design constituencies of the period—ordinarily hold cultural hegemony in their society. They belong to the group that shapes the dominant values and symbols of society. Although members never form a single historically tidy group—as a technological conspiracy theory might suggest—they reach their position of power in society because they all tend to view the world from the same perspective. Consequently, we should expect to find a set of successful technologies that, in any relatively stable era of history, embody the technological style of that society.[19] It is no accident that Ford's moving assembly line, Frederick Winslow Taylor's scientific management movement, Elmer Sperry's automatic airplane stabilizer, the introduction of tear gas for police crowd control, and the postwar consumerist advertising techniques reflect similar values. Despite their wide diversity of design, from mechanical and chemical techniques to political and advertising strategies, every one of them is based on the prevailing technological ideal. All of them represent Progressive Era America's commitment to solving problems through the centralized authority of "experts." As we shall see in some detail below, political negotiation, with its inherently messy unpredictability, had begun to lose currency and to be replaced by highly complex systems that work to control hypothetically chaotic exogenous variables, whether those variables are handcrafted artisan work habits, unruly and dissident urban "mobs," or unpredictable consumers.[20]

To be sure, the existing style of technological artifacts does not operate as the only cause of prevailing cultural values. As we have already seen, for example, Ford's paternalistic obsession with control predated his moving assembly line. On the other hand, technological style fosters as well as directs values. The host of American adaptations to the automobile exemplifies the way society accommodates itself to the designs of its successful technologies. In the process, values that fit the technology achieve societal momentum while values that do not fit diminish in importance.

2. THE MOMENTUM STAGE AND THE MAINTENANCE CONSTITUENCY

A new technology's truest measure of success appears in the array of societal responses to its design constraints. Thus, between 1915 and 1970 the United States responded to the automobile with a host of structural adaptations, from motels and suburban architecture to legislation governing highway funding, insurance, and licensing. In the process, millions of individuals and hundreds of institutions coalesced in a little-noticed social grouping that can be called the automobile "maintenance constituency." What gave them social coherence, despite their wide economic, political, and cultural diversity, was the fact that they had all come to benefit from and depend upon the increasingly popular automobile system. Automotive engineers, workers in automobile, rubber, steel, and glass plants, and proprietors of automobile-dependent small businesses, among others, depended on automobiles for their livelihood. Ordinary citizens adopted the automobile as an essential means of transportation. Examples are legion.

The very size and diversity of its maintenance constituency membership reveals the magnitude of societal momentum achieved by the automobile. When a technology becomes essential across such a broad spectrum of the body politic, it becomes nearly unthinkable for the technology to change in any substantial fashion. Imagine, for example, that the nation were to decide to shift from an automotive to a high-speed rail transport system. From an abstract technical perspective, the change might be conceivable or even desirable. However, consideration of the social turmoil and economic chaos that would result from such a revolutionary change provides a more accurate reading of automotive momentum and, at the same time, a sense of how the early flexibility of automotive technology's

design stage has been replaced by what might be called dynamic rigidity. The technology has shifted roles from a possible social option, open to a host of different futures, to a
culture-shaping and highly specified social force. This shift from
flexibility toward rigidity characterizes the movement of the
automobile from the design to the momentum stage; and it is
this same rigidity, rooted in the increasing dependency of so
many actors in society on automotive technology, that made
the mass-produced automobile such an extraordinarily powerful cultural force for the bulk of this century.[21]

3. THE SENILITY STAGE

As long as a technology's success endures, the fit between
technical design and societal context remains tight. Eventually,
however, changes occur in the larger context as new political
priorities, shifting demographics, changing tastes, ecological
transformations, or competing technological actors come to
the fore. The sweet fit between context and technology that
characterized the momentum stage begins to unravel and the
once-successful technology enters its "senility stage." Consider
a few recent examples that heralded the senility of our dominant automotive style. The American automobile, a "gas guz-
zler" stressing power over fuel efficiency, reflected the very cheap
petroleum that marked its context of origin. Beginning in 1973,
for a variety of political, economic, and religious reasons, the
Organization of Petroleum Exporting Countries (OPEC) drove
the price of petroleum to dramatic new heights and fuel-intensive
cars became less attractive. At the same time, the Ford style
of auto production in which workers make no decisions about
quality had created cars whose fit and finish suffered accordingly. Americans were so used to it that they hardly noticed.
It was understood that quality control would ultimately be
handled by the auto dealerships. But, in another contextual
change, the mid-1970s brought new competitors into the car-
selling arena. The Japanese automotive style, shaped by a radically different world view, put quality control decisions at the
point of production, and its elegant fit and finish transformed
American tolerance for the earlier Ford-style car. Finally, in the
mid-1960s people concerned about air quality began to achieve

political power. They passed laws that put constraints on yet another dimension of American auto design.

Unfortunately, the dynamic force that provided the momentum of a once-successful technological style tends to remain rigid even as a new context begins to demand change. At this point proprietors of the technology might respond in one of two ways. They can attempt a return to the radical flexibility of a new design stage, or they can use their considerable economic and political clout to try to force the context back into the sweet fit of the previous momentum stage. General Motors' Saturn project, stressing Japanese-style managerial and production techniques, exemplifies the attempt at renewed flexibility. Note however, that instead of trying to transform one of the five established divisions (for example, Chevrolet or Oldsmobile), GM started from scratch, creating an entirely new division. Remembering Ford's disastrous Edsel experiment, I asked a GM observer why the firm was risking the uncertainties of an entirely new divisional venture. He responded, "A completely fresh start gives us the chance to avoid the entrenched attitudes of much of existing GM management and the mistrust of current labor-management relations in a number of locations."[22] It would be hard to find a more apt example of the tension between flexibility and rigidity at the heart of a powerful technological enterprise. On the other hand, GM's "Mr. Goodwrench" advertising campaign represents an attempt to change the context to fit existing technological style. Mr. Goodwrench is designed to convince potential buyers that "quality GM parts" mean quality GM automobiles. It would be far easier and much less expensive to promote the image of quality than to accomplish it on the shop floor and in the managerial suite. Whether American automobile firms will achieve sufficient flexibility to respond successfully to the challenges of their changing context remains an open question.

4. The Impact Constituency

Thus far we have seen five of the constituency model's six components. It remains only to note the place of the "impact constituency"—the people and institutions who lose because of the design of the new technology. Most obvious are those who depend on competing technologies. In the automobile case, the maintenance constituencies of other forms of transport technology—from livery stable operators and blacksmiths to railroad management and workers—lost because of automobile success. A second type of impact constituency includes those who share the costs of a technology without receiving its benefits. In cities such as Detroit, whose tax revenues support freeway networks at the expense of nonautomotive transit systems, residents who cannot afford a car fall into this class. Their loss would be compounded if automotive system requirements directly harmed them, as when a freeway destroys homes, shops, and walking patterns of the neighborhood in which they live. Finally, and more subtly, almost everyone who gains from a successful technology loses at the same time. In other words, it is not only possible but commonplace for members of the maintenance constituency to be members of the impact constituency as well. For example, rush-hour drivers suffer from excessive isolation because of the atomistic individualism of the automotive forms of mass transit. Suburban architecture, leading as it does to a lifestyle without much walking, tends toward empty sidewalks and correspondingly unsafe streets.[23] The automobile, welcomed in the early part of the century as a solution to pervasive urban pollution (horse manure), became a potent source of pollution in its own right. Trade-offs abound; there is no technological free lunch.

What can we learn from this admittedly sketchy overview of the American-style automobile? Contextual history explains, in specific detail, how we have embodied a societal vision in the automotive system and, perhaps more important, how that system, with its inherent biases, influences us in return. The contextual perspective reveals the automobile not as a value-free system or an inevitable cultural force, but as the technological incarnation of a series of historically specific choices that are "political" in the root sense of the term.

II: STANDARDIZATION REPLACES NEGOTIATION

Automotive history, for all its inherent richness and complexity, cannot be understood in isolation from a larger sociotechnological context. Turning our attention to the nineteenth century, we find evidence that the decisions made by the automobile's design and maintenance constituencies were part of a much larger social process by which the nation adopted a distinctive technological style. The complete argument is too complex to be presented in this essay, but space does permit an overview of one key aspect of twentieth-century technological style in the United States, namely, the option for standardization at the expense of negotiation.[24]

Until 1870 or so the challenge of conquering the wilderness shaped the dominant technological style in the United States. As generations of men and women from Europe or the more settled eastern United States headed west, their longing for a "middle landscape," a livable place carved out of the wild, grew to be a central element of the American character. The land itself—fifteen hundred miles of virgin forest, another one thousand of prairie, the Rocky Mountains, the Sierra Nevadas, and the intervening deserts—inspired an American dream. To non-Indian eyes it was empty of history but full of both promise and danger, a manifest destiny challenging the best people had in them. Building a human place, clearing fields and rivers, constructing homes, roads, canals, bridges, tunnels, and cities preoccupied the technological imagination. Americans honored technical expertise as "know-how," a blend of often crude rules of thumb and occasional engineering elegance, together with an intimate knowledge of local terrain as the context whose constraints defined the limits of every project. Technological style, then, demanded a continual negotiation between the skills, tools, and plans of white Americans and the godlike wilderness they sought to conquer.[25] Despite their passion for freedom and individualism, Americans found negotiation a basic necessity in human interaction as well. People needed one another in an empty land.[26]

Long before this technological style fell from preeminence, however, a successor began to exert its influence. Beginning in 1815 with the U.S. Ordnance Department's commitment to standardized uniformity in weapons production, a new technical ideal gathered momentum in the land.[27] It embodied a radical shift in values. The older style's negotiation with nature and with coworkers shifted toward standardization's precision design and centralized authority. The resulting American factory system turned out a host of new products and, in the process, transformed the relationship between manager and worker from the sometimes respectful and sometimes tumultuous interaction of the early American small shop to heavy-handed enforcement of work rules coupled with the de-skilling of workers through increasingly automated machines.[28] The transformation was hardly limited to the factory. Little by little, a broad range of technological endeavors began to adopt the standardization ideal. Three examples will suggest the flavor of the new style.

Railroads evolved from a turnpike model (state-owned and supported roadbed) to a centrally owned enterprise that included roadbed and most system components. At the same time, the relationship of railroads to their surrounding context changed dramatically. J. L. Larson contrasts the design of grain shipping facilities for St. Louis and Chicago in 1860. The St. Louis design demanded bagging the grain, loading it on train cars, off-loading it at the outer edge of town where the tracks ended, teamstering it across the city, and loading it again onto river boats. The Chicago design permitted bulk loading on grain cars because the track ran all the way to the docks where it was off-loaded onto grain boats. Larson concludes his description with the following provocative sentence:

> If the Chicago system was a model of integration, speed, and efficiency, the St. Louis market preserved the integrity of each man's transaction and employed a host of small entrepreneurs at every turn—real virtues in ante-bellum America.[29]

The St. Louis arrangement required negotiation as part of the shipping process, whereas the more capital-intensive Chicago design achieved greater efficiency and permitted railroad management to ship grain without needing to negotiate with that "host of small entrepreneurs at every turn."

The geographical range and managerial complexity of the railroads fostered standardization on many levels. The railroads' need for precise timetables transformed a land of multiple local times into 1885's single system of standard time divided into our now familiar four time zones. The depot, that little building where town and rail line met, gradually evolved toward a standardized architecture that reflected the triumph of railroad system over local style. The telegraph, essential as a railroad information network, became the vehicle for nationwide, standardized news with the development of the wire services.[30]

We see the same trend in the changing character of electrical systems. If we lived in a small town in 1890 and held a town meeting to decide whether to invest in electricity, our debate could lead to a yes or a no. If yes, we would shop among the three manufacturing firms—Thompson-Houston, Edison General Electric, and Westinghouse. Once installed, the system would become a tool we had purchased to serve our needs. We townsfolk were independent vis-à-vis the technology. We could take it or leave it, and we could purchase one or another type as well. Today our little town no longer maintains this independent position. From the perspective of electrical systems management, our town serves as a functional component. We no longer "negotiate" with the electrical technology. Our dependence on electricity, together with the complex requirements of centralized generation and transmission systems, has changed the earlier negotiated relationship to one of conformity.[31]

Major redefinition of advertising extends the pattern. The first three decades of this century saw a revolution in advertising style. Mid-nineteenth-century advertisements tended to take the form of a dialogue that assumed a kind of equality between advertiser and reader. Sales were thought to result from a rational description of product qualities or a simple announcement of available merchandise. By the early twentieth century gradual changes in strategy began to coalesce in a radically new style focusing, not on the product, but on what the product could do for the consumer. Emotion-laden advertising rhetoric aimed at a consumer who was presumed to be irrational and lethargic. Roland Marchand describes the basic mentality:

> In viewing the urban masses, advertisers associated consumer lethargy as much with weak-kneed conformity as with cultural backwardness. . . . Emotional appeals succeeded because only by seeking this lowest common human denominator could the advertiser shake the masses from their lethargy without taxing their limited intelligence.[32]

The underlying rationale of the new style can best be seen a few years later at General Motors. Beginning in 1923 with the arrival of Alfred P. Sloan as president, the task of marketing new cars shifted from Ford's approach, stressing the economy and technical competence of an unchanging Model T, to fostering cyclic dissatisfaction with one's present car, the basis of "turnover buying." Continued expansion of the mass production system required turnover buying for, as the recent U.S. automotive recession demonstrated, when too many owners hold on to their cars for too long, the new car market stagnates.

GM's tactics combined two interrelated strategies. First, GM introduced annual model changes. Second, the company began to advertise its products, not as tools for transportation, but as enhancements of sexual and social-status identity. Taken together, they worked to increase consumer desire for a new car while severing the bond of affection between owner and one's present vehicle. The simultaneous messages that new means better (annual model change) and that the car enhances my inadequate sexual and social status (advertising style) teaches me an essential lesson for consumerist behavior. We might put it in the form of a logical argument: I am what I own. But what I currently own is inadequate. Therefore, twitch and buy.[33] Consumerist marketing does not work with money-conscious shoppers who tenaciously negotiate every purchase or who stay home, content with what is already there.

Consumerist advertising marks the epitome of standardization's triumph over negotiation. Whereas the U.S. Ordnance Department tried to standardize musket parts and the work patterns of skilled armorers, and centralized railroads later in the century began to standardize equipment and to expand corporate control over previously independent entrepreneurs, the new form of marketing tried to extend standardized conformity into human motivation itself.

These three vignettes indicate a radical shift of the values embedded in our normal technologies. *Technology* once meant "the tools and techniques that humans make and use for their purposes." Twentieth-century style suggests a new definition for our most complex technologies: "elegantly designed systems on which we depend for our survival." Twentieth-century systems tend to resolve the problem of peers negotiating with one another by bringing once-independent negotiators inside the system as functional components.

Three examples do not do justice to the scope of this value

shift. I have, for example, hardly mentioned our changing relationship with nature. Thus, our century-long avoidance of waste disposal problems, seen so vividly today in acid rain and toxic pollutants, reveals a consistent pattern of overriding or ignoring nature's constraints. Only recently have the majority of Americans begun to recognize that nature "has a say" in the technological endeavor.[34]

Standardization admittedly yields substantial benefits. Standardized mass production permits a much larger segment of the population to own relatively high-quality manufactured goods, improving the standard of living for poor as well as rich. Even more important, standardization fosters and rewards the virtue of precision. Living as we do in an age where sophisticated systems such as telephone networks, electric utilities, medical technologies, and computers are commonplace, we find it hard to imagine the world of 1840 where the art of making steel seemed almost magical. Precision design has joined the family of the elegant arts even as it makes possible the systems on which our communication, our health, and our productivity depend.

With its many virtues, however, standardization carries significant liabilities; most important for us is the atrophy of the ability to negotiate. Negotiation is a messy business. When mutually independent peers must find a common way of proceeding, their different world views, vested interests, and styles make the outcome unpredictable whether the people in question are skilled workers and managers, shoppers and sellers, or independent nations. In the quest for a common good no one participant's version of the best solution will be adopted. Despite its inefficiencies, the interdependence inherent in negotiation requires and therefore fosters a capacity for engagement with others not like myself and an abiding sense of the value of agendas other than my own.[35]

Of course, negotiation should not replace all conformity! In the form of simple good manners, civic duty, or a host of other pragmatic arrangements, conformity makes ordinary life possible and bearable. If we tried to negotiate each aspect of life at every turn, we would wear ourselves out with endless wrangling. Still, the tendency to replace negotiation with standardized conformity creates a serious imbalance in American society. The two societal virtues, standardization's precision and negotiation's uncertainties, seem to work best in creative tension with the other.

The argument, to this point, runs as follows. The American automobile—that is, the car, the Fordist production system and GM's consumerist marketing style—provides a typical example of the way a successful technology first embodies and later enforces a specific set of values. The case also suggests some of the ways that a once-powerful technological style might relate to its context when exogenous changes begin to diminish its momentum. Finally, an overview of America's option for systemic standardization suggests not only that the American automobile is part of a larger and older technological style but also that a diminished ability to negotiate is our most significant trade-off for the benefits of standardization.

The final section rests on a related hypothesis, namely, that excessive individualism stems not from the option for standardized systems, but rather from the atrophy of a complementary habit of negotiation. To summarize in advance, members of the three technological constituencies—design, maintenance, and impact—can engage in or evade the precise sort of political negotiation that would remedy our individualistic but publicly passive American style. To foster such negotiation without destroying the possibility of effective system design and operation is, however, a challenge that demands a certain discernment by constituency members. When does masking one's role in the success of a technology foster technological creativity? When, on the other hand, does it evade healthy negotiation? Taking each constituency in turn, let us consider the question.

III: ELUSIVE TECHNOLOGICAL CONSTITUENCIES

1. THE DESIGN CONSTITUENCY

The principle of paleontologist Teilhard de Chardin—"Nothing is so delicate and fugitive by its very nature as a beginning"—holds as much for new technologies as for living species.[36] Both the psychology and the politics at work during

the origin of a new technology make it difficult to catch designers in the act. Their penchant for privacy stems in part from
the very nature of technological creativity. Thus, although the
design *process* involves negotiation to define project goals, the
act of designing cannot occur in an atmosphere of endless discussion. At some point debate must cease, to make room for
concentration on the problems at hand. It is, therefore, perfectly reasonable to say, "We are going into hiding so that people can't get at us."[37]

Designers can also choose secrecy for a more questionable
reason, namely, to exclude some parties from design negotiation. The contrast between Japanese and American corporate
styles of new program implementation illustrates the point. The
Japanese follow the Ringi principle: a new project cannot be
approved at a higher managerial level until every affected party
on the lower level has studied it, debated it, and finally signed
off indicating their approval. At this early stage, American firms
tend to take a shortcut. Upper management can approve a project without such broad-based negotiation. Other affected parties in the firm have to adapt to it without having their say at
the beginning. There follows a long period of "working the bugs
out" that can include, among other things, enforcing company-
wide conformity on people who are angry at having been excluded from the original design process.[38]

Avoidance of negotiation trades short-run efficiencies for long-
term alienation and discontent, thus diminishing rather than
enhancing technological creativity. In short, the effectiveness
of a technical design must be measured not only in terms of
its structural efficiencies but also in terms of the durability of
its long-term relationship with the larger social context. The
principle is not limited to in-house corporate relationships,
however well they exemplify the dynamic in question. At every
level of society and in situations of cross-cultural technological transfer as well, technologies are politically effective only
to the extent that their designs reflect some basic consensus about
the goals that the technology serves.[39] In terms of the three-
constituency model under discussion, this need for consensus
raises a question about the way maintenance constituency members participate in technological consensus.

2. THE MAINTENANCE CONSTITUENCY

Those who benefit from a technology adapt to its constraints and become dependent on it. As we noted in the case of the American automobile, the number and diversity of people and institutions who depend on a technology constitute the measure of its cultural influence. They sustain its momentum precisely because they cannot get along without that particular technology. On its face, this relationship does not seem very elusive at all. Unlike designers, people who benefit from a technology do not try to avoid notice; indeed, those who preside over technological systems and those who use them often take pride in their access to the technology in question.

A closer look at the dependent character of the relationship, however, reveals its own pattern of avoidance, once again for a mix of motives. On the one hand, chronic mistrust of technical systems and excessive attention to technological constraints make a recipe for mental illness. Hyperawareness of complex technical systems, or of anything else, immobilizes the human actor. So, for very good reasons, system insiders and system users often ignore their role in maintaining system momentum and their dependence on it.

On the other hand, the maintenance relationship can be repressed because it makes us uncomfortable. If we stopped to think, for example, that the automotive system on which we rely itself depends on a normally durable, but not infallible, network of technological support systems, and that the entire system has trade-offs for society and personal life, we might become more conscious of the fragility of an essential technological system than we would like. Masking the maintenance relationship can, therefore, take the form of healthy selectivity or evasive passivity.

Two recent events suggest the political and social complexities of maintenance constituency evasiveness. In mid-January of 1986 the space probe *Voyager 2* approached Uranus almost five years and one billion miles after launch. Its computer control systems timed the encounter within one minute of the original plan while programming a rotation that permitted extraordinary photographs of this distant planetary neighbor. Several days later, before a stunned America, the space shuttle *Challenger* exploded, killing six astronauts and one schoolteacher. *Voyager*'s elegant achievement was greeted with almost blasé acceptance and so, before its launch, was the anticipated success of *Challenger*'s mission.

The gradual unfolding of the NASA *Challenger* investigation, like lawsuits such as those stemming from the disastrous design of Ford Pinto gas tanks, provide public examples of technological fallibility.[40] In such cases the tension between governmental investigators or the damaged party bringing suit, and those who disclose system failures only under duress, reveals the common tendency of insiders to cover up the vulnerabilities of their technology. At the same time, the public shift of mood in the *Challenger* disaster—from initial boredom at "another shuttle launch," to shock, grief, and fear, and finally to anger at NASA cover-ups of design flaws—tells us that it is not only insiders who tend to ignore technical fragility. One needs only contrast public nonchalance about *Voyager 2* and preexplosion shuttle missions with the rapt attention that attended the first manned moon landing to see how hard it is for the body politic to sustain attention for the complexities of familiar systems. *Challenger*'s failure and its emotional aftermath demonstrate that taking the system for granted was due not simply to confidence in normally dependable technologies but also to a form of social amnesia that takes the form of willful technological illiteracy.[41]

Such amnesia has serious consequences for civic consciousness. When we habitually suppress awareness of system complexities we treat the elegant humanity revealed in their engineering with contempt and, at the same time, grant them autonomous, godlike status that dwarfs the human person. What difference can individuals make in a world dominated by massive technologies? Are we anything more than passive drifters on the inevitable technological tide? Even the technically competent suffer these feelings of inadequacy. Outside one's area of expertise each depends on technologies too complex to comprehend. Still, democracy requires deep confidence in one's creative power. To participate in the life of the body politic citizens must believe that their judgments carry value in the social equation.[42]

For members of a maintenance constituency, then, technological literacy requires more than the simple ability to use a
technology. It includes the capacity to interpret major technologies as systems that must always be maintained by someone, that always cost money, and that always have associated
trade-offs. Still, if our every waking moment were obsessed with
consciousness of the political and technical fallibility of every
system, society would disintegrate in anxious chaos. A healthy
maintenance constituency relationship, then, balances moments
of contemplation that foster alertness to the full political and
technical dimensions of technological systems with longer periods of day-to-day system use.[43]

We turn, finally, to the most difficult political question of
all, the relationship between a successful technology and those
who lose because of the way it is designed.

3. THE IMPACT CONSTITUENCY

Paulo Freire's maxim, "No oppressive order could permit
the oppressed to begin to question: 'Why?'" and his ground-
breaking *Pedagogy of the Oppressed,* from which it is taken,
illuminate the seemingly mysterious capacity of impact constituency members to remain invisible.[44] Those who lose because of the design of dominant systems—technological, economic, or political—are most often hidden from view. Not
surprisingly, those who design and preside over successful systems tend to ignore those who lose. Industrial capitalism, in
its pure form, explains the poverty of those who lose as a result
of their own character deficiencies.[45] Freire's argument, however, while it includes a critique of the laissez-faire capitalist
position, calls attention to the oppressed themselves who tend
to evade consciousness of the systemic causes of their suffering. His "pedagogy" encourages the struggle to achieve consciousness of systemic oppression as its cornerstone.[46]

Why do the dynamics of the impact constituency generate
numbness? One story from my experience with native Americans reveals a common pattern. When I lived with the Weasel
Bear family on Pine Ridge in the summer of 1968 we depended
on our car, a twelve-year-old Ford coupé, because we had to
drive two miles for water. The Ford's trunk was sprung, the

back windows did not work, and the transmission was so bad that under five miles an hour the engine died and above fifty miles an hour the car began to shake violently. A hole in the radiator made us carry water for refills every five miles or so.

One day I asked my Indian grandmother, Rose, "What did you pay for this thing?" She said: "Five hundred dollars." I asked where she bought it and found that she had bought it from a car dealer in an off-reservation town. Reacting like the lawyer's son that I am, I said: "We've got to do something about this! We should call the Better Business Bureau." "No," she said quietly, "Suppose we got them mad; where would we get cars from?" The powerless tend not to think too hard about how systems punish them. Impotence often breeds numbness as a substitute for pain.

The "anti-Luddite" argument fosters this very mentality. The original Luddites were British textile workers who, around the turn of the nineteenth century, destroyed *some* new factory equipment, namely the machines that they judged damaging to themselves.[47] In popular progressive discourse, however, the term applies to those who break *all* new machines because of their inability to keep up with progress. Critics of successful technologies are frequently subject to the charge: "Another Luddite! You hanker for the days of untreated diseases and outdoor toilets. A romantic." Anti-Luddite rhetoric denies the very existence of impact constituencies, claiming that despite obvious costs in the present, new technologies benefit even current losers because, in the long run, progress will make life better for all or at least for the descendants of all.[48]

Finally, as we have seen, members of the maintenance constituency are themselves members of the impact constituency. The negative trade-offs of technological designs do not neatly divide a population into those who win and those who lose. Every human artifact, simple mechanism or complex system, embodies only a limited set of values and serves only limited purposes. Technologies necessarily constrain us while they help us. Thus, we noted above that automobiles give us independent mobility even as they isolate us from one another. On reflection, however, it can be seen that these limitations, inherent in the very nature of technological design, provide an extraordinary focus for healthy social critique. Every culture

writes a profile of its governing values in the benefits and liabilities of its successful technologies. By attention to impact
constituency relationships, the discerning citizen reads the signs
of the times. Contemplating society through the prism of its
normal technologies demands hard emotional work; it is never
easy to take a critical stance toward the dominant values of one's
culture. Nevertheless, the challenge of life in a highly tech-
nologized democracy calls for precisely this form of adult consciousness.

There are, of course, very constructive reasons for ignoring
the way a technology hurts us. Too much negativity immobilizes
the critic of technological oppression in the same way that excessive attention to technical fallibility paralyzes members of
the maintenance constituency. A healthy relationship with the
major technologies of our society depends on our learning to
discern the difference between healthy attention and counter-
productive obsession. It should be clear by this point, however,
that submission to the ideology of autonomous progress leads
us to trade active citizenry for passive drifting and eviscerates
any effort at such discernment.

This is not to say that any society will ever completely free
itself from negative effects. Technologies necessarily arrange
reality so that some things go better while others go worse,
and increased consciousness about how we relate to our technologies will not lead to a technological "pie in the sky" whereby
we eventually reform the world so that there are no more impact constituencies.

CONCLUSION

Why, then, make the effort to sort out the politics of technology? Why endure the discomfort that necessarily attends contemplation of successful technologies and our multiple relationships with them? Put most simply, contemplation is the price
of technological and democratic adulthood. As I try to demonstrate in this essay, designing and maintaining successful technologies constitutes one of the most powerful forms of political
activity in our present social life. Far from being "value-neutral,"
successful technologies exert enormous force that shapes the

lives of those who depend on them. But the values they foster throughout the years of their power originated in decisions that, as our brief sketch of the Ford Motor Company design constituency suggests, are quite believably human in scale. We must retrieve that humanity before we can hope to engage in their politics.

Civic hope has made great demands in every culture that has ever existed. Still, it seems that the courage of contemplation may be more important today than at any time in our nation's history. We face a contemporary technological malaise:

> There is a widespread feeling that the promise of the modern era is slipping away from us. A movement of *enlightenment and liberation* that was to have freed us from superstition and tyranny has led in the twentieth century to a world in which ideological fanaticism and political oppression have reached extremes unknown in previous history. *Science,* which was to have unlocked the bounties of nature, has given us the power to destroy all life on the earth. *Progress,* modernity's master ideal, seems less compelling when it appears that it may be progress into the abyss.[49] (emphasis added)

Because of our inherited language of autonomous progress we are tempted, in the late twentieth century, to worship at the shrine of our own creations, for when we ascribe an inevitable force to the technologies we make, we relinquish our role as citizens in what may be the most important single dimension of contemporary life. Renewing human society cannot happen in this technologically complex society without the very adult awareness that *someone's* designs will be adopted, that *someone* will make decisions about the allocation of resources, and about which lines of research to pursue and which to ignore. Technological style, with all its nobility and liabilities, remains the work of human beings.

If the foregoing analysis is correct, the price of adult citizenship calls us to two interrelated responsibilities. We must, on the one hand, abandon the rhetoric of autonomous technological progress in favor of a politically more realistic form of technology talk. On the other hand, we must work to restore the balance between large-scale standardized systems and the political negotiation that they have tended to preempt. The

former task will help us with the latter. A renewed technological language, revealing as it does the human and political drama
of our relationships with successful technologies, can serve us
well as we engage in similar decisions about our future technologies. The stories of successful technologies show us how
to be noble and elegantly creative at the same time that they
warn us of our violence and injustice. To run the risk of becoming engaged in the political debate means, when seen from
this perspective, learning to sort the tangled strands that are
continually woven and rewoven as members of society embody
their values and world view in technologies that reflect and then
reshape a vision of the common good.

NOTES

1. U.S. Department of Commerce, Bureau of the Census, *Historical Statistics of the United States: Colonial Times to 1970* (Washington, D.C., 1975), vol. 1, series D 1-10. I have chosen a conservative
figure. Unemployment in some industrial cities reached a level of 80
percent.
   In this essay I will frequently, and reluctantly, follow common practice and use the terms *American* and *America* to refer to the United
States and its citizens. Although I am aware of the implicit insult—
for citizens of Latin America—involved in this parochial use of the
expressions, I have yet to find an alternative that is not inordinately
clumsy.
2. *Official Book of the Fair* (Chicago: A Century of Progress,
Inc., 1932), 21.
3. Ibid., 11. I am indebted to Lowell Tozer's "A Century of Progress, 1833–1933: Technology's Triumph Over Man," *American Quarterly* 4 (Spring 1952): 78–81, for first calling my attention to the Exposition and to Cynthia Read-Miller, curator of photographs and prints
in the archives at the Henry Ford Museum and Greenfield Village,
for copies of the *Official Book* and photographs of the iconography
referred to below.
4. Lenox R. Lohr, *Fair Management: The Story of A Century
of Progress Exposition* (Chicago: Cuneo Press, 1952), 96.
5. *Official Book*, 11. For photographs of the statues and text from
the Guidebook see Appendix.
6. Cited in James W. Carey and John J. Quirk, "The Mythos
of the Electronic Revolution," *The American Scholar* 39 (Spring/

Summer 1970): 411. *The American Scholar* does not use source nota-
tion and neither I nor Dr. Carey has been able to track the original
source of the text.

7. Historians at least as far back as Frederick Jackson Turner
have wrestled with the same question. See Frederick Jackson Turner,
"The Significance of the Frontier in American History" in *The Frontier in American History,* (New York: Henry Holt & Co., 1920), 1–
38; Henry Nash Smith, *Virgin Land: The American West as Symbol
and Myth* (Cambridge, Mass.: Harvard University Press, 1950); Leo
Marx, *The Machine in the Garden: Technology and the Pastoral Ideal
in America* (New York: Oxford University Press, 1964), and John F.
Kasson, *Civilizing the Machine: Technology and Republican Values
in America, 1776–1900* (New York: Penguin, 1976).

8. Carey and Quirk, "Mythos," 420–21.

9. Ibid. Carey, after the manner of Henry Adams in "The Virgin
and the Dynamo," focuses almost exclusive attention on electricity
to explain American technological style. As will be evident, I differ
slightly, seeing electronic technology as one major strand in a larger
cultural pattern of standardized systemic technologies.

10. David Potter, "Abundance and the Turner Thesis," in *History
and American Society: Essays of David M. Potter,* ed. Don E. Fehren-
bacher (New York: Oxford University Press, 1973) addresses the same
point in his critique of the frontier hypothesis as articulated by Turner
and Walter Prescott Webb. For Potter, Turner and Webb attribute too
much influence to the ideal of wilderness America and "did not recognize that the attraction of the frontier was simply as the most ac-
cessible form of abundance" (127). In so arguing, he overlooks the
mythic role of Nature as a "feminine" principle of renewal over against
a more "masculine" technology and science. For this distinction and
its long roots in Western culture, see Carolyn Merchant, *The Death
of Nature: Women, Ecology, and the Scientific Revolution* (New York:
Harper and Row, 1980).

11. The ideology of autonomous progress is considerably more
complicated than this brief sketch indicates. For a more detailed study
of the origins, development, and implications of the rhetoric described
here see my "Perils of Progress Talk: Some Historical Considerations,"
in *Science, Technology and Social Progress,* ed. Steven Goldman (Beth-
lehem, Pa.: Lehigh University Press, in press).

12. Robert Bellah et al., *Habits of the Heart: Individualism and
Commitment in American Life* (Berkeley: University of California
Press, 1985), chap. 2. Hereafter referred to as *HH*. On their description of individualism as the "first language" of Americans today see
pp. 20 and 334. On their call for the creation of a new first language

more broadly based on individualism and the republican and biblical traditions, see p. 292. Thomas C. Cochran notes the same patterns, especially in chapter 5, "Bureaucracy," of his *Challenges to American Values: Society, Business and Religion* (New York: Oxford University Press, 1985).

13. On Bellah et al.'s analysis of the four national traditions (republican, biblical, utilitarian individualism, expressive individualism) see *HH,* chap. 2.

14. John M. Staudenmaier, S.J., *Technology's Storytellers: Reweaving the Human Fabric* (Cambridge: MIT Press, 1985), esp. 95–103, 134–48, and chap. 5. Hereafter referred to as *Storytellers.*

15. Ibid., 192–201.

16. The exact chronology of Ford's shift from the traditional shop floor arrangement where supervisory personnel made up 2 percent of the workforce to their 1917 arrangement when the supervisory share had increased to 14.5 percent is not altogether clear. Stephen Meyer finds fragmentary evidence for the traditional style as late as 1913. See Meyer, *The Five Dollar Day: Labor Management and Social Control in the Ford Motor Company, 1908–1921,* (Albany: State University of New York Press, 1981), 50–51.

17. For details of Ford's labor policies during the period see Meyer, *Five Dollar Day.* For similar assessments of contemporary fear of chaos see John Higham, *Send These to Me: Jews and Other Immigrants in Urban America* (New York: Atheneum, 1975), esp. chaps. 1, 2, and 6. See also Michael Schudson, *Discovering the News: A Social History of American Newspapers* (New York: Basic Books, Harper Torchbooks, 1978), 127–34.

18. For a definitive study of the nineteenth-century tradition, see David Hounshell, *From the American System to Mass Production, 1800–1932,* (Baltimore: Johns Hopkins University Press, 1984). For a detailed treatment of the technological supports required in the design stage see *Storytellers,* pp. 61–69. See pages 40–45 for a treatment of invention and pages 45–50 for development.

19. On cultural hegemony see T. J. Jackson Lears, "The Concept of Cultural Hegemony: Problems and Possibilities," *The American Historical Review* 90 (June 1985): 567–93. See also *Storytellers,* 192–201.

20. On Taylorism see Edwin T. Layton Jr., *The Revolt of the Engineers* (Cleveland: Case Western Reserve University Press, 1971; reissued Baltimore: Johns Hopkins University Press, 1986), 134–53. On Sperry's control style of inventions see Thomas P. Hughes, *Elmer Sperry* (Baltimore: Johns Hopkins University Press, 1971), 45–46, 283–85. On tear gas see Daniel P. Jones, "From Military to Civilian

Technology: The Introduction of Tear Gas for Civil Riot Control,"
Technology and Culture 19 (April 1978): 151–68. On consumerist
advertising styles see note 32 below.

In the following trenchant observation the authors of *Habits of
the Heart* make the same point about Progressive Era politics. "This
desire for a more 'rational' politics, standing above interest but based
on *expertise rather than wisdom and virtue,* moved American political discourse away from concern with *justice,* with its civic republican echoes, toward a focus on *progress* — a progress defined as material abundance" (*HH,* 261; emphasis added).

21. Historical shifts are notoriously hard to fix in time. Design
and momentum stages of a technology typically overlap. The technology begins to achieve societal acceptance and a correlative increase
in cash flow before it has reached what hindsight will reveal as its
mature form. Inventive activity and developmental changes characteristic of the flexible design stage often mark the early momentum stage.
Thus, for example, the mid-1920s General Motors' marketing strategy significantly modified the Ford automotive style more than a decade after it had entered the momentum stage. On General Motors'
marketing strategy see below.

22. My source requests anonymity. He also noted that the GM-
Toyota joint venture — New United Motor Manufacturing Incorporated
(NUMMI) — has adopted a "production team" concept reminiscent
in some ways of the early-twentieth-century, fixed-work-station style
that predated Ford's moving assembly line.

23. See Parker J. Palmer, *The Company of Strangers: Christians
and the Renewal of America's Public Life* (New York: Crossroad, 1981)
38–39, 46–48, where he argues that these patterns have fostered political apathy in twentieth-century America.

24. I am presently working on a book-length version of this interpretation. For a still brief, but slightly more complete, analysis see
my "United States Technology and Adult Commitment" in *Studies
in the Spirituality of Jesuits* 19, no. 1 (January 1987): 1–37.

25. Carolyn Merchant's *Death of Nature* traces the gradual shift
in western Europe from *Nature* defined as the goddess who sets the
rules and boundaries for human enterprise to a still feminine but
newly passive entity destined for exploitation and conquest. Roder-
ick Nash, *Wilderness and the American Mind* (New Haven: Yale
University Press, 1967), studies the complementary theme of *wilderness.* He finds its earliest meaning — wild, chaotic and often evil
darkness — shifting in nineteenth-century America to a romantic and
nostalgic source of regeneration. As early Americans encountered
the virgin wilderness they found their dreams of conquest tempered
as much by nature's raw power as by the crudity of their tools. For

other discussions of the middle landscape see Marx, *Machine in the Garden;* Kasson, *Civilizing the Machine;* and Thomas Merton, *Conjectures of a Guilty Bystander* (New York: Doubleday, Image Books, 1968), 33–39.

26. Lest we idealize the American conquest of nature we should note that the myth of the middle landscape had a special place for native Americans and blacks. Native Americans were seen as part of the wilderness, godlike in their ability to live in the forbidding terrain and subhuman at the same time, lacking both culture and history. Blacks, on the other hand, were part of the tools that white Europeans used to conquer the wilderness. Neither image, of course, is even close to the self-image of these two peoples.

27. On the drive toward standardization in the Ordnance Department see Merritt Roe Smith, "Military Enterprise and Innovative Process" in *Military Enterprise and Technological Change: Perspectives on the American Experience,* ed. M. R. Smith (Cambridge, Mass.: MIT Press, 1985).

28. The most helpful source on nineteenth-century labor-management tensions over work rules remains Herbert Gutman, "Work, Culture and Society in Industrializing America," in his *Work, Culture and Society in Industrializing America* (New York: Random House, Vintage Books, 1966).

29. J. L. Larson, "A Systems Approach to the History of Technology: An American Railroad Example" (Paper delivered at the annual meeting of the Society for the History of Technology, Toronto, Ontario, Canada, October 18, 1980), 17.

30. Carlene Stephens, *Inventing Standard Time,* (Washington, D.C.: Smithsonian Institution, 1983); Mark Duluk, "The American Railroad Depot as Technological Vernacular Architecture," *Dichotomy* 5 (Spring 1982): 10–15. On the early history of the wire news services, see Daniel J. Czitrom, *Media and the American Mind: From Morse to McLuhan* (Chapel Hill, N.C.: University of North Carolina Press, 1982) esp. chap. 1: "'Lightning Lines' and the Birth of Modern Communication, 1838–1900"; Richard Schwarzlose, "Harbor News Association: The Formal Origins of the AP," *Journalism Quarterly* 45 (Summer 1968): 253–60; and Robert L. Thompson, *Wiring a Continent: The History of the Telegraph Industry in the United States, 1832–1866* (Princeton, N.J.: Princeton University Press, 1947).

31. For a definitive study of electrification in the United States, Germany, and Great Britain, see Thomas Parke Hughes, *Networks of Power: Electrification in Western Society, 1880–1930* (Baltimore: Johns Hopkins Press, 1983).

32. Roland Marchand, *Advertising the American Dream: Making Way for Modernity, 1920–1940* (Berkeley: University of Califor-

nia Press, 1985), 68–69. See also p. 10 and passim. See also Daniel Pope, *The Making of Modern Advertising,* (New York: Basic Books, 1983). For an analysis of the new advertising style similar to *Habits'* "expressive individualism," see T. J. Jackson Lears, "From Salvation to Self-Realization: Advertising and the Therapeutic Roots of the Consumer Culture, 1880-1930," in *The Culture of Consumption: Critical Essays in American History, 1880–1980,* ed. Richard Wightman Fox and T. J. Jackson Lears (New York: Pantheon Books, 1983), 1–38.

33. The GM strategy was, in fact, more complex than we have time to discuss. For a more complete presentation, see Emma Rothchild, *Paradise Lost: The Decline of the Auto-Industrial Age* (New York: Random House, Vintage Books, 1973), chap. 2.

34. On early-twentieth-century avoidance of evidence indicating ecological damage from technical systems, see John Burke "Wood Pulp, Water Pollution, and Advertising," *Technology and Culture* 20 (January 1979): 181–84.

35. For an interpretation of contemporary U.S. society that exactly matches these observations see Palmer, *Company of Strangers.*

36. Teilhard de Chardin, *The Phenomenon of Man* (New York: Harper and Row, 1959), 120.

37. These few lines summarize and dramatically oversimplify the tangled subtleties found in real cases of emerging technology. *Storytellers* (chap. 2, "Emerging Technology and the Mystery of Creativity") treats the matter in greater detail. See also N. John Habraken, *The Appearance of the Form: Four Essays on the Position Designing Takes between People and Things* (Cambridge, Mass.: Atwater Press, 1985), 135–39, for a provocative discussion of negotiation's complexity during the design process.

38. For a comparison of the Japanese and American styles see Masaaki Imai, *Kaizen (Ky'zen): The Key to Japan's Competitive Success* (in press). Studies of labor-management conflict due to lack of negotiation make the same point. See, for example, Meyer, *The Five Dollar Day;* Merritt Roe Smith, *Harpers Ferry Amory and the New Technology: The Challenge of Change* (Ithaca: Cornell University Press, 1977); and David Nobel, *Forces of Production* (New York: A. A. Knopf, 1983). For a survey of recent literature see *Storytellers,* 114–18, 176–77, 189–90.

39. A number of recent best-selling books indicate increased awareness of the difficulty and importance of consensus negotiation. Roger Fisher and William Ury's *Getting to Yes: Negotiating Agreement Without Giving In,* ed. Bruce Patton (New York: Houghton Mifflin, 1981), appears to be the best. For another example, see Herb Cohen, *You Can Negotiate Anything* (New York: Bantam, 1980).

40. For a summary of NASA and Morton Thiokol coverups in

the Challenger project, see David E. Sanger, "How See-No-Evil Doomed Challenger," *New York Times,* 29 June 1986, Business Section. On the Pinto case see Richard T. De George, "Ethical Responsibilities of Engineers in Large Organizations: The Pinto Case," *Business and Professional Ethics Journal* 1 (Fall 1981): 1–14.

41. Langdon Winner's discussion of the problem of technological ignorance in contemporary society's situation of "manifest social complexity" provides a helpful general discussion of what I am calling "willful technological amnesia." See his *Autonomous Technology: Technics-out-of-Control as a Theme in Political Thought* (Cambridge, Mass.: MIT Press, 1977): 279–87.

42. The harsh treatment often meted out to "whistle blowers" is a particularly acute form of such individual intimidation. Bucking the system normally carries a high price tag. In addition to the Morton Thiokol–Challenger case noted above see Rosemary Chalk, "The Miners' Canary," *Bulletin of the Atomic Scientists* 37 (February 1982): 16–22, and the special issue on whistle blowing and engineers in *Technology and Society* 4 (June 1985): 2–31 for multiple examples.

43. One thinks here of Hocking's concept of "alternation," that shifting of focus and attitude from time to time for the sake of a balanced perspective. See John R. Stacer, "The Hope of a World Citizen" in this volume.

44. Paulo Freire, *Pedagogy of the Oppressed,* trans. Myra Bergman Ramos (New York: Herder and Herder, 1972), 74.

45. Laissez-faire capitalism disposes of technological "losers" with a complex argument. Poverty results from personal character deficiency, and human creativity can only be guaranteed within society at large when the penalty for defective behavior is so severe that it serves as a driving motive for individual and competitive advancement. Thus, in Herbert Spencer's unforgettable prose: "The poverty of the incapable, the distresses that come upon the imprudent, the starvation of the idle, and those shoulderings aside of the weak by the strong, which leave so many in shallows and in miseries, are the decrees of a large, far-seeing benevolence" (Spencer, "The Sins of Legislators," in *The Man Versus the State* [1892; reprint ed., Indianapolis: Liberty Classics, 1981], 107–8).

46. Karl Marx's famous aphorism, "Religion . . . is the opium of the people," makes the same point. Insofar as organized religion suppresses awareness of systemic oppression it works to numb the consciousness of the impact constituency. Marx ignored, or perhaps had little contact with, religious traditions which, beginning at least with the Old Testament prophets, foster Freire's type of consciousness. For a striking example see Herbert Gutman's study of working class Protestantism in late nineteenth-century America, "Protestantism and the

152

American Labor Movement: The Christian Spirit in the Gilded Age," in his *Work, Culture, and Society*, 79–118. The texts he cites are remarkably similar to recent Latin American liberation theology. See, for example, José Miranda, *Marx and the Bible: A Critique of the Philosophy of Oppression,* trans. John Eagleson (Maryknoll, N.Y.: Orbis, 1974). For the relationship between Marx and Christianity see Arthur F. McGovern, *Marxism: An American Christian Perspective* (Maryknoll, N.Y.: Orbis, 1980).

47. For the interpretation of the Luddite argument given here see David F. Noble, "Technology's Politics: Present Tense Technology," *Democracy* (Spring 1983): 8–24; and Adrian J. Randall, "The Philosophy of Luddism: The Case of the West of England Woolen Workers, ca. 1790–1809," *Technology and Culture* 27 (January 1986): 1–17.

48. Of course laissez-faire capitalism, in its crudest form, would argue that the worthless poor should die, preferably without offspring, so that the race might excrete its unfit members. Thus, for example, "Well, the command 'If any would not work neither should he eat,' is simply a Christian enunciation of that universal law of Nature under which life has reached its present height—the law that *a creature not energetic enough to maintain itself must die.* . . . Moreover, I admit that the philanthropic are not without their share of responsibility; since, *that they may aid the offspring of the unworthy, they disadvantage the offspring of the worthy*" (Spencer, *Man Versus State,* 23–24; emphasis added).

49. *HH*, 277.

APPENDIX

The Chicago 1933 Exposition
Photographs and Text

On the following page is an illustration of the Administration Building with two sculpture figures on either side of the entrance symbolizing science and industry from a catalog: *Chicago and Its Two World's Fairs, 1893–1933* (Geographical Publishing Co., 1933). From the collections of the Henry Ford Museum and Greenfield Village. With permission.

The next illustration is of the fountain in the Hall of Science with the sculpture "Science Advancing Mankind" (Louise Lentz Woodruff) from: *Official World's Fair in Pictures: A Century of Progress Exposition, 1933,* (Chicago: Reuben H. Donnelley, 1933). From the collections of the Henry Ford Museum and Greenfield Village. With permission.

Also reproduced is a page of text from *Official Book of the Fair* (Chicago: A Century of Progress, Inc., 1932).

Theme of Fair Is Science

As two partners might clasp hands, Chicago's growth and the growth of science and industry have been united during this most amazing century. Chicago's corporate birth as a village, and the dawn of an unprecedented era of discovery, invention, and development of things to effect the comfort, convenience, and welfare of mankind, are strikingly associated.

Chicago, therefore, asked the world to join her in celebrating a century of the growth of science, and the dependence of industry on scientific research.

An epic theme! You grasp its stupendous stature only when you stop to contemplate the wonders which this century has wrought.

Science Finds—Industry Applies—Man Conforms

Science discovers, genius invents, industry applies, and man adapts himself to, or is molded by, new things. Science, patient and painstaking, digs into the ground, reaches up to the stars, takes from the water and the air, and industry accepts its findings, then fashions and weaves, and fabricates and manipulates them to the usages of man. Man uses, and it effects his environment, changes his whole habit of thought and of living. Individuals, groups, entire races of men fall into step with the slow or swift movement of the march of science and industry.

There, in epitome, you have a story that A Century of Progress tells you, not in static, lifeless exhibits, but in living, moving demonstrations of beauty and color. Science, to many of us, has been only a symbol of something mysterious, difficult, intricate, removed from man's accustomed ways. So few of us realize that in virtually everything that we do we enjoy a gift of science. A Century of Progress undertakes to clothe science with its true garb of practical reality and to tell its story of humanly significant achievement so that even he who runs may read.

Exhibits of Action and Life

Other great expositions have shown, most often in settings of splendor, the achievements of man as exemplified in the finished products of general use; of dwellings and clothes; of packaged and labeled foods and other commodities; and of the machines and tools and instruments with which they were made—parade of products and devices displayed for ribbons and prizes.

But when the plans were in the making for the exposition of 1933, the thought came that Chicago's Centennial celebration should be used to help the American people to understand themselves, and to make clear to the coming generation the forces which have built this nation.

One night, President Rufus C. Dawes sat at dinner with Prof. Michael Idvosky Pupin, noted American scientist and inventor, and he

Beyond the Melting Pot:
An Essay in Cultural Transcendence

Carl F. Starkloff, S.J.

As an ethos, individualism typifies white middle-class Americans. This essay journeys into another world — the world of racial minorities. It does so by examining a problem that thrusts itself into one's consciousness with a reading of North American history. I refer to the failure, especially of the United States dominant culture, to welcome and articulate its own diversification; that is, America has remained a "melting pot" in its attitude of assimilation of foreigners,[1] and the foreigners happen to include the earliest settlers of this continent, the "Indians." But let us begin our discussion by looking at four such native persons who have proved "unmeltable."

FOUR NATIVE NORTH AMERICANS

Dominic Eshkakogan is a Canadian Ojibway in his late fifties who lives in a village on one of the many Ontario reserves. He has for many years served in local politics as well as on committees dealing with national problems; he has held various administrative positions within his native band. Dominic's children are now grown, but he and his wife, Gladys, are deeply involved with the concerns of their extended family and especially with their grandchildren. Dominic is a deeply religious Roman Catholic, and while he has experienced many conflicts with different priests and other mission personnel, his relationship with the church is strong. So strong is it that Dominic has completed a formation program and has been ordained a deacon. At present he is local administrator and to all practical purposes pastor of his village church, where a priest and a sister visit weekly for a "full" eucharist and adult catechetical training. Dominic is also a "charismatic" Catholic and now participates with other native persons in a music and healing ministry.

Dominic is, moreover, a traditional native person; he is fluent in the language, and while he has not been a practitioner of tribal ceremonies, he is familiar with them and has recently undertaken to study them. He has acquired skills in religious analysis and discernment as a means of ministering to his people in their concern over how to be "Indians" while also being Christians. Like so many of his fellow native ministers, Dominic is also a recovering alcoholic and regularly participates in healing ceremonies and therapeutic gatherings, especially Alcoholics Anonymous, both for his own health and as part of his ministry.

As a native Christian, Dominic has never been in a position to insulate himself—as most Euro-Americans can do—from impinging foreign culture, and thus he has spent his life dealing with it. While he has passed through periods of anger over his people's loss of land, over the poisoning of their environment, and over the devastation of their culture, his own strength lies in his strong and serene determination to help native people build and administer their own native church within the Catholic communion. He desires to work, not against white people, but with them, and hopes to see the day—"hopefully while my wife is still alive too"—when he can be ordained to the priesthood.

Jim Dumont is also an Ojibway, now in his early forties, who comes from a Protestant Christian family and has received a master of divinity. He has a brother who is an ordained minister in the United Church of Canada. Jim typifies many of the middle-generation native persons who grew up apart from the strictly traditional native life but who now turn to that life in the search for wholeness and as a way to serve their people. Jim too has gone through anger at his church but has now passed beyond that anger into a more creative stance toward church, native tradition, and the dominant culture.

Jim has joined his own immediate family with a dozen or so other native families in an area of an Ontario reserve, to pursue a planned process of revitalization of native life. They are obtaining the help of tribal elders and spiritual and political leaders in order to build a modern Indian community around contemporary and traditional models of the Ojibway customs. The children are receiving a more traditional Indian education in a school set up by the families, until they are ready for high school. While Jim and his compatriots seem to have little bitterness toward the church and hospitably received me on one occasion into one of their "sweat" ceremonies, they insist on maintaining their independent position vis-à-vis white society and the mainstream church.

Vivian Juan is a Papago woman in her late twenties, a graduate in business administration and education now pursuing a master's degree in related areas. She was chosen Miss Indian America in 1982. Like most of her people, who live on a large reservation in Arizona, Vivian is a practicing Roman Catholic with roots in a very indigenous form of Catholicism as well as in tribal ways that have developed over three centuries. In recent years Vivian has become a powerful leader among Indian youth all over the United States, where she travels extensively on behalf of the Tekakwitha Conference—a Catholic organization, some five thousand strong—of native people and other church workers.

While Vivian too has had to struggle with frustration and anger, she never seems to dwell on the matter, preferring to carry her message of self-confidence and hope to native youth and to further a solidarity network of Indian people both in society and in the church. Vivian has from her earliest years received family and tribal support in her efforts to deal constructively with her people's problems. Her source of strength is her culture, and, having her feet firmly planted within it, she can reach out to other cultures.

Dick Ortiz is a Wyoming Arapaho in his early thirties, the son of a Northern Arapaho mother and a Mexican-American father. While Dick and his one brother and three sisters have experienced the problems of reservation life, the parents have raised the family in an off-reservation town and have given the children good opportunities for education and growth. The family is Catholic, and the parents are especially devout practitioners. Dick himself has gone through a period of serious questioning and has moved into a closer relationship with the church. He is married to a white woman and has one young son.

Dick has obtained a master's degree in business administration and has returned to help in the work of community development on the reservation, although he might now find more lucrative employment. He too has served in the past as head of the youth task force in the Tekakwitha Conference, organizing workshops of reconciliation between native young people and church leaders. Dick by now has identified strongly with his mother's people and has become involved in the Sun Dance tradition and the Arapaho way. He sees this involvement as compatible with his Catholic life and is resolved to witness to the dialogue between the two.

The persons I have described above are real people, and two are close friends and associates. They do not typify their people, who suffer many trials and much brokenness, but they have shown how many native persons and even communities are coming to grips with cultural crises. They can serve as examples to instruct our often rootless white middle class in the ability to relate to alien cultures, because they are very much examples of people who live in "communities of memory"[2] that are becoming "communities of hope."

The native people of this continent can serve as a witness to the present generation of assimilated immigrant peoples in four ways. They are an example, first, of the enduring tribal value of solidarity, not because they are altruistic, but because tribal people know that they cannot survive without solidarity. Second, they put a word of caution to the most pervasive Euro-American ideology—that of progress. If ideology is a justificatory and apologetic defense of an established order, the word *progress* might well describe our cultural ideology.[3] Third, Indian people live with an instinctive sense of culture as a total experience. Finally, their own history has forced them to come to terms with other cultures, much as the biblical Israelites had to do.

Apropos of these points, Raimundo Panikkar attributes the exhaustion of the entire Western Christian tradition to its failure to cross-fertilize and mutually fecundate with other cultural and religious traditions. His thesis may be even more applicable to the United States, where significant European shortcomings have been magnified—for reasons to be discussed in this essay.[4] The present series of essays, of which this article is a part, endeavors to confront the problem of American individualism. This further involves a concern with the decline of American "civil religion." In this light we must also deal with the problem of public philosophy and its importance to a nation.[5]

In addressing the issue of individualism, I shall propose a fundamental question for reflection by Americans in general and for the churches in particular. The question is based on a belief that self-transcendence is the essence of spiritual motivation and moral consciousness even while the moral subject remains firm in adhering to a primary vision and strives to achieve an equilibrium between the solitary self and the submerged self. Thus, we ask, can there be a strong, spiritually creative culture that is incapable of entering into dialogue with other cultures and of recognizing their spiritual values?

We discover a tension in any culture between universality and particularity, between inclusiveness and exclusivity; but culture in the United States exhibits a notable inconsistency between the ideals of freedom and national solidarity, on the one hand, and their practice, on the other.[6] In this essay I will expand the discussion of this aspect of the problem of American spirituality and morality in the light of the need recognized by many contemporary thinkers: that is, to seek an overarching spiritual motivation that might furnish hope for more universal common meaning among nations and cultures. In this context, I shall examine the themes of civil religion, individualism, and cultural pluralism as we find them played out in the relationship between American Christian missions and American Indians. To this purpose, I shall investigate the ideology of Manifest Destiny as it won over and then utilized the churches and missions. My concluding statements will deal with a pastoral theology and spirituality of culture as it might emerge from a dialogue between North American mainstream culture (led by the churches) and the oppressed societies of the continent.

THE BROKEN COVENANT

As Robert Bellah has noted in *The Broken Covenant,* utilitarian individualism does not express the fundamental religious and moral conception of America. Rather, the United States had its spiritual origins in an "imaginative religious and moral conception of life that took account of a much broader range of social, ethical, aesthetic and religious needs than the utilitarian model" (*BC,* xiv). Contemporary American individualists have lost the original "civil religion" of this nation, which is "that religious dimension, found . . . in the life of every people, through which it interprets its historical experience in the light of transcendent reality" (*BC,* 3).

The founders of this nation looked upon themselves as a chosen people, but America as a whole has not yet emerged from the situation of deuteronomic Israel (a tribe bound tightly by law) into that of prophetic Israel (a community challenged by the message of mature moral integrity), and it certainly has not entered into Jesus' awareness of universality that gradually permeated the apostles and the early Christian community.[7] Moreover, America's Calvinist roots (the pristine spiritual inspiration of the "covenant" that the founding ancestors believed they had from God) eventually sprouted into a distorted version of the work ethic and individual progress—the equation of salvation with personal success. The liberation of individuals failed to bring with it an ethic and spirituality of responsibility to the wider society. This failure bore along with it the inevitable disillusionment faced by egocentric aspirations for success.

Nativism in United States white society also echoes the xenophobia that seems to have characterized much of Israel in its postexilic era, when its own civil religion tended to become largely an "external covenant" (*BC,* 142). This combination of radical individualism and Anglo-Saxon nativism has led inevitably to the paranoic fear of socialism and communism now so closely identified with United States political life. Every form of communalism (including, be it noted, tribal concepts of living), now languishes under the same taboo in the collective American psyche. This seemingly paradoxical combination of individualism and collective rigidity was explained perceptively by Alexis de Tocqueville. He suggested very early in American history that such extreme individualism might eventually work at counterpurposes to its intent, as a populace loses any authoritative communal resistance to whatever tyrannical ideology might come along.[8] Then the nation faces the task of creating a new myth of solidarity and moral authenticity.

HABITS OF THE HEART

In *Habits of the Heart* Robert Bellah and his collaborators took their title from Tocqueville, who equated the phrase with mores, which he described loosely as notions, opinions, and ideas that "shape mental habits" and as "the sum of moral and intellectual dispositions of men in society."[9] In their extensive interviews of middle-class (and white) Americans, Bellah and his team found everyone they interviewed trapped in some form of individualism (utilitarian or expressive) whether he or she exhibited concern for success and self-satisfaction, on the one hand, or for the general social welfare, on the other. In all cases, the individualistic conscience lacked a language, a "public philosophy," that would allow it to transcend individualism and the narcissistic entrapment of the "therapeutic mentality." In Walter Lippmann's words, one sees here "the growing incapacity of the large majority of the democratic peoples to believe in intangible realities."[10] Even within evangelical or more socially concerned churches, especially in the churches of the civil rights movement, the problem arises of transforming the habitual attitudes of individualistic Americans enough to create a new social ecology.

The failure of American individualists to retain belief in intangible realities is not unique in history; in fact, it would seem to be the pattern of all societies. The people of Israel, in their history of becoming a people, continually experienced the tension between understanding their homeland as a divine gift—to be used only in stewardship and not in ownership—and grasping at that land as an object of control, forgetting its spiritual origin in Yahweh's care for the people. This interpretation would also seem to indicate that it is not only individuals who must transcend themselves, but nations and cultures as well.[11]

Without burdening the reader with autobiographical details, it occurs to me that there is some value in noting how my own perception of American social and cultural history has changed with six years of residence and work in Canada. To be sure, the two countries share many common characteristics and problems along our three-thousand-mile-plus border, especially in our relationships to the native peoples. But it is also noteworthy how, after sharing a common colonial history up to the American Revolution (which, I suggest, continued until after the War of 1812), our countries developed a number of subtle differences in our conceptions of progress and national identity. The United States developed within the ideology and overarching horizon of Manifest Destiny, with its imperative to absorb all that stood in the way of frontier progress. Canadians, at least those of English background, have retained much identification with Britain even into the present, and their transition to national sovereignty has contained no such mighty rallying cry. There has been no powerful sense of election to translate the will of God into terms of national identity.[12] To be sure, strong disputes still exist between English and French Canadians, and growing immigration will present increasing problems of orderly transition into the multicultural society espoused in political rhetoric. But Canada, even in its own westward expansion and subjugation of the Indians, has retained a stronger sense of pluralism, social welfare, and collectivism, generally free of the bloody violence that prevailed south of the border. Whether there is here a practical lesson to be learned by Americans is a question worth investigating, and it is in the interest of both countries to pursue the multicultural question. The context of that discussion in this essay will be the history of our Euro-American ancestors, joined to that of those peoples over whom they walked in their search for either national or self-realization.

Vine Deloria, Jr., devotes two chapters of his book *God Is Red* to a description of religion in America and to a survey of the relationship between tribal religions and contemporary American culture.[13] Since lawyer-philosopher Deloria is one of the foremost spokespersons within and for the native community, his work is a perfect example of a native person emerging from oppression and leading his people in writing its own history and theology.

More significant here is the assistance furnished by Deloria to a self-understanding by North American Christians of their place within the social fabric that this continent has become. One can see qualifications that need to be made in Deloria's argument (*GR,* chap. 9) that Christianity ceased to be a truly viable religion when it departed from its original cultural moorings in the Near East. Nonetheless, it can be argued that what Christian apologists have always maintained to be the great strength of Christianity—its potential for transcending all cultures even while living in all cultures—also presents the greatest threat. That is, how do whole societies of Christians manage to live and practice such a reflective and intellectual brand of spiritual motivation? Every Christian group that settled North America, whether it brought with it the Lutheran doctrine of the two kingdoms, the Calvinist idea of the Christian commonwealth, or the traditional Roman Catholic perfect-society model of church, eventually identified with the prevailing national ideology. In Canada's case, this was a benign form of European culture-Christianity, none the less arrogant for that, determined as it was to bring Indians in dignified fashion into the ranks of the civilized. In the United States, it was a self-righteous and violent history that trampled all who stood in its way, leaving blood on the hands of generations to come. As a result, is it so far-fetched that Deloria is able to show us such a sideshow of religiosocial aberrations?

MISSIONS AND THE NEW WORLD DREAM

The history of our problem can be described, given the nature of this essay, in two sections: there is the period of early colonization, when the mission and colonial efforts were both part of a new world European movement; then there is the period leading into our own era when the ideology of expansion took on its own American identity.

The fundamental responses of Europeans, whether colonists or missionaries, to the phenomenon of Indian culture are remarkably similar. In his treatment of the French conquest, which most historians will agree was the most benign and least ethnocentric of all the European conquests, Cornelius Jaenen situates the European mentality in the then-current thinking of the philosophes, who sought the pure primeval culture of the noble savage, unspoiled by modern society, over against another contemporary representation of Indians as depraved barbarians bent on bloodshed, living in every form of perversion. Missionaries, first the Franciscan Recollets and then the Jesuits, found themselves attempting to discern the truth between these conflicting theories. The Jesuits, with extensive classical training, developed into excellent linguists and, within the limitations of their age, ethnologists. Jaenen credits the latter with some skill in entering into the cultures of the Indians, but they did so only in order to bring them around to a conformity to French civilized ways and to the rigid Roman Catholic theology and religious discipline of the time.[14] It is ironic, one might add, that the French Jesuits were unable to imitate the work of their brethren in South America and separate the natives from rapid European acculturation, precisely because of the less violent and cruel policies of the French. The barbarities of the conquistadors left little doubt in the minds of the Jesuits to the south that the natives must be given a refuge away from their conquerors.

As the French and Indian cultures, except in the case of intermarriage, drew farther apart into the segregated condition of the present day, native societies became increasingly disorganized and tended to absorb the worst elements of European culture (*FF*, 194). French society was able to stabilize itself economically and militarily, even though it proved to be incapable of integrating with the Indians. A distinct white Canadian culture did emerge, along with a growing ethnocentrism, the identity of which depended on an interaction of culture and religion. Thus the pattern of the Canadian "cultural mosaic" was begun, but the mosaic development was controlled by the dominant European politics and economics. Canada would go on to experience its own tensions between the conquering English and subjugated French, but in the process would learn to deal much more open-mindedly with ethnic differences, to tolerate and even encourage distinctive cultural pockets within the nation. Sadly, this process proved to be of little benefit to the native Indian inhabitants, whose cultural integrity had been so badly damaged.

James Axtell detects in the Jesuits what might be called a certain primitive countercultural methodology in their efforts first to establish villages in which Indians might be settled and weaned from their nomadic habits, but later, with greater political savvy, to segregate the Indians from the "frenchifying" plans of colonial rulers.[15] The Jesuits made efforts to accommodate their teaching and discipline to native culture as they became more sophisticated anthropologically. But with all this, North America was already beginning its total submission to European conquest, and the Euro-American ideology was already becoming a "structure" in itself, in spite of many good intentions of missionaries and settlers. The conquering culture was incapable of recognizing the spiritual values in cultures so different from itself.

United States culture eventually surrendered to the melting pot ideology and to a determination, at times fanatical, to suppress cultural dissent. In his treatment of English Protestantism, Axtell concedes to those staunch Puritans the same conviction as that of the French. Those colonists granted that Indians were indeed capable of being touched by the gospel, but their belief was tinged by the conviction that the Indians were in a condition of barbarism that was an "infinite distance from Christianity" (*IW*, 133). Their strange ways were representative of that depravity that Cotton Mather could describe as a state of miserable animals and "idiots" without the use of reason (*IW*, 133). By now, not only had European culture determined the criteria of decency and civility, but nothing in Indian culture could be allowed any semblance of spiritual value—a teaching that even John Calvin might have hesitated to expound. For the first time here we can detect that spirit of the holy crusade that Bellah will establish as the basis of American civil religion.

An important historical phenomenon is related to this cultural naivete and perhaps presages the later cultural crises among individualistic North Americans. I refer to the case of the "white Indians." These were Europeans captured by natives and put through an acculturation and adoption into tribal life—persons ranging in age from infancy into adulthood. Many more of these later captives chose to remain as Indians, or left their adopted families unwillingly, than was true of Indians in white custody.

Even those who did return to their own people without resistance
generally recalled the years of their Indian residence with fond-
ness. Axtell points out: "They stayed because they found Indian life to possess a strong sense of community, abundant love,
and uncommon integrity—values that the European colonists
also honored, if less successfully."[16]

Already we can detect the decline of the white civil religion
and the breaking of the covenant. The colonists were losing
confidence in the conviction that their transplanted European
idealism alone represented the will of God for the new world.
Relatively few Indians became devout Christians in America,
largely because the example of the colonists taught them the
vices of Europe and few of its virtues. Already in the mid-
eighteenth century the injustices were mounting and the native
ideals of resistance and revitalization were greater than the moral
and religious ideals offered them by European Christianity. This
resistance troubled, as it does today, the more perceptive among
the Christians, who saw that the new dream was not winning
over the Indians. Yet Axtell voices a sentiment that may well
be echoed by missiologist and social critic alike when he comments on the rising doubts of white colonists at their failure
to win over the Indians: "We can only regret that the invaders,
stripped bare and defenseless, did not seize the moment for self-
understanding, tolerance, and true humiliation" (*IW*, 333).

The history of the American Southwest and northern Mexico reflects similar basic patterns over three eras of domination,
first by the Spanish, then by the Mexicans, and finally by Anglo-
Americans. In each case, however, there are significant differences, and in the third era we find the typical patterns of Anglo-
American frontier and missionary activity.

The Spanish phase of conquest, which lost its hegemony with
the great Pueblo liberation rebellion of 1680, is again typical
of the muscle flexing of an adolescent European nationalism.
Missionaries, military men, and colonial administrators took
seriously their duty to civilize the natives, a campaign that generally took the form of acculturation into specific elements of
the Spanish culture of the period, including obedience to the
King of Spain and the Roman Catholic form of Christianity.[17]
Edward Spicer notes, however, the efforts of many Jesuit missionaries, especially Eusebio Kino, to respect and enter into

the Indian cultures. Missionaries were indeed slowly learning, as the tragedy of Paraguay would demonstrate, the true nature of church-state partnership.[18] Nevertheless, the pattern of enforced acculturation proceeded generally unhindered except for the Pueblo revolt.

Mexican domination, assuming hegemony in the early eighteenth century, differed from the Spanish in its modernized developments—individualized landholding by Indians, democratic and constitutional forms of government, and an actual institution of the hitherto unpracticed principle of Indian equality in citizenship. Mexico did not enforce any form of religion, true to its historical struggle against clericalism. The Mexican conquest, however, featured scarcely any more creative analysis of or dialogue with native culture, except insofar as Mexican culture in general is a spontaneous synthesis of European and native American cultures.

The Anglo-American era began differently in this region, commonly called Northwest New Spain: at first there was no desire or effort to change the native cultural life, but rather the practice was to get them onto reservations and into isolation from the rapidly flowing American mainstream. Soon enough, however, the more altruistic quality of the American ideology began to surface. The newcomers sought to civilize the Indians with the English language, American agricultural technology, elementary schools with religious instruction (generally Protestant), and, perhaps most significant, the holding of land by individual title—a policy laced with much deeper ideological implications than in the Mexican version.[19]

Spicer's account of the rise of native revitalization religions (new movements seeking to preserve the true values of the past) and the persistence of the tribal religions again shows us that this form of idealism remained more vital for the Indians than did Euro-American beliefs and practices.[20] The broken covenant that already characterized so much of America's frontier life was evident in the churches' failure to capture the native imagination and in their lack of prophetic power to resist the political and economic submergence of native tribes. As Tocqueville observed with remarkable perception for his day, the Indians who survived the harshness of the Spaniards at least managed to adapt their religion and customs and settle down to the business of living. But the Americans, he noted, continued to destroy the natives with all the formulations of law. "It is impossible," he wrote, "to destroy men with more respect for the laws of humanity."[21] At this point, our horizon opens out onto the problem of ideology.

If America has indeed lost the authentic covenant fidelity of its civil religion, this loss can be interpreted in the light of a degeneration into a combination of merely "anthropological faith," and a commitment to values constricted within the immanent order.[22] Such a form of social religion can easily develop a rationale for an established and corrupt social order, which is what happened in the case of the ideology of manifest destiny.

CHRISTIAN MISSION AND MANIFEST DESTINY

We can divide this discussion into two categories, the first being a description of the ideological process in frontier history, and the second being the resultant praxis, which it is perhaps more fitting to call "antipraxis," if I may be permitted this form of Greco-Latin barbarism. Thus, if praxis is the reflective integration of theory and practice, antipraxis is the haphazard and headlong practice of an ideology gone out of control, leading into actions and policies that no longer answer to any legitimate source of conscience in the transcendent order. I do not mean to depict all missionary activity in such a demonic light; here we are wise to attend to Bernard Lonergan's advice on "perspectivism" in historical research, realizing that there are no "raw facts" in history but that every generation somehow "changes" the data in the light of its own ideas and world views.[23] There has been much heroism and sanctity, as well as wisdom, in mission work. But insofar as it lost the self-critical skills of Christian discernment, mission became tragically involved with the dominant culture's breaking of the faith with its original covenant. Christian mission had been domesticated.

Robert F. Berkhofer traces the development of America's "grand object" (the ideal of a uniquely American christianization) from the point of the Second Great Awakening in the 1790s. Berkhofer sees this as "responsible for so much of the organized benevolence, especially Congregational and Presbyterian, throughout the next century."[24] He also makes mention of a further significant point which highlights the difference between United States and Canadian frontier history. After the War of 1812, a certain "nationalistic current" joined the wave of pietism and altered the course of American history (*SS*, 1). It is indeed at this point that United States and Canadian history diverge, subtly but significantly, in a matter related to mission and to contemporary religiocultural critique.

A less painstaking reading of Canadian mission history reveals little that differs from history south of the United States–Canadian border. One finds this clearly evident in the studies of Grant and Price, which reveal a similar history of cultural invasion by church and state.[25] But there is one significant difference that marks the advance of Euro-Canadian domination, as it differs from the lawless violence that often marked the United States frontier advance. Canada continued as a British dominion long after the War of 1812, identifying its fortunes rather intimately with those of the Commonwealth rather than engaging itself in the wholesale campaign to find a new frontier identity. It even seems that the less violent Canadian history can be attributed to the advance-guard presence of the Royal Canadian Mounted Police on the frontier, while United States expansion quickly shattered the restraints of governmental control.

The intense Anglo-French rivalry does indeed constitute much of Canada's history of cultural crisis, but this very crisis, along with a much less intense perception of itself as a new nation with a divine mission, has given Canada a certain national sensitivity to ethnic differences within its boundaries and a tendency to emphasize a "cultural mosaic" (rather than a "melting pot") with companion social programs to encourage this. If Canada plays its cards well, especially in a just treatment of the aboriginal rights question, it may be hoped that there will develop a more equitable solution to racial and cultural crises. Canada may even be able to build itself into a greater nation on the platform of cultural diversity than it could on an individualistic quest for power and national security. In other words, Canada may perhaps become an example of a solution for its southern neighbor.

Returning to the burgeoning American frontier craze after the War of 1812, we see a vivid development of church-state ideology. In one sense, the transcendent message of the gospel was accentuated all the more, as mission leaders voiced their determination to bring the natives the Word of God. But in another sense, the gospel and Christian institutions such as the Sabbath were to be the primary means of civilizing the natives through an interesting fusion of a theocentric ethic with cultural behaviorism (*SS,* 5). "Civilization" and "Christianity," in the minds of these missionaries, reveal a form of anthropological faith subtly growing within the primitive covenantal thought of the early colonists. Civilization became "an upward unilinear development of human society with the United States near the pinnacle" (*SS,* 6). It was part of the nation's manifest destiny that, as the Rev. Stephen Riggs proclaimed, "as tribes and nations the Indians must perish and live only as men" (*SS,* 7). Only in this way could they fall in with the Christian civilization that was destined to cover the earth. Truly, nothing of the savage culture could possibly contribute to the evolutionary process of survival of the fittest culture; it had "no chambers of commerce, no insurance companies, no banks, no joint stock associations" (*SS,* 9). The more tender affections and the forms of mutual aid and interest depended entirely upon the diffusion of Christianity.

The plan for education of the Indians was to fit the common American pattern of character development through moral training, and the creation of a boarding school environment in which all savage examples and behavior were eliminated was the sole means of a total reconditioning and acculturation. The theological moorings of this system lay in the doctrine of redemption from total depravity, as it was manifested in the habits and practices of these "heathen" wherever they differed from American mainstream morality (*SS,* 55). Tribal life, which scholars today recognize as an integrated system of culture, was to the church persons of that period no more than a "gehenna" of confusion.

It should be pointed out here that most Protestant missionaries of the period, like the French Jesuits of an earlier century, explicitly eschewed all forms of racism, and fully believed in the basic equality of Indians and whites.[26] There was no viewpoint here similar to that belief under debate in the sixteenth-century Spanish courts, so shocking to us today, that Indians did not even have human souls and the corresponding rights. But to the strong Calvinist tradition, the natives' depravity and graceless condition was manifest in their thinking and behavior.

It is easy to understand how missionaries could seize upon the culture known to them as symbolic of the life of the redeemed. As Michael Coleman points out, the early and mid-nineteenth century, even given the Civil War, which taught "lessons of wisdom," was a time of unbridled optimism for the United States.[27] Especially out on the frontier, the settlers could observe little of the growing corruption in politics and the misery of the cities that would eventually sting Americans toward self-critical reform movements such as the Social Gospel. Church workers and leaders harbored no self-deceptions about the fact that many of their own kind, with their drunkenness, debauchery, lying, cheating, and cruel treatment of the Indians, were a bad example to their converts. The missionaries knew that much had yet to be done in their own household—but *how much* they did not suspect.

The concepts of "culture" or of "structure" were of course foreign to the people of frontier America, and even to the intelligentsia. The dangers latent in civil religion as a modern form of Christendom were not evident. Thus it is not far off the mark when Ronda and Axtell propose their thesis that missionaries, primarily presenting themselves as laborers for the eschatological salvation of the Indians, were actually cultural revolutionaries who aimed at a total transformation of native culture.[28] It was hard for missionaries in the nineteenth century to detect these subtler racist tendencies in their society, as for example an outsider like Tocqueville could do.[29] At this period the demonic nature of conquest was not evident in the way it so quickly became to the Jesuits of Latin America and even of French Canada. Only in the late nineteenth century did reformist historians like Helen Hunt Jackson attempt to prod Americans into staring in horror at the savagery of the white American frontier experience.[30]

In the area of praxis and antipraxis, the pattern is consistent; it can be illustrated through examples of historical policies intended as developmental for the future of Indians and indicative of the nobility of the American experiment. These cases illustrate a weaving together—a "context"—of education and political action into a fabric of church-state collaboration intended to model the ideal society into which the Indians must enter and to which they must accommodate themselves.

American school policies toward Indians followed a consistent pattern lasting from the late nineteenth century until the mid-twentieth century, when native culture began to assert itself. Henry Bowden describes it well in saying that, in the minds of the missionaries, "anything that threatened national homogeneity had either to be converted or removed."[31] This assimilationist principle was expressed by Congress in 1819 when it established a "civilization fund" that furthered Indian education in agriculture, literacy and "other beneficial pursuits." There developed a fourfold pattern, changing its order of priority according to differing interpretations, typified by the words "primer, hoe, plow and Bible."[32] It is a further historical irony that the interweaving of an individualism growing out of Christian respect for the human person meshed with the isolation of the person that developed from the industrial revolution. The insights and recommendations of the Hocking Commission on missions in the 1930s are among the first to address this ideological problem.[33]

In the first half of the nineteenth century, the Grand Object was of an almost totally Protestant character, as Catholics were occupied in overcoming nativism and establishing themselves as true Americans. This historical process in itself is an ironic development, given the common Catholic church-state theories holding that a rigid adherence to the "perfect society" model of church would always allow the church to resist absorption into the state. Bowden indicates the crack in the Catholic armor that would soon make Catholic mission work little different in its school practices from mainstream Protestant America. When President Grant's Peace Policy came into effect in 1869, some seventy-three Indian agencies were distributed to the various mission groups, and the Catholic Church was given only seven of these. As a consequence, the Bureau of Catholic Indian Missions was formed for the purpose of combating anti-Catholic prejudices and strengthening Roman Catholic missions and schools.[34] The struggle of the Roman Catholic Church in

America for federal contracts led to a gradual triumph over anti-Catholicism in government education policy.[35]

Unfortunately, in this campaign Catholics joined the trend of other American Christians both in their treatment of Indians and in the melting pot theory. Anyone who has worked closely with American native people (or, for that matter, with native Canadians, for the outcome is almost identical in this case) is painfully aware of how the term *boarding school* or *residential school* has come to represent North America's frontal assault on Indian culture. Whatever benefits the schools operated by the religious orders may have brought, they all tended to join with the mainstream in reducing the Indian children to clones of their white counterparts. The greater irony here is that in this campaign the Roman Catholic Church lost much of its countercultural potential by combining its rigid pre-Vatican II liturgical and catechetical norms with the prevailing American mystique of progress. In this light it is small wonder that Catholics in the United States exhibit no distinctive identity in their views on individualism.

The Peace Policy of 1869 deserves special mention here, serving as it did to further reduce Christian mission activity to a function of secularized civil religion. The policy was conceived on a principle, valid in the abstract, that missionaries could be best situated to deal with Indians in a local context. Moreover, it was first introduced through discussion with Quakers, whose commitment to nonviolence and countercultural lifestyle contrasted sharply with an American frontier mentality. One of the most influential Quakers of the period, Albert Smiley, though he never took active part in the Policy itself, had established a benevolent program to aid the Indians and to assimilate them with less violence into American life.[36] Thus President Grant established the plan (not without opposition from many sectors) to allot the aforementioned agencies to various churches, with church personnel, generally clergy, as the local agents. The fact that so many things went wrong with the program need surprise no one, given the growing corruption in American politics and in the Grant administration especially. More importantly, this plan stands out as the epitome of church-state compromise both to engage in a "gentle genocide" of the Indians and to identify itself with forces that would contribute so powerfully to the gradual secular domestication of the original spiritual covenant.[37]

The gradual corruption of so many ecclesiastical Indian agents is not startling in light of the conditions under which they had to work. In fact, in spite of all this, there were indeed many talented and dedicated persons among them. More troublesome is the fact that mission thought and practice inadvertently became allied with an America caught up in the social obtuseness of the Gilded Age and a pragmatic interpretation of social Darwinism. In a paradoxical political effort, the churches joined in the fight to defend individual Indians against the ravages of a might-makes-right expansionism but were unable to transcend the idea that more than one culture might be entitled to survive into a mature Christianity.

On the dissenting side were a few church leaders who demonstrated a highly advanced cultural sophistication in their work for the native people. Presbyterian Cyrus Byington stands out in early nineteenth-century history for his cultural and linguistic creativity and for his concern to preserve a distinctive Indian identity.[38] This concern led him to an early awareness that a discernment between the gospel and the dominant cultural interpretation of it was important. A similar figure was the Jesuit Joseph Cataldo in the Northwest, who, even though doubting that Indian culture could survive, lived out the Jesuit principle of accommodation, formulating and implementing policies that accepted local native customs. Cataldo was eventually recognized as a "new DeSmet" in his imitation of that great missionary-defender of the Indians. Cataldo's desire was to enable Indians to live as Christians in American society without yielding their whole culture to its melting pot ideology.[39] Cataldo viewed the Peace Policy as a disaster, since he had struggled to build a type of "reduction" system redolent of the Paraguay missions, to impede the advance of white civilization into Indian country[40]—a development DeSmet had hoped for in vain a half-century earlier.

TOWARD A RENEWAL OF INTEGRITY

It is a matter of debate whether or not such a "conservative" policy as attention to the preservation of Indian culture was the best direction to follow. Yet modern insights drawn from anthropology and sociology would indicate that there was a principle operative in both the common practices and the protests of some missionaries that was overlooked by the prevalent theories of progress: that a society's (or church's) moral and spiritual greatness may be discovered in its capacity to encourage cultural diversity within its boundaries, not simply out of tolerance, but from the desire to benefit from the spiritual power latent within each authentic culture. The vital point here is that when a society and its churches are capable of encouraging cultural pluralism, they indicate an awareness that cultural vitality is not a mere given but must be remade or renewed continually. To be able to accept such ongoing contributions into its own larger structure is a sign of integrity and maturity in a culture.

One may speculate that it is such integrity that Walter Lippmann had in mind in his search for a renewal of natural law theory in public philosophy. Lippmann, as we have seen, considered it to be one of the great weaknesses in modern Western democracies that their people had lost the capacity to believe in intangible realities.[41] Thus he called for a dialectical method for elucidating the ever-changing manifestations of the classic values of truth, morality, and justice.[42] That is, a society could effectively live a praxis of the public philosophy if it could grow spiritually and ethically through an interface with the many forces within it.

I have already indicated how native peoples in North America have formed their own culturally based revitalization religions as a source of inspiration against oppression by an imposed foreign cultural system. To show the urgency of this cultural awareness for a nation's renewal and spiritual vitality, I propose three points for a social and spiritual renewal: first, that a genuine culture is a vital spiritual reality; second, that the moral integrity of a democratic society is tested by its ability to recognize and respect the values of its minorities; third, that North American Christians can grow in their own spirituality through a permeation by such values into the larger social structures.

1) According to Gerardus Van der Leeuw, power—the quality of vitality and effectiveness as opposed to flaccidity, passivity, and futility—is the fundamental reality in all religious experi-

ence.[43] From the earliest primal ritualistic societies down to the contemporary world religions, power is manifested as the element that vitalizes a community. Power is that quality of strength and effectiveness that joins with *will* and *form* in constituting the entire object of the investigation of religion. That is, where power is most effective for believers, it is the quality of will or personality possessed by the sovereign deity (perhaps by other spirits) that removes power from the domain of magical manipulation and places it within the realm of grace. Here authentic religion is set in relationship to a God whose intention all worshippers must strive continually to discern.

Where a ceremony, a symbol, a religious group, or a whole culture is expressed as a locus of power, one then understands *form* to be present. The whole becomes an empowered configuration or *gestalt* that appeals to the deepest imaginative and spiritual aspirations of its members and motivates them to labor for the continuance of that form. To be sure, a form can grow corrupt in its embodiment of power, as happens whenever power is perceived as no more than a source for individualistic profit. An authentic spiritual gestalt can exist only where the whole and all its members are enabled to benefit from a power that is given as a gift by a personal benefactor. A case in point would be the loss of the transcendental power-as-covenant given in the nobler aspirations of the American dream, and the deterioration from a sense of grace to the efforts of individuals to retain power without consciousness of the good of the whole. An insight into the nature of cultural-religious gestalts helps to further grasp the significance of the remark of Bellah that "we lack a way of making moral sense of significant cultural, social and economic differences between groups. We also lack means for evaluating the different claims such groups make" (*HH,* 207).

A culture is not merely an aggregate but has a certain organic integrity and power in itself.[44] This concept of culture can contribute to theology, missiology, and social philosophy a sensitivity that was unavailable to our predecessors. They were not in a position to appreciate the fact that every culture, whatever its moral or spiritual lacunae, is basically animated by a spiritual-ethical power and thus merits a respectful regard. Concomitantly, these early missionaries also lacked the skill for a sociological critique of their own cultures. Christian theology has yet to tap its own doctrine of the Holy Spirit as the unfolding essence of the Church, and the Church's right to interpret that essence, to remind Christians that they must seek an ongoing renewal in their relationships with the world and culture.[45] The pneumatological aspect of theology must accompany any effort at Christian social and cultural renewal.

Such collaborative interpretation of culture is exemplified in the communications specialty of Bernard Lonergan with its key concept of "common meaning."[46] Only through the self-transcendence necessary in this process can we in the churches and in society overcome the individualism that renders us merely an aggregate rather than a community. Many early missionaries were possessed of a certain kind of self-transcendence that inspired them with courage to endure hardships that would daunt most of us today. But perhaps it is our gift in this age to be able to develop and contribute a new form of transcendence that manifests not only a religious conversion but also a new intellectual conversion and a better-informed moral conversion. Efforts to dialogue with other cultural forms of spirituality will tap new sources of imaginative energy that can strengthen community both locally and internationally. Ethnocentrism and narrow religiosity resist contributions from other cultures and in so doing demonstrate either their immaturity or their effeteness.

2) We return here to the quest for a new integrity that reaches beyond individualism. As I observed at the outset of this paper, the quest is based on the self-transcendence just described in the example of persons and communities learning to appreciate and reverence the spiritual power enlivening another culture or religion. There are precedents in mission history for this. Pope Gregory the Great in the late seventh century seems to have recognized this principle even from afar, in his pastoral instructions to missionaries in Britain. Francis of Assisi seems to have acknowledged it in the Sultan with whom he visited and shared spiritual conversation. The Jesuit Matteo Ricci in sixteenth-century China and twentieth-century Protestants there under Hudson Taylor are better-known examples of this openness. Roberto di Nobili in seventeenth-century India embodied the same principle of accommodation and inculturation, while Bartolome de las Casas acquired the same virtues in his impas-

sioned sixteenth-century struggle for the Indians of Latin America. So too, perhaps, the Jesuits of Paraguay and some of those in New France saw the spiritual vitality within local cultures. Today, Catholic and Protestant missionaries in many areas are operating from a renewed sense of cultural respect among the tribal and world religions, and in the process becoming richer themselves.

But the integrity gained through interreligious dialogue requires a deeper praxis that Christianity must acquire as a habit if it is to teach cultural transcendence to modern nations. No society can retain its own vitality if it fails to appreciate the sources of vitality in another culture resident within it. Further, it is the test of a democracy to be capable of recognizing and protecting the spiritual sources of rights claimed by the minority cultures, and in respect for these sources to be able to incorporate them into its system of justice.

A current example to test this democratic potential is one that has been with the Americas from the beginning of the explorations and is now confronting all the democracies of the hemisphere. I refer to the question of the rights of native peoples and their influence or lack of influence on national legislation. The case of aboriginal rights has been argued ever since the epic struggle of Las Casas to gain equal status for the Indians and has made its way into North America in the courts of the British Commonwealth and in the United States. The most graphic illustration of the problem is presently occurring in Canada, because of the repatriation of the Canadian Constitution from England to Canada, rather than in the United States. While America has incorporated equal rights into its own constitution, however imperfect the recognition, Canada is still facing the vexing problem of the meaning of this "aboriginal rights" principle—deeply rooted in the native peoples' spirituality.[47] While Canadian courts have employed the services of anthropologists to help determine "aboriginal occupancy" in land title claims, the final decisions are still based entirely on principles of British law. In the United States, similar problems exist around the determination of land, water, hunting, and fishing rights.

It would be naive to think that there is any facile solution to such problems. However, it must be asked of those democratic societies composed largely of immigrants whose coming is relatively recent, whether they are worthy of the name of democratic if they cannot in a significant manner honor the spiritual basis of the rights of their minorities. This recognition would demand acknowledgment of the foundation of such rights in the beliefs held by these cultures. It must have a grounding sounder and deeper than a primitivistic romanticism. The principles of such grounding are available in the shared needs of native and white society alike: conservation, pollution control, family solidarity, and communal belonging, to mention the most important. A certain reciprocal missionary effort, undertaken with typical reticence by native people but now welcomed by many white North Americans, is informing our society with a new appreciation of lasting values in traditional cultures.

3) When we were in the process of translating liturgical texts and prayers into the native idiom some ten years ago, an Arapaho elder said to me, "Remember one thing: we can't go backward; we have to go forward!" There is no future, literally, in nostalgia! However, there are deep values in all traditions that have to be kept in living memory and applied to new contexts, thus maintaining the authentic aspects of old cultures and enriching the new ones' development. We must consider the possibilities of a new synthesis in the encounter between cultures, dynamically shedding the old trappings of one age and acquiring new forms and dynamic symbols for preserving the "intangible values."

This struggle is illustrated theologically in the Acts of the Apostles[48] as well as in the letters to the Galatians and the Romans. Jewish religion and culture were in a crisis of identity within the hellenistic world when the coming of Jesus and a new spiritual community complicated the question even more. Not only did the narrower meaning of the law have to yield to a gospel of freedom, but the cultural religion had to change in order to permit the membership of Gentiles in this new religious faith with its universal aspirations. The struggle of the Jewish Christians, as Bellah has suggested, is paradigmatic for all Christians, and, I propose, for all members and groups within a society. Each world view must hold fast in faith to its basic tradition but be able to live in an overarching faith and ethic that can animate a world society. This new kind of faith within pluralism must be the new civil religion, the stuff of the new covenant, and it now seems that it has become a matter of the greatest urgency not only nationally but also internationally.

The racial and cultural minorities in North America may well serve as role models for us in the search for common meaning. In some seventeen years of working at dialogue between Christianity and native spirituality, I have witnessed the growth of native groups such as the Tekakwitha Conference and the Canadian Amerindian Conference. In a strangely poignant way it has been a heartening experience to pass from holding positions as a resource in these groups to the role of an engaged participant or even simply an interested spectator, as native people have assumed their own charge of inculturating the gospel in contemporary Indian life. Here too one encounters many more persons with histories similar to the four accounts given at the beginning of this paper.

Currently, this renewal takes the form of ministry training programs that prepare native lay persons, deacons, and priests to minister within their own cultures and even to the non-Indian community. As such groups enthusiastically engage with the Word of God and the Church, their instructors, such as myself, are discovering small groups of dedicated Christians who believe passionately that they have a covenant from God. The similarity here to the Latin American basic ecclesial communities is not accidental! It is clear in their interpretations of Scripture and theology. It is present in their interpretation of the conflict between imported and indigenous law when they discuss the second chapter of Romans; it is touchingly revealed when native homilists liken the Hebrew exile period to the cultural exile of the Indians and call for a peaceful revolution in the thinking of their own people. It comes home powerfully to the non-Indian witness when these persons compare the native peoples' search for identity to the wandering of the Hebrews and ask, What are the idols in this modern wilderness that draw our people away from God and from their deeper values?

TOWARD A PASTORAL PRAXIS

The renewal of a national covenant in North America can come only through the mutual collaboration and respectful engagement of all the struggling societies of the continent in their search for common meaning within cultural pluralism. The critical factor here is dialogue, with its fruits manifested in political and ecclesial forms. The means of effecting this dialogue are found through spiritual and intellectual discipline, while the vivifying principle is the Holy Spirit. The entire process is one of intellectual, moral, religious, affective, and political conversion.[49] In this light, it may be of help to conclude this essay with a brief proposal for a vision and program for North American parish life.

Ecclesial communities in North America, given the conversions mentioned, are in a position to mediate the tension between individual and community and between single cultural groups and the wider community. The churches must, in this light, carry on campaigns to build respect for particular differences within an appreciation for the whole. In the spiritual life of the churches, the vitality to inspire persons and groups beyond their own pragmatic needs must become more evident, alerting them further to the transcendental capacity to grasp enduring values as evidenced in the various cultures.

North American Christianity has been a continuation of expatriate European aspirations to "diffuse" the Christian gospel, especially in its imperative of respect for human dignity. The vocation of the gospel, however, calls for the ability—or the "grace"—to transcend, without renouncing, the cultural forms through which this stewardship manifests itself. Only in this way can the internal and external covenants—the laws of the heart and the book—continue with the strength to constitute a vital civil religion.

The vast potential in North American parishes, as these parishes become increasingly multicultural, and in native missions as well in their interface with mainstream churches, presents hope that we have grounds here for a powerful social praxis. But such collaboration can happen in the churches only when they are ready to undertake cross-cultural programs based on a sound theory of mission. The logic of Vatican II, that the Church is missionary by its very nature, can come to realization only through behavior that flows from that nature. And when mission is unidirectional it is truncated behavior; each local Christian mosaic has its own values to share.

Transformed by such a spirit of gospel inculturation, the

churches further acquire strength to continue the critique of the wider society, and they lend further credence to official church social statements on the economy, peace, and racial justice. The problem of individualism must of necessity give way to such a campaign, which, to use the old Scholastic equation, converts "habits of the heart" into "virtues of the heart."

NOTES

1. An excellent case study of this problem, although entirely absorbed with the immigrant question, is John Higham, *Strangers in a Strange Land: Patterns of American Nativism, 1860–1925* (New Brunswick, N.J.: Rutgers University Press, 1955).

2. Robert N. Bellah et al., *Habits of the Heart: Individualism and Commitment in American Life* (Berkeley and Los Angeles: University of California Press, 1985), 152–55. Hereafter referred to as *HH*. Bellah's use of these terms is drawn from Josiah Royce. See the essay by Frank Oppenheim in this volume.

3. This is a working definition for the present paper. For fuller treatment, see Clifford Geertz, "Ideology as a Cultural System," in his *The Interpretation of Cultures* (New York: Basic Books, 1973), 231; Juan Luis Segundo, *Faith and Ideologies,* trans. John Drury (Maryknoll, N.Y.: Orbis Books, 1984). Hereafter referred to as *FI*.

4. See Raimundo Panikkar, *The Intrareligious Dialogue* (New York: Paulist Press, 1978), 61.

5. See Walter Lippmann, *The Public Philosophy* (New York: New American Library, 1956).

6. Robert N. Bellah, *The Broken Covenant: American Civil Religion in Time of Trial* (New York: Seabury, 1975), 88. Hereafter referred to as *BC*.

7. On the subject of the biblical universalist-particularist process, see Donald Senior, C.P., and Carroll Stuhlmueller, C.P., *Biblical Foundations for Mission* (Maryknoll, N.Y.: Orbis Books, 1983).

8. See Alexis de Tocqueville, *Democracy in America,* 2 vols. (New York: Vintage Books, 1945), 100, cited in *HH,* 36–37.

9. Tocqueville, cited in *HH,* 37.

10. Lippmann, *Public Philosophy,* 49.

11. See Walter Brueggemann, *The Land: Place as Gift, Promise and Challenge in Biblical Faith* (Philadelphia: Fortress Press, 1977), esp. chap. 4.

12. This being said, we should note that Canadians have consistently criticized Canada's own history of racism and ethnocentrism.

See (from a native Canadian perspective) George Manuel and Michael Posluns, *The Fourth World: An Indian Reality* (Don Mills, Ont.: Collier Macmillan Canada, 1974); David R. Hughes and Evelyn Kallen, *The Anatomy of Racism: A Canadian Perspective* (Montreal: Harvest House, 1974), esp. 65–214.

13. Vine Deloria, Jr., *God Is Red* (New York: Grosset and Dunlap, 1973), chaps. 14–15. Hereafter referred to as *GR*. It is also worth noting that the theme of land is developed here, in chap. 6, much along the lines of Brueggemann's work cited earlier. See also Vine Deloria, *Custer Died for Your Sins* (New York: Macmillan, 1969), chap. 2.

14. Cf. Cornelius J. Jaenen, *Friend and Foe* (Toronto: McClelland and Stewart, 1976). Hereafter referred to as *FF*.

15. James Axtell, *The Invasion Within* (New York: Oxford University Press, 1985), 70. Hereafter referred to as *IW*.

16. Ibid., 327. It must also be noted, however, that Axtell's documentation comes from the middle of the eighteenth century and even the early nineteenth century, after many changes of attitude had also taken place within Indian cultures — some having become Christian. There is ample evidence (see Jaenen, *Friend and Foe,* chap. 4, for an example) that earlier white captivity among many Indian tribes was characterized by cruel torture and cannibalism. Axtell at times seems to typify here the revisionist guilt of the white North American!

17. Edward H. Spicer, *Cycles of Conquest* (Tucson: University of Arizona Press, 1981), 5.

18. The Paraguay "reductions" were native settlements led by the Jesuits, where Indians might be shielded from the slave trade and the general colonial greed of the Spanish and Portuguese. They endured for nearly two centuries. See Philip Caraman, S.J., *The Lost Paradise: The Jesuit Republic in South America* (New York: Seabury, 1976).

19. See Spicer's summary in *Cycles of Conquest,* 7–8.

20. I have attempted elsewhere to construct phenomenological and theological studies of the native religious revitalization movements. See Carl F. Starkloff, "Religious Renewal in Native North America: The Contemporary Call to Mission," *Missiology* 13, no. 1 (January 1985): 81–101; "New Tribal Religious Movements in North America: A Contemporary Theological Horizon," *Toronto Journal of Theology* 2, no. 2 (Fall 1986): 157–71.

21. Tocqueville, *Democracy in America,* 369.

22. For greater detail on this concept, see Segundo, *Faith and Ideologies,* 50–70.

23. Bernard J. F. Lonergan, S.J., *Method in Theology* (New York: Herder and Herder, 1972), chap. 9, 214–20.

24. Robert F. Berkhofer, *Salvation and the Savage* (New York: Atheneum, 1972), 1. Hereafter referred to as *SS*.

25. See John Webster Grant, *Moon of Wintertime* (Toronto: University of Toronto Press, 1984); John Price, *Indians of Canada: Cultural Dynamics* (Scarborough, Ont.: Prentice-Hall of Canada, 1979).

26. See Michael C. Coleman, *Presbyterian Missionary Attitudes toward American Indians, 1837–1893* (Jackson: University of Mississippi Press, 1985), chap. 7.

27. Ibid., 47.

28. James P. Ronda and James Axtell, *Indian Missions: A Critical Bibliography* (Bloomington: Indiana University Press, 1978), 4.

29. Tocqueville, *Democracy in America,* chap. 18.

30. See Helen Hunt Jackson, *A Century of Dishonor* (New York: Harper and Row, 1881).

31. Henry Warner Bowden, *American Indians and Christian Missions* (Chicago: University of Chicago Press, 1981), 165.

32. Ibid., 167.

33. See William Ernest Hocking, *Rethinking Missions: A Layman's Inquiry after One Hundred Years* (New York: Harper and Row, 1932), chap. 11.

34. Bowden, *American Indians and Christian Missions,* 192.

35. See Francis Paul Prucha, *The Churches and the Indian Schools, 1880–1912* (Lincoln, Neb.: University of Nebraska Press, 1979), 205.

36. See Clyde Milner, II, and Floyd A. O'Neil, *Churchmen and the Western Indians, 1820–1920,* (Norman, Okla.: University of Oklahoma Press, 1985), chap. 5.

37. See Robert H. Keller, *American Protestantism and United States Indian Policy, 1869–1882* (Lincoln, Neb.: University of Nebraska Press, 1983), chap. 8. The principle "Christianization and Americanization are one and the same thing," used as a goad to the assimilation of immigrants, became a principle for native tribes as well. See Higham, *Strangers in a Strange Land,* 261.

38. See Keller, *American Protestantism and United States Indian Policy,* chap. 1.

39. See Milner and O'Neil, *Churchmen and the Western Indians,* 139.

40. Ibid., 126.

41. Lippmann, *Public Philosophy,* 49.

42. Ibid., 97.

43. See Gerardus Van der Leeuw, *Religion in Essence and Manifestation,* trans. J. E. Turner (New York: Harper and Row, 1963), esp. chaps. 1 and 9.

44. For one of the earliest insights into this point, see Ruth Benedict, *Patterns of Culture* (Boston: Houghton Mifflin Co., 1934, 1959).

45. On this point, see Karl Rahner's pivotal address, "Towards a Fundamental Theological Interpretation of Vatican II" in *Theological Studies* 40, December 1979, 716–27.

46. See Lonergan, *Method in Theology,* chap. 14.

47. This problem is discussed in detail in Peter Cumming and Neil Mickenberg, *Native Rights in Canada,* 2nd ed. (Toronto: General Publishing Co., 1972).

48. Acts 10 and 15.

49. I am using the term employed by Donald Gelpi elsewhere in this volume.

The Hope of a World Citizen: Beyond National Individualism

John R. Stacer, S.J.

A pastor whom I know invited his well-educated parishioners to read and discuss *Habits of the Heart*. They did not enjoy the book; it tells their own story too pointedly, names their own problems too clearly. Does utilitarian individualism's goal of getting ahead or expressive individualism's quest of feeling good guide us to live meaningfully? Do we in fact live by ideals broader than those of individualism? Do we have language to talk about these important values? To aid our reflection the authors recall some of the religious, moral, and political values on which our nation is founded.

Moreover, the authors invite others to join their moral discourse. In thinking about the invitation, I wondered what one question I judged most worth adding to their examination of conscience. *Habits of the Heart* tells the story of those who are locked within their individual selves or their lifestyle enclaves and calls them to break out through commitment to family, city, or national communities; yet the book mentions world community only a little. Thus my additional question: How can we resist national individualism?

The term *national individualism* may sound jarring. It suggests that responsibilities toward a world community resemble responsibilities toward smaller communities. Individualistic Americans need to experience liberation from the solitary confinement of personal interests. In this essay I strive to free us from the larger prison of one nation's interests. I include myself among those who need liberation; *we* in this chapter refers to you the readers, to me, and to our fellow U.S. citizens. It is difficult to live in our country without undergoing the subtle influences of national individualism's spirit of competition and its concern for "survival," attitudes opposed to a spirit of co-operation and a concern for solidarity that urge our commitment to building world community.

Like personal individualism, national individualism has both utilitarian and expressive aspects. Utilitarian national individualism, for example, may prompt us to win in economic competition, win even by profiting unjustly from the inexpensive labor of people from the Third World. Expressive national individualism may fuel our quest to feel better about ourselves and more secure, even if it involves looking down upon other cultures.

Resisting national individualism does not discourage concern for the common good of our nation. An unhealthy concern limits our focus to national problems and separates us from the rest of the world, but a healthy concern for the nation helps unify us so that our country's diverse cultures nourish one another within one organism. Moreover, just as periods of solitude help us examine our consciences so as to resist personal individualism, so some reflective solitude helps develop the broad vision of a world citizen who resists national individualism. We need to be present with those of other nations in order to hear their challenges, but we also need times of solitude to integrate the challenges into our understanding of the world and freely decide to respond in a way which promotes the world-wide common good.

We in the United States have a special need to develop concern for coming generations.[1] Since we move easily and inhabit relatively young cities or towns with only recent architecture, our memories rarely go back many generations. It follows naturally that our hopes rarely go forward many generations. We act wisely to nourish our long-term memories by reading history and our long-term hopes by reading about environmental sciences and international relations.

When Dr. Martin Luther King, Jr., made the difficult decision to risk support for civil rights at home in order to oppose the Vietnam War publicly, he acknowledged the responsibility of a world citizen—"invoking biblical and republican themes and emphasizing the economic and social dimensions of full citizenship on an international as well as national level" (*HH*, 213). Our national memory includes other prominent world citizens. Woodrow Wilson spoke a language of world community as he promoted the League of Nations. If more had listened, World War II might have been avoided. George Marshall served as a citizen of the world in helping former enemies as well as former allies get back to their feet after that war. For his service to the United Nations we think of Dag Hammarskjöld less as a Swede than as a world citizen. Many U.S. citizens who serve with the Peace Corps, the State Department, the media, and the international business community experience world citizenship. Promoters of "Live Aid" and other concerts brought food to the hungry and challenged the consciences of the affluent. Members of groups such as Bread for the World, Amnesty International, and Pax Christi serve worldwide causes and build world community. Remembering them fuels our hopes and invites our commitment.

Among such world citizens we may number William Ernest Hocking (1873–1966), a philosopher who chose *The Coming World Civilization* as the title for a book which he considered his "conspectus of a life's work."[2] A native of the United States, his international experience surpassed that of his principal teachers, Josiah Royce and William James. The elder thinkers recounted their experiences and encouraged Hocking to study abroad. Royce in particular inspired Hocking with his ideal of the Great Community of all persons, an ideal that Frank Oppenheim sketches earlier in this volume. On his way to a Harvard Ph.D., Hocking studied for a year in Göttingen, Berlin, and Heidelberg. In 1931–32 he prayed in oriental monasteries and temples as chair of a lay commission evaluating Christian missions; his ideas on missionary inculturation came about forty years ahead of their time. In 1936 he gave the Hibbert Lectures at Oxford and Cambridge, in 1938 and 1939 the Gifford Lectures at Glasgow. In 1947–48 he taught at Leiden in Holland. His books include *The Spirit of World Politics, Re-Thinking Missions,* and *Living Religions and a World Faith.*[3]

Today relatively few U.S. citizens experience other nations in an affirmative manner. For many the term *international* triggers negative thoughts and feelings about the arms race, wars,

terrorism, and trade deficits. Our "losses" in economic or political "competition" and the growing insecurity symbolized by
our weapons give much international experience a sour taste.
Hocking himself helps us understand how his life and his writings offer more positive experience of world citizenship and thus
may strengthen our resistance to national individualism. He
reflects autobiographically that "*solipsism is overcome . . . when
I can point out the actual experience* which gives me the basis
of my conception of companionship" (*CWC*, 35; Hocking's emphasis). Hocking moved beyond solipsism's extreme personal
individualism and grounded his conception of personal companionship in an experience of sharing memories and hopes
with Agnes Boyle O'Reilly, a person very different from himself
with whom he came to make a commitment that led to fifty-
five happy years together. Hocking moved beyond national individualism and grounded his conception of worldwide companionship first in vicarious experience of other cultures through
persons such as Royce and James, then in his own experience.
National individualism imitates personal individualism; we
move beyond it through experience, often at first vicarious and
later direct. Hence today we are called to let persons such as
Hocking recount their experiences of companionship with people of other nations, experiences such as we too have had or
can have.

To this chapter's moral discourse Hocking contributes three
major positive reflections, which I will combine with objections
and responses. In the first place, worldwide problems call for
a worldwide social movement. However, fear of world conquest
by a single power raises an objection, which Hocking meets
by explaining that world community does not require a world
state but rather an attitude of world citizenship. Second, building world community requires that we communicate about values and engage in an intercultural moral discourse that simultaneously broadens and deepens our consciousness of values
through a process which Hocking calls "reconception." A concern that in assimilating values from others we lose genuine
values specific to our national culture is met by recalling some
experiences of religious, political, and economic ecumenism.
Third, an ideal of world citizenship functions as a moral imperative challenging us to act with reverence toward all persons.

The objection that an attitude of respect could undermine freedom of choice is met by appreciating that moral ideals reorientate our affections; they function not by coercion but by persuasion. A concluding objection arises from a feeling of despair; many people have little experience of world citizenship and few ideas about how to solve world problems. To meet the objection we recall a further experience of Hocking's forming some world community and summarize his wise guidance about solving some world problems.

In what follows I will present Hocking's major reflections in the most challenging language possible; some might call it idealistic. I do not seek to provide an overly upbeat scenario for world reform. Rather I aim to call our attention to what is at stake when we, like Hocking three decades before us, wrestle with the inevitable consequences of world citizenship. This chapter, then, aims to help us examine our consciences, paying attention to our opportunities as well as our doubts in the critically important struggle to work toward a world community.

WORLDWIDE PROBLEMS CALL FOR WORLD CITIZENS, NOT A WORLD STATE

What problems most concern us when we take a worldwide and future-oriented perspective? War, starvation, ignorance, pollution of the environment, and depletion of resources rank high on any reasonable list. To meet these world problems, worldwide social movements are now developing: the peace movement, the movement to combat starvation, the ecological movement. A moral concern that animates these movements offers hope that they may succeed. As the authors of *Habits* write in their conclusion: "The morally concerned social movement, informed by the republican and biblical sentiments, has stood us in good stead in the past and may still do so again. . . . Our problems today are not just political. They are moral and have to do with the meaning of life" (*HH*, 295). These worldwide movements include a spiritual dimension, an appreciation for justice and solidarity that motivates us to work directly for the common good and thus indirectly render our

individual lives meaningful. A long tradition of Western philosophy affirms that we human persons are inherently social,
political, and moral—related to one another by shared human
nature and responsible to work for the common good. Thus
commitment to others naturally enriches a person's life, whereas
an individualistic lack of commitment to others conflicts with
the self's own nature. "Making America great makes you great"
expresses an important truth, yet one that calls for an addition. Since the universal common good is the good of all persons everywhere and at all times, we may affirm more broadly:
Making the world great makes America great; making the world
great makes you great.

Hocking implies this same broad truth through the titles and
contents of his most mature books. Working toward *The Coming
World Civilization* brings about *Strength of Men and Nations*.[4]
Only a misguided way of serving as a world citizen would
weaken the individual person. The worth of commitment to
a community includes its good results for each individual's
character: "The natural devotion of the individual to the 'community of memory and of hope' carries with it a docility to
personal discipline such as any whole view imposes on sporadic
impulse" (*CWC*, 2).

Likewise, a nation's devotion to the development of other
nations disciplines and thus strengthens the nation that so commits itself. Only a misguided exercise of world citizenship would
threaten a particular nation. A world community requires not
a world state but rather a worldwide attitude of respect for basic
human rights. "In his essay on *Perpetual Peace,* Kant suggested
not a world State but a group of republics of such character
that a traveler would everywhere find, certainly not his own
state, but *statehood.* He would be accorded certain minimal
rights of civilized treatment" (*SMN,* 173; Hocking's emphasis). Like Kant, Hocking and I call for "world citizenship, im-
plying a thin, common fabric of legality pervading all nations,
. . . needing no support of overall sovereignty" (*SMN,* 173).
Common rights are best guaranteed not by one state but by
all states. On the high seas various states collaborate to protect
the rights of all. No one state has overall sovereignty; each state
can be everywhere. "As state-interests and domains interpenetrate on the high seas, so their destiny is to interpenetrate

throughout" (*SMN,* 173–74). Interpenetration of state interests suggests that a world community is partly a spiritual reality, established and maintained because all world citizens and all nations share the same most basic interests such as peace, justice, and the preservation of life.

Those who act as world citizens participate in a worldwide social movement, a spiritual reality able to interpenetrate both with national movements, such as for civil rights, and with other international movements, such as for peace and for conservation. An ideal of world community enlivens all who commit themselves to become world citizens, but each centers attention on some well-defined movement. The traditional principle of subsidiarity states that work toward any specific common good should be directed by the lowest social or political authority able to direct the effort and undertaken by the smallest social or political unit able to achieve the good. This principle respects the three values of practicality, use of intelligence, and exercise of free choice. Thus subsidiarity dictates that individual world citizens use energies wisely by collaborating with groups of appropriate size who work to solve particular problems. Collaboration is motivated in part by a desire to develop the world as a whole and all its citizens, but collaboration is directed by persons close to particular problems who have undertaken a sufficient study of those problems.

To take the perspective of world citizens and bring our nation more fully into the community of nations, we need freely to discipline our use of free choice so that other persons and nations may also exercise freedom. This suggests that we become less managers and more collaborators; it requires that we focus less on techniques and means, more on values and ends. We are called to share "democracy," not as too specific a form of government but rather as any form that encourages an active participation of those governed proportionate to their developing capacities for such participation. Democracy's "strength lies in its development of the electorate, its awakening, encouraging, educating, lifting power, through the gift of responsibility. This gift . . . develops capacity by assuming it . . ." (*SMN,* 115). To give responsibility involves promoting health and education worldwide, then trusting persons different from ourselves to use their own intelligence and freedom in choosing the forms of political representation and of social and economic direction that they find appropriate to their varied gifts, circumstances, and stages of development. They, not we, live nearest to the relevant facts.

At this point an objector might well pose several questions: Do we not risk too much in assuming that others will develop a capacity they might not develop? Is it not prudent to prevent them from making mistakes? Does not the United States need to use its best human intelligence and other resources for defense? Is not subsidiarity too idealistic a principle to apply when the USSR threatens world conquest and an exercise of world sovereignty that might leave no room for subsidiarity?

Is it not risky to assume that others will develop a capacity for self-government that they might not develop? Yes, but is it not riskier to assume they will not develop it? Both assumptions tend to be self-fulfilling. The assumption of development normally reaches fulfillment in actual development, as parents and educators experience repeatedly. The contrary assumption, whether stated explicitly or implied in action, provokes a what's-the-use attitude in would-be developing countries: "If our attempts to use intelligence and free choice will have no significant results because the First World controls our economy and uses economic power to control us politically, then why should we bother to be awakened or become educated?" To promote development in others requires that we resist utilitarian individualism's tendency to control and that we thus grow in the ability to cooperate.

Is it not wise to prevent others from making mistakes? Not as this has been attempted in our nation's recent international practice. Taking the principle of subsidiarity into account, the United States seems more likely to make mistakes or to provoke mistakes than to prevent them. We do not live close enough to the various local histories. Acting compulsively under the influence of expressive individualism's desire to feel good by feeling secure, we too easily interpret conflicts in East-West terms rather than in North-South terms or local terms. Unlike people-oriented statespersons and like machine-oriented technicians, we expect results more quickly than do people in most parts of the world. We tend to manipulate for short-term results and to alienate over the long term. Recent fashioners of U.S. Central American policy, for example, seem unwittingly to follow Karl Marx's scenario; they widen the rift between rich and poor and thus provoke the poor of the entire region to revolt. A utilitarian individualistic need to win seems to push us toward losing.

Are we not called to use our best intelligence and other resources for defense? Yes, but only if we understand this to mean strengthening ourselves morally, deepening our awareness of values, and learning to communicate with regard to values. No, if we imagine that we need to devote great resources to weapons. Excessive U.S. defense spending and exporting a defense mentality divert our resources and those of other nations from their proper use in providing food, health, and education for those who need them. When denied access to resources, the destitute feel desperate and thus driven to commit crime, engage in terrorism, and wage war. Hence resources are misused when they go to fabricate excessive weapons that occasion fear and hatred—fear and hatred that bring greater ignorance, further inhibit development, and thus make the world more dangerous rather than more secure. Hocking rightly understands that "ignorance, poverty, disease, political passivity" inhibit development (*SMN,* 143) and that development is *"definitely a world problem,* toward which every nation in the well-favored areas has a certain responsibility" (*SMN,* 148; Hocking's emphasis). The United States and the USSR would both act wisely to cooperate as leaders in meeting that responsibility.

But does not the USSR threaten to conquer the world and then exercise world sovereignty in a way that might conform little to such principles as subsidiarity? In 1959 Hocking agreed with Walter Lippmann that "the Soviet leadership is more concerned with winning the uncommitted peoples of Asia and Africa to its side than with any direct contest with the USA, which, if it took military form, would involve destruction of its primary programs; it neither wishes nor contemplates war" (*SMN,* 163). Today Mr. Gorbachev appears wiser than did Mr. Khrushchev in 1959, more likely to advance the USSR's "primary programs." Even were it somehow established, moreover, a world state could accomplish little by coercion. If people throughout the world come freely to espouse an attitude of world citizenship, subsidiarity still demands that local and national governments retain a large measure of authority. "World conquest" cannot be achieved by war, nor can "world sovereignty" be maintained by police. Breaking the two myths and dropping the two combinations of words from human language would help people of both the United States and the USSR to call forth the best will from people of the other country, a will to create on a worldwide scale and not to destroy.

Significantly shifting resources from weapons toward worldwide development means taking "a *risk from strength*. . . . There must be a break-through, and such break-through must have its risk, as all life-giving has its risk" (*SMN*, 166; Hocking's emphasis). Furthermore, "because the statecraft of the USA . . . is built upon a tradition of faith in the moral factor of the Process of History, it is this nation that is called upon to take the step" (*SMN*, 166). History demands that we "create not security but solidarity" (*SMN*, 218). Not by building weapons but by communicating values do both individuals and nations develop authentic and recognizable strength.

Many scenes make our strength visible in the Third World: members of the Peace Corps teach farming, carpentry, and hygiene. On the other hand, a missionary returning from Africa told me about one scene that made our national weakness visible. "Before his family's palm-leaf shelter stood a teenage boy, stark naked, his almost visible bones and distended stomach telling of starvation. His right hand and left shoulder supported an M-16 rifle. I thought I heard Christ say in the boy's weak voice, 'I was hungry and you sold me a rifle.'"

Yet is not fear too great an obstacle to our changing how resources are used? Hocking acknowledges the power of fear when he discusses the origins of that "double-morality" that he considers "the most pervasive enemy to national strength" and to world community (*SMN*, 79). In times of solitude individuals more readily reflect at the sole natural level of morality, a level at which all persons are motivated by values shared worldwide. Living with singleness of purpose, they spontaneously affirm universal moral principles that urge them to act with reverence for the life, health, intelligence, and freedom of all. A second and artificial level of motivation arises and "double-morality" results when one group comes to feel that some other group threatens it. Toward those within their own group, people still relate by the Golden Rule. Toward the feared other group, they act compulsively by the leaden rule: do unto others as you fear they will do unto you, only do it first.

> The situation is intrinsically absurd: socialism must be destroyed because, for socialism, capitalism must be destroyed; and, vice versa, capitalism must be destroyed because, for capitalism, socialism must be destroyed! The most vicious of vicious circles. (*SMN*, 128–29)

Members of a fear-driven group imagine that "moral self-defense" allows or even commands them to kill, oppress, and deceive members of some feared group. Actions that strong reflective individuals correctly identify as vices come to be named "virtues" by weak members of a fear-swept crowd.

Fear becomes most destructive when allowed to control international relations. "Fear is the worst counselor for a constructive foreign policy, . . . a chronic liar, and an assured source of weakness to the nation admitting it" (*SMN*, 162–63). To reflective persons in other nations, the arms race and exporting arms symbolize intellectual, moral, and political weakness on the part of both the United States and the USSR. The excessive weapons signal that too many influential people in both superpowers believe the propaganda they are fed about the other country's supposed plans for world domination or about the alleged effectiveness of costly weapons for maintaining world peace. Such influential people seem to have forgotten that Hitler became powerful by similar propaganda and that during World War II those who profiteered from selling weapons were considered criminals.

Can influential people resist fear and its lies? In fact, many have not resisted. To help, Hocking makes a recommendation that seems poignantly relevant at a time when some U.S. officials refuse to accept responsibility for their actions and try to justify themselves by appealing to the actions of others. "What our practical democracies most need is a definite provision for every official to get away from the noise of all groups and be alone with himself" (*SMN*, 193–94). Persons who live mainly in a crowd easily fall prey to manipulation by utilitarian individualists who sell products that are not needed or by politicians who make unreflective expressive individualists feel good but who destroy the common good.

On the other hand, "the foundation of all national strength lies in the conviction of the individual thinker. The value of that conviction comes from the normal universality of private judgment: the truth for the solitary thinker is the truth for all" (*SMN,* 193). Often we say to others, "Don't pressure me. Let me think this over for myself." We may add, "I'm the one who must explain this to the world, not you." Paradoxically, we resist personal and national individualism partly by seeking reflective solitude from time to time; for such solitude enables us to focus again on those great values we share with all persons — ideals of life, justice, truth, and freedom that belong to that authentic, single-minded morality followed by the strong and the courageous.

This first main section has helped us examine our consciences through naming some motives, attitudes, and acts by terms that indicate their reality. The term *national individualism* alerts us to an attitude whereby we care too little about other nations and their people. In conversing or remaining silent on international matters, we may speak or keep silence compulsively because we are driven by fear, the chronic liar. Profiteers or potential war criminals may tempt us to countenance the country's weakness of participating in the arms race or selling arms to those who need food. We may indulge in that weak double morality that operates by the leaden rule and justifies itself by a vicious circle. Becoming alert to these dangers urges us to practice enough reflective solitude so that we may use and develop intelligence to act with responsible freedom of choice and not be swept along by a crowd. Thus we can better resist the propaganda of those who talk much about security but little about solidarity and creative risk from strength. We are encouraged to drop from our vocabulary word combinations like *world state, world conquest,* and *world sovereignty* and speak instead of *world citizens, world social movement,* and *world community.* In accord with the principle of subsidiarity, we recognize that we can move toward the broad goal of world community by working for more particular goals such as those of the peace movement or the ecological movement.

MORAL DISCOURSE, AIDED AT TIMES
BY "RECONCEPTION," ENABLES DIVERSE CULTURES
TO STRENGTHEN ONE ANOTHER'S VALUES

Moral authority rather than police unifies and directs a social movement. Moral authority functions through moral
discourse, through the communication of values. By *values*
Hocking and I mean such worthwhile ideals as respect for life,
mutual understanding, beauty, justice, peace, and preservation
of the environment. If a person considers these ideals in an unbiased way, then their worth naturally urges the person to live
so as to embody the values in action. Through moral discourse
persons aid one another's unbiased consideration of values.

Now, is such moral discourse possible among the diverse
members of a world community? Technologies used for transportation and communication contribute to making worldwide
communication of values possible. The jet plane and television
with satellite links enable contemporary cultures to interpenetrate on the level of consciousness and nourish one another's
appreciation of values. As Hocking puts it, "The making of
a single civilization is contained in the two concepts, the universal and the unlosable, plus the simple existence of the arts
of unlimited human communication" (*CWC*, 51). The terms
universal and *unlosable* refer to values. Values such as truth,
justice, and peace do not disappear; even a declining civilization can communicate its genuine values to other civilizations.
"Our present period is one of general and reciprocal osmosis
of thought, technique, art, and law. The assimilation proceeds
from both sides; though the West is only beginning to realize
its potential property in the unlosables of the East" (*CWC*, 51).

Osmosis of values among cultures occurs naturally provided
that persons and nations communicate naturally, that they dialogue in a way that reveals their authentic values. In one of the
earlier essays in this volume, John Staudenmaier recognizes that
the capacity of U.S. citizens for moral discourse has decreased
because standardization discourages negotiation and because
control over nature enables us to evade sufficient dialogue with
persons. Those in other nations criticize us for our failure to
know our own values and to talk about them, so we need to
give special attention to the communication of values. To make

our best contribution to world community, we need to shift from controlling as technicians toward conversing as states-persons.

The osmosis by which values are communicated among cultures involves interpenetration of cultures; it does not involve melting. In another earlier chapter, Carl Starkloff criticizes the tendency of the United States to destroy cultural diversity in its "melting pot"; he recommends a "cultural mosaic" as a symbol of greater respect. Attempting to form world community in a melting pot would destroy many diverse embodiments of values that are now actualized by different cultures. Looked at in any single instant, a healthy world community takes the form of a cultural mosaic, made beautiful by its contrasts. Looked at in its process of development, the coming world community takes the form of a kaleidoscope or a colorful sunrise.

The Orient exemplifies this process of osmosis in its long tradition of openness to the ideals of other cultures. Thus by interaction with Christianity Hinduism and Buddhism have grown in depth, as in a repudiation of the caste system. Moreover, in the West many have made their own some of the un-losable aids toward increasing attention to others and toward experiencing inner peace that are found in Zen and other oriental wisdom.

Within intercultural moral discourse this osmosis is often aided by "reconception," a process by which a given culture simultaneously broadens and deepens its consciousness of values through interaction with another culture. In *Living Religions and a World Faith* Hocking sketches its exemplification in religion; reconception occurs also in politics, economics, technology, art, and other aspects of civilization. (See below, page 202.) For simplicity the second figure assumes only the perspective of religion A; telling the full story would require a third figure drawn from B's perspective. The third apex would be labeled B′; the line beyond it would lean left and be designated B″. Together the three figures would symbolize the fact that reconception benefits the two religions, as both Hinduism and Christianity have grown through their interactions.

Moreover, the figures bring out that reconception involves more than addition and broadening. A deepening of A must occur for it to assimilate B without losing its own form; con-

Inclusion by Reconception

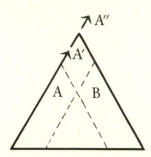

| Two religions, A and B, are represented as being partly coincident or overlapping in their present teaching and character. | The apex of the cone A, its conceived essence, moves upward, until without distortion the cone A includes what is valid of B, and indefinitely more, as self-understanding deepens. (*LR*, 194–95) |

nective values not hitherto esteemed by either of the two must be appreciated for assimilation to take place, and still further values may come to be esteemed during later reflection on what has happened. Thus, for example, the values espoused by capitalism and socialism have been reconceived through their interaction. Capitalism moved toward A′ by adopting the values of social security; socialism moved toward B′ by adapting pay scales to a worker's performance as well as need so as to incorporate values of greater incentive. Neither of these worthwhile patterns had been exemplified in earlier, "purer" forms of capitalism or socialism. Some ways of moving toward A′ and B′ may practically coincide, as when both the United States and the USSR come to actualize the value of trust in ways not yet experienced by either. Beyond point A′ or B′ extends the line A″ or B″, symbolizing that there are as yet unthought-of patterns for embodying values such as healthy cooperation between the United States and the USSR to help other nations develop.

At this point an objector might well ask: Is not reconception an ideal process that can occur very little in the actual world? Perhaps it can work in religion, but can it work in economics and politics? Will not attempting to actualize it in economics bring either world conquest by capitalism such as that warned against in *Global Reach*[5] or world conquest by socialism such as that advocated by Marx? In politics will it not lead to a world state dominated either by the United States or by the Soviet Union?

In politics, we argued earlier that world conquest would be extremely difficult to achieve and world sovereignty almost impossible to maintain. In economics, significant changes already move both capitalism and socialism closer to one another. Hocking and I favor conquest neither by capitalism nor by socialism. We anticipate that their advocates will continue to reconceive both economic theories as they observe their practice in a world community strengthened by the availability of more than one theory to guide diverse peoples in different stages of development.

In the 1930s many challenged Hocking's ideal of religious reconception. They feared losing authentic values of their own religions by communicating about values with those who practiced other religions. Gradually over the last fifty years Hocking's ideal has come to inform more and more the actualities of missionary and ecumenical practice. In October of 1986 his ideal was clearly exemplified when religious leaders from all around the world gathered in Assisi to pray for peace. These included the Pope, the Archbishop of Canterbury, the Dalai Lama, and leaders of Orthodox and Protestant Christianity, Judaism, Islam, and major oriental, African, and native American religions. They formed a community of memory and of hope, thanking God for gifts received and petitioning the gift of peace for which all hoped.

The prayer shared at Assisi provides a striking illustration of what Hocking calls "consociation." "As the recognition of kinship between different faiths becomes general, while the call of historical loyalty remains strong, occasional acts of co-worship may develop freely into what I have called 'consociation'" (*CWC*, 157). The value of a community of memory implies that we not throw aside historical loyalty to a particular religious group as we pray within a more universal community of hope. We do not deny memories of difference as we share hopes of unity. Thus "consociation, as a limited union between faiths for work and worship, is a definite step toward making the visible institutions more truthfully express the realities of identity within difference, moving toward difference within identity" (*CWC*, 158). In Assisi each religious leader prayed in his or her own way; "difference" characterized their prayer's mode. Yet all prayed for peace; "identity" characterized their prayer's intention. A similar identity has characterized many of the causes for which people of different religions have worked together in ecumenical groups such as Bread for the World and Amnesty International.

The title of Hocking's book, *Living Religions and a World Faith,* was vividly illustrated at Assisi. On the one hand, as leaders of major world religions, those who prayed were members of different religious groups. On the other hand, as praying with a shared faith, confident at least that prayer for peace was worthwhile, those who prayed were all members of one faith community. Likewise, members of Amnesty International work for specific causes as citizens each of his or her own country, yet in so doing all work together as world citizens for the general cause of amnesty. Religious people recognize that membership in one faith community of prayer for peace interpenetrates well with membership in different specific religious communities. Those who work for amnesty recognize that world citizenship expressed through cooperation within an international organization interpenetrates well with national citizenship; it even enables them to gain a broader perspective on how to exercise national citizenship responsibly.

Today ecumenism helps many people of different religions feel at home together in the world faith they share. Travel, international business, student and cultural exchange help many feel at home in foreign countries. Today people feel left out and are left out more for economic reasons than for religious or political ones. The unemployed are left out from lack of active contribution; they and their children experience hunger, sickness, and little opportunity to take advantage of the world's educational resources or to participate in its political processes. To build world community we need not only religious ecumenism but also political and particularly economic ecumenism. Our memories of success with regard to religious ecumenism can nourish our hopes and direct our striving for political and economic ecumenism.

Hocking's appreciation for world religions made him a better Christian. It enabled him to "reconceive" Christianity so as to embrace more values; broadening his experience of other religions deepened his experience of his own, as he symbolized in the preceding figure. In a similar way appreciation for some socialist values invites ideas for improving capitalism, and appreciation for some capitalist values invites ideas for improving socialism. For centuries prior to World War II western European countries had experimented with national individualism, but negative results such as the two world wars motivated them to develop a more ecumenical stance toward one another. Now their interactions within the Common Market have improved both their economic and their political patterns at home. Statespersons who have lived with sufficient reverence in other cultures have returned to nourish their home cultures with the diverse values of the other cultures.

Today the task of political or economic reconception appears more difficult than that of religious reconception. It seems that many missionaries more readily experience the needed motivation; they attend more easily to values whose sharing brings trust. "The true mystic will recognize the true mystic" (*CWC*, 142). Yet do not true statespersons also recognize true statespersons? Granted that both the United States and the USSR presently infect each other with xenophobia, have not western Europeans learned to interact with increasing trust? Do not tourists experience some trust when they visit other countries, students and teachers experience considerable trust when they live for some time in other countries? Conductors, musicians, dancers, and athletes become enthusiastic world citizens, as do those who collaborate in Amnesty International or Pax Christi. So also do many receptive persons in foreign service, the media, and international business who have lived long enough in other cultures to esteem diverse values because their own lives and their home cultures have been nourished by those values.

This second section has suggested language that may help us build world community by engaging in intercultural moral discourse. This discourse involves our shifting from the style of a manager or technician into that of a statesperson. We have noticed our national inclination to bring diverse peoples together in a melting pot where minorities are manipulated into conformity with a controlling majority. On the contrary, we may be motivated to strive for the unity of a cultural mosaic in which contrasts make the whole more beautiful. Communication about values may lead us eagerly to engage in religious, political, and economic reconception — processes of dialogical reflection in which our appreciation of values grows not only by our assimilating the values of others but also by our developing needed connective values and by our opening ourselves indefinitely to further growth. Communication about values is furthered by consociation, a coming together of persons from different traditions in order to work or pray for common hopes in a spirit of religious, political, and economic ecumenism.

AN IDEAL OF WORLD CITIZENSHIP
ACTS AS A MORAL IMPERATIVE,
NOT BY COERCION BUT BY PERSUASION

Intercultural moral discourse, aided when need be by reconception, makes it possible for us to live as world citizens and to build world community. But is it worth the trouble? Does the ideal of world citizenship obligate us to be concerned about all persons and about all genuine values? Hocking's answer is clear: "Deliberate narrowing of the range of idea, in one's occupation with the part, is the essence of *sin.*"[6] From Hocking's perspective, we have an "idea" that embraces the whole of reality — a "whole-idea" closely associated with a valuing, a concern. Our natural human "range" of idea and concern embraces all reality, including all persons and all genuine values; it can be narrowed only through a deliberate choice by some person. Hocking recognizes that such narrowing is immoral; it deprives other persons and physical nature of the individual's concern and of the respectful acts that express that concern, and it also reverses the natural growth of the individual whose range of concern is narrowed.

We easily detect temptations to develop an immoral attitude of personal individualism, even if we fail to resist them. As a consequence, on the issue of individualism we need a collective examination of conscience. In response personal individualists might excuse themselves by claiming that others caused

their narrowness, yet few would deny that deliberately narrowing one's range of concern is immoral. Temporarily narrowing
one's present focus of attention so as to learn about the particular does not narrow the whole range of idea and concern;
at times this centering is healthy, not immoral. The personal
individualist, however, narrows the whole range of idea, and
consequently the range of affection and action; thus only the
self is thought about, loved, and developed. Such an individualist has flagrantly narrowed the range of idea in a preoccupation with the self, clearly a very small part of the whole
universe.

We do not easily notice temptations to develop an immoral
attitude of national individualism. Fear-driven double morality may even name that attitude a virtue. Yet the nation is small
compared with the world, and the national individualist has
narrowed the range of idea in a preoccupation with only part
of the world community. It is wrong arbitrarily to exclude those
outside the nation from our thought, love, and action. We too
easily excuse ourselves by saying that manifestations of national
individualism are not deliberate on our part. On the contrary,
each of us has an opportunity and an obligation to become
informed, reflect, and make responsible choices. These choices
govern our votes, conversations, letters, and other acts that can
and do influence national attitudes and policies.

When a national government's policies do violence to other
members of the world community, its own citizens may protest
as did U.S. citizens during the Vietnam War. Rightly a national
government's "freedom of action is limited to courses which
do not massively violate the consciences of its people" (CWC,
47). Today reflective consciences are violated by the ways in
which having and exporting a defense mentality occasions starvation, unemployment, crime, and poor education at home and
abroad. Profiteers would isolate our consciences, have them constricted by fear or by luxury so that we do not notice the effects
that come from the fact that limited resources of human intelligence and limited natural resources are used so much for
weapons and luxuries and so little for food, health care, and
education. Many serious thinkers—among them the Roman
Catholic bishops in their letters on peace and on economic justice[7]—strive to liberate our consciences from narrowness so

that we can resist the profiteers. These thinkers offer a sign of hope and invite us to join them in working to end the government's violation of our consciences.

Individual consciences are naturally endowed with a broad "range of idea" concerned about all members of a world community, endowed with "a disposition close to the essence of all civilization which we may call *reverence for reverence* — something far away from toleration" (*CWC*, 154; Hocking's emphasis). This reverence invites us not merely to tolerate but actually to promote the value-enhancing activities of persons very different from ourselves. Hocking learned from and encouraged the reverence which he found among devout Hindus and Buddhists; today we could follow his example by learning from and encouraging the "respect" for persons and nature that is highly valued by native Americans.

An objector may ask whether focus on reverence or respect does not undermine freedom of choice and thus indirectly undermine morality. Are not reverence, respect, and other ideals taught and repeatedly reinforced by instilling fear of punishment in this life or after death? Does not such fear inhibit a balanced and mature use of intelligence and a responsible exercise of free choice? Hocking and I respond that reverence and all moral ideals function not by coercion but by persuasion. We admit that some religious groups have employed psychological and physical coercion in a misguided attempt to manage the activities of others. Some even wage "religious wars" and "holy wars." To counteract the misunderstanding that moral ideals can be enforced by coercion, Hocking discusses how values guide us by reflecting first on a lesson from the Orient and then on the separation between church and state.

"Missionaries from the Orient" (*CWC*, 81) to the West teach us nonviolence and *satyāgraha*, "truth force which is love force," important values for both Mohandas Gandhi and Martin Luther King, Jr. We have argued that world community cannot be built or maintained by coercion; hence reasonable persuasion must provide its foundation. This persuasion focuses on important truths such as the deep kinship by which all persons are related, truths that naturally motivate us to act with reverence for one another.

National individualism involves an orientation of affections so centered upon the national group that we do not easily commit ourselves to others beyond that group. When we focus on the kinship of all persons, truth force which is love force reorientates our affections so that they reach beyond ourselves and our group. Donald Gelpi explains earlier in this volume that conversion has affective, intellectual, moral, religious, and sociopolitical dimensions. Thus reorientation of affections motivates actions and makes it possible for us to answer the challenging question, "How can we accomplish deeds which further the cause of world community?"

> The answer cannot be found in the idea of duty; it must lie in a disclosure of the nature of the world. For a demand upon feeling calls for a transformation of desire; and desire, formed in us by nature, can be transformed only by a vision of unsuspected beauty and meaning in the heart of things. If man can somehow fall in love with the Real, as source of life, he may fall out of love with his self-absorbed self; and it is hard to see how else he can be "reborn" in the orientation of his affections. (*CWC*, 92)

"The Real" for Hocking refers to God, whose vision of unsuspected beauty involves finding God present in our human brothers and sisters everywhere. Yet explicit faith in God is not required for a person to catch sight of beauty in every member of our human family. The truth of universal human kinship that invites love for all persons can be appreciated by any who take time to reflect and to overcome biases that might obstruct their natural vision.

The reorientation of affections, changing habits of the heart, involves

> seeing the neighbor now as what he is—not only, with Kant, as a free being, hence requiring respect; and not alone as an object of divine regard, hence calling out love and service; but also as having something of the divine in him—"ye have done it unto me"—hence worthy of reverence, "even the least of these." (*CWC*, 94)

Recognizing something of the divine in every person urges us to commit ourselves to every person. Our commitment responds to an experience, a vision of truth, not primarily to a command.

The truth that we see motivates us to labor for the common good of all persons. Today's media of communication, transportation, and flow of currency enable an influential person to affect every other person throughout the world. Like it or not, we are influential persons because we can reflect, converse, write, and vote within an influential nation. Our influence gives us the responsibility to use it well in working toward the coming of world community.

Reverence invites us to influence one another only by persuasion, not by coercion, which would restrict the range of idea. Most of us have been "pressured" at times; we may recall how our natural perception of values was clouded by an apparent opposition between the value of intelligent free choice and some other value or seeming value that the pressurer pushed. We may even have done something unwise because in the circumstances it seemed more important to express personal freedom of choice than to make the too-strongly-demanded contribution to order.

The separation of church and state makes it easier for truth force which is love force to operate within individuals. Separation urges both church and state to exercise persuasion and not coercion, thus encouraging the individual to use intelligence and free choice responsibly.

> As the church has released its claim upon . . . the secular state, the state *ipso facto* has released the church to define its own province. But since that province is the revealing to individual souls of the way to their own integration, the state in freeing the church accepts the *freedom of individuals to define their own ultimate loyalties.* The central motivation of each individual is thus placed beyond the reach of the state, with the state's consent, and at the same time beyond any but the persuasive power of the church. What is genuinely universal in the field of will-aims is thus enabled to rise before the mind to its due level at the time and in the way suited to the life pilgrimage of each person. (*CWC*, 132; Hocking's emphasis)

If undue coercion prevents a person from acting on some value, it is hard for him or her to acknowledge that value. Both undue subservience to a coercive state or church and undue reaction-formation against a coercive state or church obscure the recognition of genuine values and weaken the natural motivation to act in accord with them. On the contrary, values are best appreciated by persons who can choose freely whether or not to actualize those values. Hence appropriate efforts to build world community respect the freedom and thereby the intelligence of all persons.

Today many reflective persons suffer when they notice misuse of power by those in authority within the state or the church. Those less reflective may ask, "Why suffer? Why not simply pay no attention to authorities who misuse their influence?" "Because we take authority seriously," the sufferers reply. Misuse of authority tends to divide the community. We all have limited intelligence; at times we need to trust the judgment of others. Now when persons whom we ordinarily trust or would trust try to impose opinions regarding which they have not reflected enough, then the community divides. Those on one side think little and follow the authority, even if it be into error or into destructive action; those on the other suffer from having to choose between two needlessly complex combinations of good and evil. Because we esteem community we suffer from misuse of authority.

On the other hand, some people suffer because they think that state and church should punish more severely; some even advocate the death penalty and excommunication. They say that "toughness" teaches a greater respect for ideals. From Hocking's perspective and mine, however, excessive punishment betrays a weakness that may be associated with both kinds of individualism. Like the utilitarian individualist, the one who uses coercive punishment seeks to control others. Like the expressive individualist, the one who punishes excessively may do so in order to feel self-righteously good. Yet the victims of excessive punishment and those who feel compassion toward them may notice the punisher's individualism and refuse any education that the punisher might otherwise offer. Far from bringing respect for ideals, excessive punishment brings disrespect because it inclines many to make false connections. In response to coercive punishment, people make false connections between the genuine values that the punisher seeks to enforce and the despotism he or she uses to enforce them; hence people come to disrespect the values. Thus, for example, the ideal of appropriate sobriety suffered rather than grew during the period of

Prohibition. "Banned in Boston" once served as inexpensive advertising for movies no one would have bothered to see except
for the ban. Because we esteem genuine values, Hocking and
I oppose any attempt to impose them by coercive punishment.
What is a proper use of authority in dealing with terrorists
and other persons or nations who have committed destructive
acts? To be universal, reverence should extend even to a person
or nation needing rehabilitation. A people who tolerate the death
penalty and the bombing of Libya may well be challenged by
a quotation from Sir Winston Churchill and by Hocking's last
two paragraphs of *The Coming World Civilization*. Churchill
commented:

> The mood and temper of the public with regard to the treat-
> ment of crime and criminals is one of the most unfailing tests
> of the civilization of any country. A calm, dispassionate recog-
> nition of the rights of the accused, and even of the convicted
> criminal against the state; a constant heart-searching by all
> charged with the duty of punishment; a desire and an eagerness
> to rehabilitate . . . ; tireless efforts toward the discovery of crea-
> tive and regenerative processes; unfailing faith that there is a
> treasure, if you can only find it, in the heart of every man. These
> are the symbols which . . . mark and measure the stored-up
> strength of a nation . . . proof of the living virtue in it.[8]

On this Hocking reflected,

> The "constant heart-searching" of the punisher . . . the
> "rights of the accused even against the state" . . . "the unfail-
> ing faith that there is a treasure in the heart of every man" . . .
> these do indeed represent a strength stored up, not in a day,
> and not by an accumulated mass of mental measurements, but
> in the long reflections of a people upon their deeper insights
> of human possibility. Clearly, these reflections are not achieved
> by the political power itself; nor are they as yet universal. They
> can enter the structure of law in the coming world civilization
> only as a certain "spirit of the laws" first permeates its fabric.
> It is a spirit which arises from a severe and resolute confidence
> in human nature, a confidence which refuses to discourage by
> asserting limits set by circumstance. . . .
> The historical sources of that spirit remain an unfailing

spring, whose potency makes and will make for the healing of the nations. (*CWC*, 187)

When we reflect, we will to rehabilitate nations as well as individuals. We now regret that too many in the United States refused to share in Wilson's will to rehabilitate Germany after the Kaiser. On the other hand, most of us did share in Marshall's will to rehabilitate Germany and Japan after Hitler and Tojo. The strength of our nation manifested itself in those rehabilitations. They did produce good results such as normally follow from moral acts, but would we have accomplished them with merely utilitarian motivation? Were we not moved at least partly by a feeling that we shared world citizenship with the ordinary people of Germany and Japan? Do we not share world citizenship also with the ordinary people of the USSR, of Nicaragua, of Libya and Iran? Wisely we restructure debts to heal Mexico and other nations economically. If we devoted more of our intelligences and other resources to "the healing of the nations," then the weakness of our individualistic manipulation and fear would yield to the strength of cooperation and solidarity with other peoples.

Upper- and middle-class Americans suffer from the "poverty of affluence." "We are finally defenseless on this earth. Our material belongings have not brought us happiness. Our military defenses will not avert nuclear destruction. Nor is there any increase in productivity or any new weapons system that will change the truth of our condition" (*HH*, 295–96). Following Churchill and Hocking, we might just as well speak of "the impotence of coercion" and counter it with "the strength of persuasion."

Nations develop strength through their citizens. Individuals build and maintain a practical intellectual and moral strength partly through a healthy shifting of focus between what is public and what is private, between the community and the individual, between the outer and the inner. Failure to shift focus soon enough brings partial paralysis, a lack of vitality exemplified by both forms of individualism. Utilitarian individualists get stuck more in the outer world that they strive to control; they need to shift at times toward the inner. Expressive individualists get stuck more in the inner self about which they strive to "feel good"; they need to shift at times toward the outer.

The utilitarian outer focus helped develop technology that can provide for better nutrition and overall health care, for worldwide communication and distribution of life's necessities. Yet getting stuck in this outer focus prevents us from reflecting enough about values, thus depriving us of direction and incentive: "With this abandonment of man's native rapport with the whole, the nerve of worth in his own living and acting silently ceases to function" (*CWC*, 23). Hocking joins Dewey, Whitehead, Einstein, Lorenz, and others who challenge us to develop ethical wisdom apace with scientific technology. This value-centered practical wisdom, rather than any compulsive hunt for mere year-at-a-time profits, offers valid incentives for ecologically sound planning that guides our providing for a world habitable by our generation's grandchildren and great-grandchildren.

The expressive inner focus helped develop psychology that can guide personal growth in sensitivity to others and in self-awareness. Hocking joins James, Royce, Marcel, Lonergan, and others for whom the exploration of our inner selves opens us to different varieties of interiority and thus prepares us to understand persons from all around the world. Yet getting stuck in this inner focus distracts us from attending to other persons or to the outer objects and shared values on which friends naturally focus in conversation. A therapeutic mentality inhibits conversation by narrowing its focus; talking too much about how we feel occasions our talking too little about important events outside us — events we may also avoid because they are painful, and because demagogues have made "feeling good" seem more important than it is. Thus excessive inner focus tends to decrease our dialogue generally; it may tempt us to become weak spectators who passively watch television fantasy rather than strong participants who actively develop an actual world that needs our creativity.

This third section offered further language for an examination of conscience. We have recognized how destructive it may be deliberately to narrow our range of concern in our preoccupation with the nation, a relatively small part of the world. We have been alerted to possible violation of our consciences by profiteers or by narrow-minded persons within the government. We can guard against the poverty of affluence and the impotence of coercion by allowing truth force which is love force to guide our actions. We can deal with other persons through persuasion that is informed by a spirit of reverence, a spirit of respect much appreciated by native Americans. When people have acted destructively, we can be eager to rehabilitate, concerned for the healing of persons and for the healing of nations.

CONCLUSION: HOCKING'S EXPERIENCE AND GUIDANCE GROUND OUR HOPES FOR WORLD COMMUNITY AND CALL US TOWARD COMMITMENT

One further objection needs to be faced. Have we not recounted ideals that many despair of attaining? If we think about these ideals and consequently about how far we are from reaching them, will we not become discouraged? Does not pessimism paralyze our efforts toward achieving such ideals? As the researchers of *Middletown Families* discovered,

> Contemporary Middletowners are more pessimistic than any of their predecessors, back to the first settlers. . . . What people of all ages see as they look into the future is nuclear war, environmental pollution, inflation, exhaustion of resources, and a general deterioration of the quality of life. . . . They are not at all sure that the world will last. . . .[9]

The multiplicity and complexity of world problems tempt many to despair. MX missiles, Star Wars fantasies, and starving boys with M-16s symbolize such despair and the suicidal tendencies that may accompany it.

Few succeed without hope of success. Without hope few even make a commitment to try. The term *hope* must not connote merely utopian dreams. Hope aims to motivate striving, action that turns a particular hope into a memory. Moreover, the principle of subsidiarity applies not only to planning and striving but also to hoping. If we center only on worldwide hopes, we may become discouraged by the fact that so much remains to be done. Hence we need to shift focus both toward smaller goals and toward memories of goals attained. One who hikes up a mountain looks ahead and also looks back; so do we who

step by step ascend the mountain on which we change hopes
for world community into some actualities of world community.

We find courage in knowing that we are not alone on the
mountain. Reflective persons all around the world share common hopes for world peace, for an end to starvation, for an
end to environmental breakdown. Such persons include many
thinkers whom Hocking influenced. A group of these offers us
a striking example of world community in the pages of the
Festschrift published in Hocking's honor, a cultural mosaic
whose authors come from ten countries and ten academic fields.
The writers whose diverse personal modes of thought Hocking both encouraged and clarified include the French philosopher Gabriel Marcel, the Lebanese Secretary General of the
United Nations Charles Malik, and the President of India Sar-
vepalli Radhakrishnan. In "Solipsism Surmounted," Marcel
thanks Hocking for liberating him from the suffocating prison
of solipsism by showing that through sharing a common external world we actually do experience persons different from ourselves. Malik considers the ecumenical movement "the greatest
event of this century";[10] he challenges us in the West to learn
deeper social and personal values from the East and to manifest
all our values in our deeds and our discourse. In "Fellowship
of the Spirit," Radhakrishnan recounts how the impact of Christianity brought a religious awakening among Hindus; he suggests that a similar awakening would enable us in the West to
live with greater reverence, wonder, and loyalty.

The immense task confronting a worldwide social movement
toward world community may seem so overwhelming as to discourage commitment. In accord with the principle of subsidiarity, would we not commit ourselves effectively to world community by participating actively in limited movements such as
those for peace, for feeding the hungry, and for preserving the
environment? U.S. citizens are frightened to think about a world
state in terms of world sovereignty achieved by the USSR through
world conquest. Are such thinking and its language reasonable?
Can we resist them and with an attitude of world citizenship
commit ourselves and our resources to cooperate in working
for worldwide development in food, health, and education?

Making any commitment implies that we have explicitly noticed values that we share with the persons to whom we com-

mit ourselves or with whom we commit ourselves to some goal. Do we develop sufficient skills in communicating about values? Can we learn to reconceive values so that the values of others nourish us without destroying our genuine values? Have we looked to accomplishments in religious ecumenism to guide and encourage our practice of worldwide political and economic ecumenism?

Commitment cannot be coerced but must be invited. Does reverence guide all our dealings with others? Do we reflect enough to recognize that every person is related to us within one human family? Does this realization reorient our affections so that we deeply desire to commit ourselves to our distant brothers and sisters? Does the range of our concern extend to all, even to those persons and nations in need of rehabilitation?

Hocking would not want us to be discouraged if we do not yet answer all these questions as fully committed world citizens. *The Coming World Civilization* and *Strength of Men and Nations* were his most mature books, not his first. Hocking himself had first to find the trail along which he would now guide us. As a world citizen he did find that trail and reach its summit vista of a world community. The description he leaves communicates a vision of unsuspected beauty that calls for our commitment to follow, our minds enlightened and our hearts filled with hope.

NOTES

1. Robert N. Bellah et al., *Habits of the Heart: Individualism and Commitment in American Life* (Berkeley: University of California Press, 1985), 158. Hereafter referred to as *HH*.

2. William Ernest Hocking, *The Coming World Civilization* (New York: Harper and Brothers, 1956), xiv. Hereafter referred to as *CWC*.

3. William Ernest Hocking, *The Spirit of World Politics: With Special Studies of the Near East* (New York: Macmillan, 1932); *Re-Thinking Missions: A Layman's Inquiry after One Hundred Years* (New York: Harper and Brothers, 1932); *Living Religions and a World Faith* (New York: Macmillan, 1940)—hereafter referred to as *LR*.

4. William Ernest Hocking, *Strength of Men and Nations: A Message to the USA vis-à-vis the USSR* (New York: Harper and Brothers, 1959). Hereafter referred to as *SMN*.

5. Richard J. Barnet and Ronald E. Muller, *Global Reach: The Power of the Multinational Corporations* (New York: Simon and Schuster, 1974).

6. William Ernest Hocking, *The Meaning of God in Human Experience: A Philosophic Study of Religion* (New Haven: Yale University Press, 1912), 415; Hocking's emphasis.

7. National Conference of Catholic Bishops, *The Challenge of Peace: God's Promise and Our Response* (Washington, D.C.: National Conference of Catholic Bishops, 1983), and *Economic Justice for All: Catholic Social Teaching and the U.S. Economy* (Washington, D.C.: National Conference of Catholic Bishops, 1986).

8. Winston Churchill, *Probation,* cited in *CWC,* 186.

9. Theodore Caplow, *Middletown Families: Fifty Years of Change and Continuity* (Minneapolis: University of Minnesota Press, 1982), 37.

10. Charles Malik, "It Is Time to Tell the West," in *Philosophy, Religion, and the Coming World Civilization: Essays in Honor of William Ernest Hocking,* ed. Leroy S. Rouner (The Hague: Nijhoff, 1966), 403.

Afterword

Robert N. Bellah

I speak for all five of the authors of *Habits of the Heart* in welcoming with pleasure the appearance of *Beyond Individualism.* The John Courtney Murray group has done much more than respond to issues raised by *Habits of the Heart.* They have in some cases amplified our themes, in other cases helped to make up for our deficiencies, but above all they have significantly advanced the discussion of public philosophy and public theology to which we sought to contribute in *Habits.* In this effort they are true followers of John Courtney Murray, a central member of that group of writers, which includes John Dewey, Walter Lippmann, and Reinhold Niebuhr among others, who kept public discourse alive in America in the middle decades of the twentieth century. Murray's work helped to maintain an atmosphere which made *Habits of the Heart* possible, and we are happy to acknowledge our indebtedness.

While on occasion the authors of *Beyond Individualism* challenge assertions made in *Habits,* I do not take their work as primarily critical, and beyond indicating that I think most of their objections are justified, I would rather use these remarks to indicate the ways in which these essays significantly move the discussion forward.

Donald Gelpi begins the book with a salutary reference to Jonathan Edwards, who stands near the beginning of the American intellectual tradition and who spoke for the Puritan component of that tradition, which even today informs our culture more than we might imagine. Conversion is a fundamental theme in biblical religion and one central to Puritan theology.

Gelpi quite rightly discerns the theme of conversion in *Habits,* implicitly in the whole project and explicitly in the concluding chapter. The conversionist theme in *Habits* has undoubtedly helped the reception of the book in a variety of American religious communities, including significantly the evangelical community. But Gelpi, partly with Edwards's help and partly by moving beyond him, shows us how to recover a broader and deeper meaning to conversion than we have often assumed. Recognizing that the religious element in conversion is basic, he develops a multiple understanding of conversion which includes affective, intellectual, moral, and sociopolitical dimensions as well. By indicating that conversion must always be personal, but that it must also be cultural and sociopolitical, he strengthens the argument of the concluding chapter of *Habits.* By suggesting that conversion is not the result of moralistic guilt-tripping but occurs through openness to the beauty of true virtue, as Edwards would have put it, Gelpi shows how we can avoid the pitfalls of the traditional Protestant jeremiad—a genre which *Habits* does not altogether escape, a point to which I will return below.

It is part of the culture of radical individualism to believe that "we are perfect just as we are." To suggest even the possibility of conversion, much less the necessity of it, in this cultural context, requires the wisdom of serpents. Gelpi's reflections on the complex possibilities in the conversion motif enrich the possibility of bringing this theme into contemporary discussion.

Stephen Rowntree's essay argues for a richer understanding of romantic love than that provided in *Habits,* where, he argues, we assimilated it too quickly to a therapeutic model. Rowntree sees romantic love as leading beyond a narcissistic preoccupation with oneself and into a network of connections that includes not only the beloved but also the children that may fulfill the love relationship if it is consummated in marriage, and the larger community involvements that the raising of children, in turn, necessitates. Even if we may wonder whether the near idolatrous obsession with finding the one perfect other, which is often what romantic love means in our culture, necessarily has these richer implications, we are certainly prepared to admit that it sometimes does. A genuine commitment to even one other person, provided it moves beyond narcissistic fantasy and involves a real moral claim, can break the solipsist implications of radical individualism, even though apotheosizing the dyad can lead to a new form of isolating individualism, that of the couple rather than the individual. But in Rowntree's view romantic love at its best leads individuals into widening circles of care and concern, and where that is the case we would certainly want to affirm it.

Rowntree's paper raises a larger question, at least implicitly, to which I would like to respond. Romantic love might well be interpreted as falling under the rubric of expressive individualism. There are those who have pointed out that the treatment of expressive individualism in *Habits* is not entirely fair in more than one way. We move too quickly, it is said, from Whitman and Emerson to the therapeutic culture and so present expressive individualism more in collusion with utilitarian individualism than as a challenge to it. But historically expressive individualism often arose as a revulsion against the claims of instrumental reason to dominate all cultural life. Nor did it lack the capacity to form and nurture community. Emerson was devoted, it is pointed out, to the cause of antislavery. Whitman gave years of his life to the care of the wounded in the Civil War. Given that "communities of memory" have in fact often been narrow and oppressive, those unwilling to take the utilitarian route, but unable to affirm loyalties that they justly found too confining, attempted through some version of expressive individualism to find a new way. It is true that in *Habits* we do not take seriously enough this phenomenon. Perhaps the one exception is near the end of chapter 9 where we argue that religious individualism, a form of expressive individualism, presents a serious challenge to the established churches and sects. We indicate there the institutional fragility of religious individualism, and the same is true of expressive individualism generally, yet we take it seriously as a social phenomenon. But we should have made the point more generally and thus been fairer to the culturally positive possibilities in expressive individualism.

Drew Christiansen expands on a theme that is important but undeveloped in *Habits,* namely, the theme of the common good. As many have pointed out, *Habits* is more a diagnosis of our condition than a prescription for it. We point to un-utilized resources in the biblical and republican traditions but we do not often even begin to spell out their concrete applications. To some extent we are attempting to remedy that situation in writing a successor book to *Habits* that we are tentatively entitling *The Good Society*. As the very title implies, we will be much concerned with issues of the common good in the new book. Christiansen's chapter is a much needed aid in that effort. He is particularly helpful in pointing out the ways in which traditional Anglo-American political philosophy and the common good position of modern Catholic social thought might be brought together in a fruitful dialogue. Catholic social thought, by moving from a natural law to a human rights framework, opens up significant relationships with the Anglo-American rights tradition. But the new situation is not one of simple harmony, for human rights in the Catholic tradition, by significantly expanding the scope for the application of rights, raises questions of substantive justice that the Anglo-American tradition has preferred to ignore. The issues here are complex and need to be argued not just in the abstract but in relation to concrete cases. Christiansen has, however, opened up a range of issues that deserves a great deal of further attention.

Frank Oppenheim in his essay draws our attention to the exhilarating perspective that the philosophy of Josiah Royce offers to the problems posed by *Habits of the Heart*. I was embarrassed to discover that our own memory had lapsed in that the authors of *Habits* did not credit Royce with the terms "community of memory" and "community of hope" which play a central role in our argument. Royce was in the background of several of us but we did not return to him in the period when we were writing *Habits,* and Oppenheim's essay suggests that it would have been better if we had. Oppenheim suggests that Royce's concern for the universal community, his unwillingness to stop short of any community that does not embrace the human race, might have expanded our horizons beyond the American middle class. He recognizes that there was good sociological warrant for our concentration (though others have questioned even that—more on this later) but that our argument suffers from the narrowness of our empirical base. Our empirical focus was strategic and we were certainly aware that none of the problems we were describing could be solved except in a global perspective, something that we tried to indicate in the last pages of the book. Yet a world perspective is critical today and we will try to make that clear in the successor volume. With respect to some of Oppenheim's other points, we may ask whether a sociological work can deal adequately with the philosophical and religious questions about the deeper meaning of community and the essential role of atonement in the life of genuine community that full attention to Josiah Royce's thought would require.

John Staudenmaier in his essay raises still another major topic that we only touched on briefly in *Habits,* namely, technology. Staudenmaier's essay is remarkably judicious in an area where much writing is either mindless apologetic or apocalyptic prophecy of doom. By reminding us that decisions about technology are made by human beings, that Science and Technology are neither demigods nor demons that control us against our will, he helps to reassert the essentially political context within which technology develops and calls us to a more ethically sensitive political discourse through which we might think better about the decisions we do make. Staudenmaier's paper, like most in this collection, is both a complement to *Habits* and an aid in the next phase of our work. *The Good Society* must clearly say more about technology than *Habits* did and do so within the context that Staudenmaier develops.

Carl Starkloff's essay provides a valuable counterpoint to arguments made by Frank Oppenheim. Both begin by a concern that the empirical focus of *Habits* on the white middle class is too narrow. Oppenheim pushes us in the direction of a greater emphasis on the universal community, though reminding us of Royce's polarity between provincialism (used in a positive sense) and universalism. Starkloff presses us for a greater recognition of cultural particularity; and he insists that the test of any culture is its capacity to transcend itself in recognizing the value of other cultures and thus—from the other direction, so to speak—to attain Royce's ideal of universality. Starkloff uses as his primary example the most poignant of all minority cultures in North America, the native Americans. This is indeed the test. Starkloff is kind enough to recognize that I did address this issue, along with cultural pluralism generally, much

more satisfactorily in *The Broken Covenant* than we did in
Habits of the Heart. But the issue, though not sufficiently salient in *Habits,* is very much in the mind of the authors and
will receive more attention in the successor volume.

Just how important Starkloff's challenge is is brought home
to me at the moment I am writing as I glance at today's *San
Francisco Chronicle* (1 June 1988). I am gratified to read that
President Reagan in Moscow proclaimed that his characteriza-
tion of the Soviet Union as the "evil empire" is now outdated
but appalled to see him on the same day say that we "humored"
the Indians in putting them on reservations: "Maybe we should
not have humored them in that, wanting to stay in that kind
of primitive lifestyle. Maybe we should have said, 'No, come
join us. Be citizens along with the rest of us.'" It is useless to
ask what kind of world Ronald Reagan lives in — unfortunately
it is the world of most white North Americans. The heroic and
tragic saga of an outnumbered and beleaguered people defending the form of life that gave them their very identity, their
genocidal treatment at the hands of government and majority
citizens alike, the long history of broken treaties and broken
promises and the desperate conditions that now exist — all this
is blotted out. For these are dangerous memories, to use Jo-
hann Baptist Metz's term, that call our very civilization in question. I agree with Starkloff that our churches and our whole
society are being tested by the issue of cultural pluralism. I further agree with him that in the end we can solve that problem
only by cultural transcendence, only by the effort genuinely to
participate in the cultural experiences of others. This effort is
necessary especially in the cases of those who have been de-
spised and rejected, whose personal dignity has been violated,
because we, whether through ignorance or malice, failed to find
in them the neighbor that we are to love as ourselves.

John Stacer fittingly brings the volume to an end with an
essay on world citizenship. His focus on William Ernest Hocking complements Oppenheim's reflections on Royce, for Royce
was Hocking's teacher and Hocking's emphasis on "the coming world civilization" is clearly a development of Royce's ideal
of the universal community. Stacer continues and develops the
concerns in Starkloff's paper with the problem of cultural particularity by appreciating Hocking's effort to encourage a genu-

ine dialogue between the great religions, and, more, a mutual participation in the lives of the several religious communities.

As the twentieth century comes to a close Hocking appears truly prophetic. For the nation-states are no longer in command, not even the strongest of them, as they have been for most of modern history. The big problems in our world—nuclear armaments, the international economy, the global pollution of the environment—require international agreements and a structure of international institutions if we are to avoid physical or moral destruction. World citizenship, a world public philosophy, are not merely ideals; they are actually taking shape. If in *Habits* we did not emphasize this enough, we certainly will in the next book, thanks in part to the prodding of the John Courtney Murray group.

I would like to conclude with a passage that Stacer quotes from Hocking. It is deeply Platonic and an excellent admonition against a Protestant proclivity to moralize (some have noticed that my proclivity to the jeremiad form was significantly mitigated in *Habits* by the fact that I am the only one of the five authors who has a Protestant background). Stacer quotes Hocking as asking, "How can we accomplish deeds which further the cause of world community?"

> The answer cannot be found in the idea of duty; it must lie in a disclosure of the nature of the world. For a demand upon feeling calls for a transformation of desire; and desire, formed in us by nature, can be transformed only by a vision of unsuspected beauty and meaning in the heart of things.

And that, of course, is a description of conversion. We return to the beginning of the book, to the concerns of Donald Gelpi, and we see how beautifully integrated this collection is. It is itself an effort to describe the vision that can transform us. The authors of *Habits* are honored to have provided the occasion for such a rich body of reflection. In turn, we are instructed and encouraged in our own continuing efforts.

Index